X-TREME X-MEN

Storm
The Arena

Writer
Chris Claremont

Pencils
Igor Kordey

Inks
Scott Hanna with
**Sandu Florea,
Igor Kordey,
Mark McKenna,
Andrew Pepoy,
Norm Rapmund,**
and **Josef Rubinstein**

Colors
Transparency Digital

Letters
**Virtual Calligraphy's
Rus Wooton**

Cover Art
Salvador Larroca

Assistant Editors
Stephanie Moore and
Cory Sedlmeier

Editor
Mike Marts

Collections Editor
Jeff Youngquist

Assistant Editor
Jennifer Grünwald

Book Designer
Meghan Kerns

Editor in Chief
Joe Quesada

Publisher
Dan Buckley

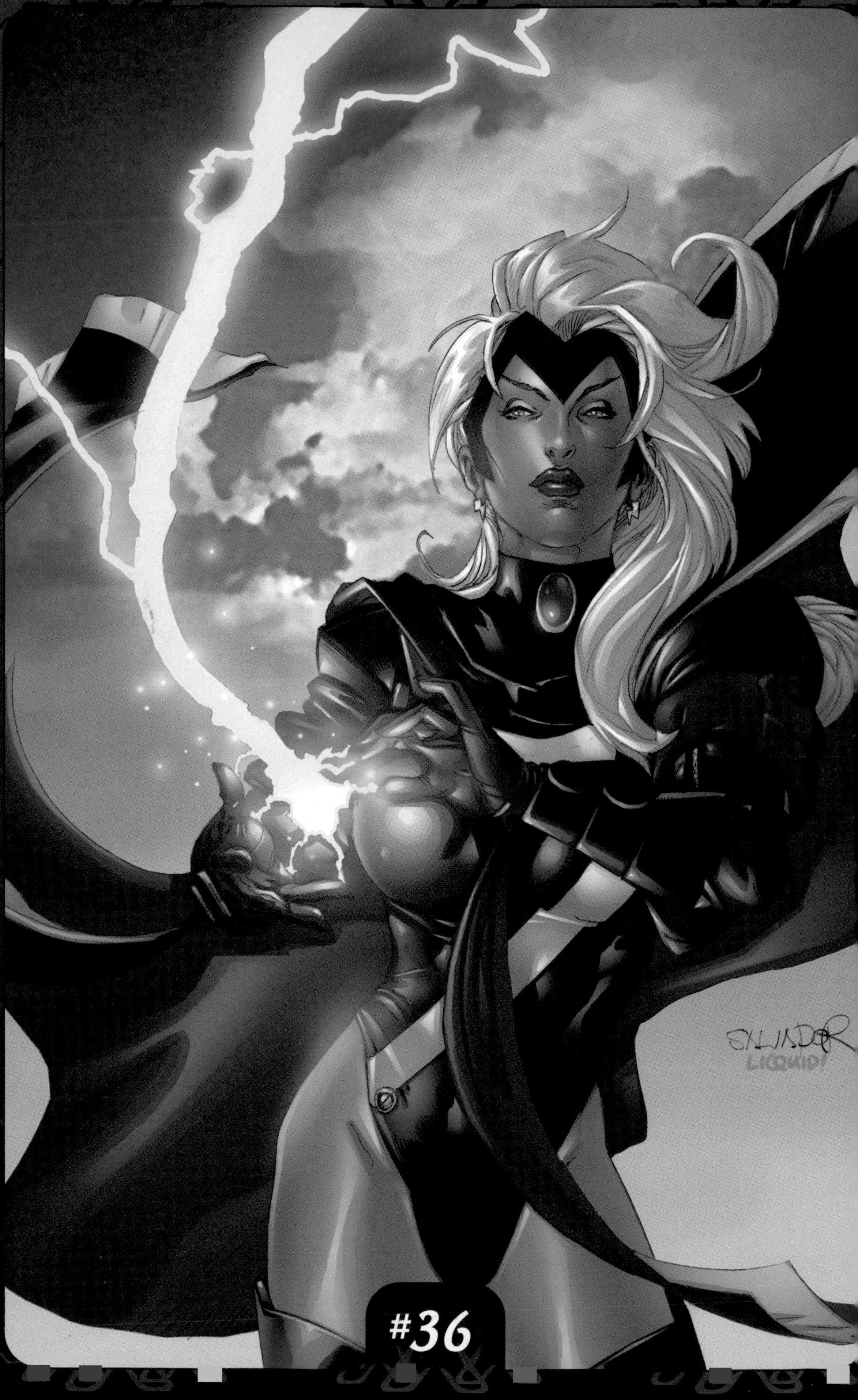

#36

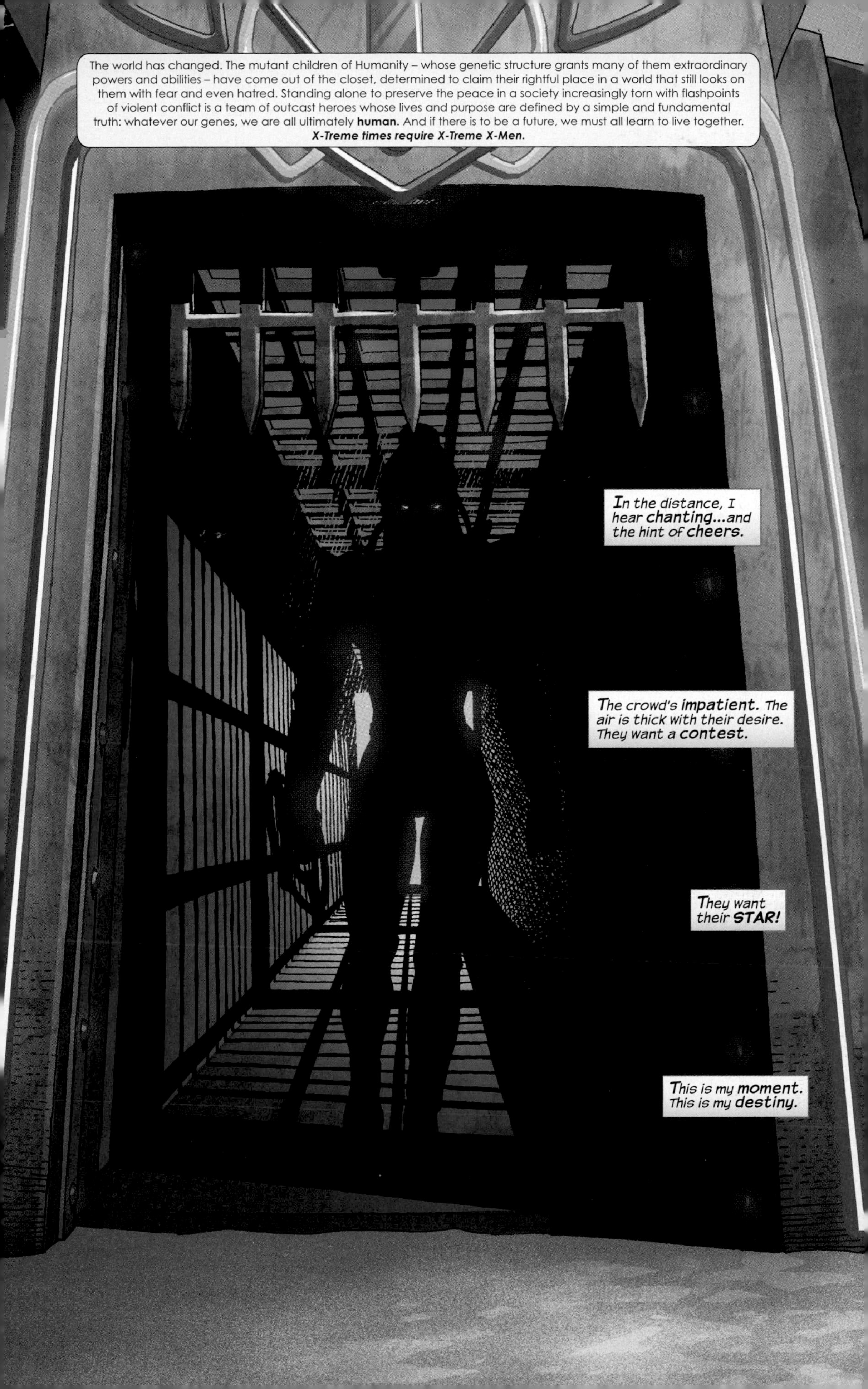
The world has changed. The mutant children of Humanity – whose genetic structure grants many of them extraordinary powers and abilities – have come out of the closet, determined to claim their rightful place in a world that still looks on them with fear and even hatred. Standing alone to preserve the peace in a society increasingly torn with flashpoints of violent conflict is a team of outcast heroes whose lives and purpose are defined by a simple and fundamental truth: whatever our genes, we are all ultimately **human.** And if there is to be a future, we must all learn to live together.
X-Treme times require X-Treme X-Men.
In the distance, I hear chanting...and the hint of cheers.
The crowd's impatient. The air is thick with their desire. They want a contest.
They want their STAR!
This is my moment. This is my destiny.

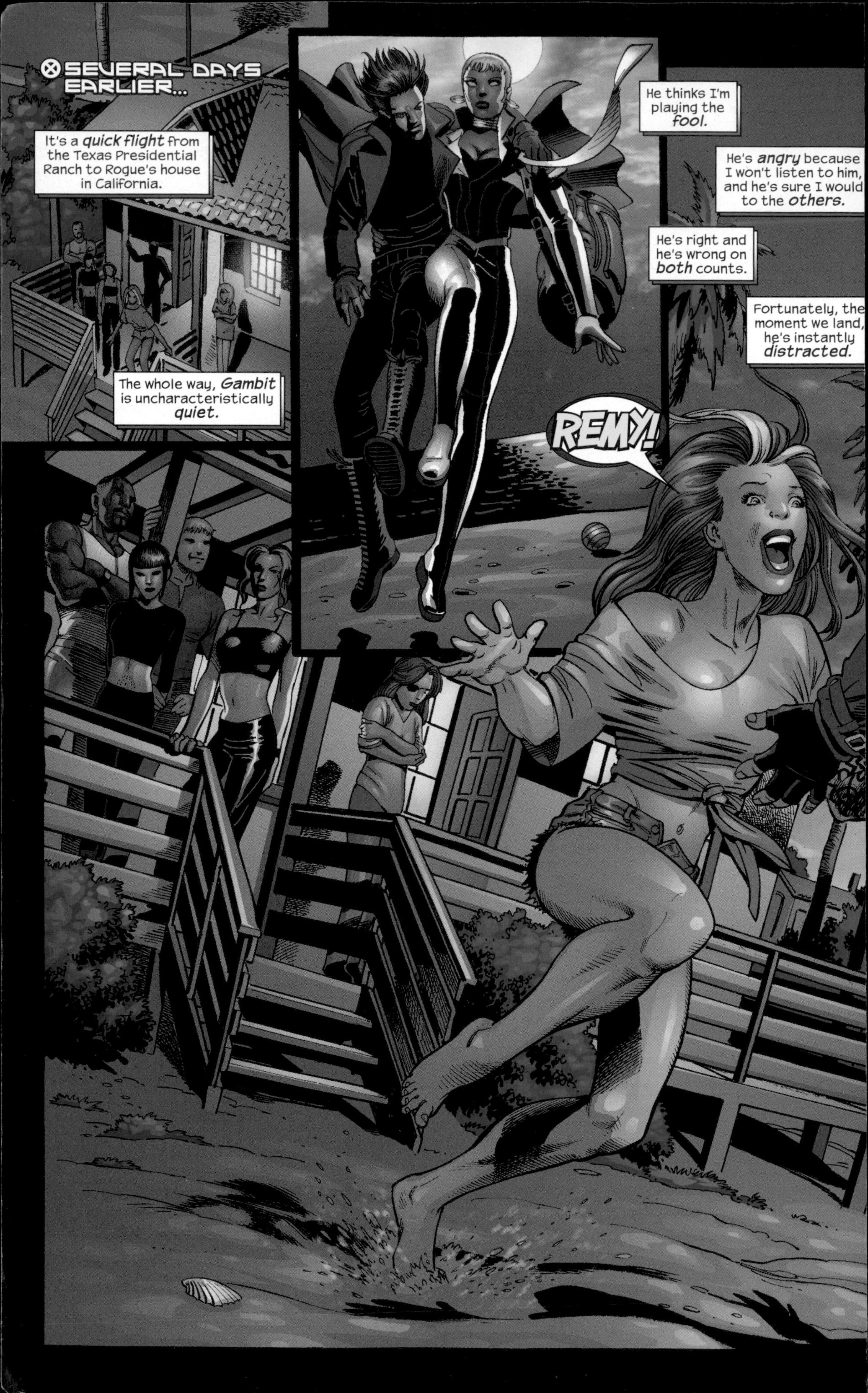
SEVERAL DAYS EARLIER...
It's a quick flight from the Texas Presidential Ranch to Rogue's house in California.
The whole way, Gambit is uncharacteristically quiet.
He thinks I'm playing the fool.
He's angry because I won't listen to him, and he's sure I would to the others.
He's right and he's wrong on both counts.
Fortunately, the moment we land, he's instantly distracted.
REMY!

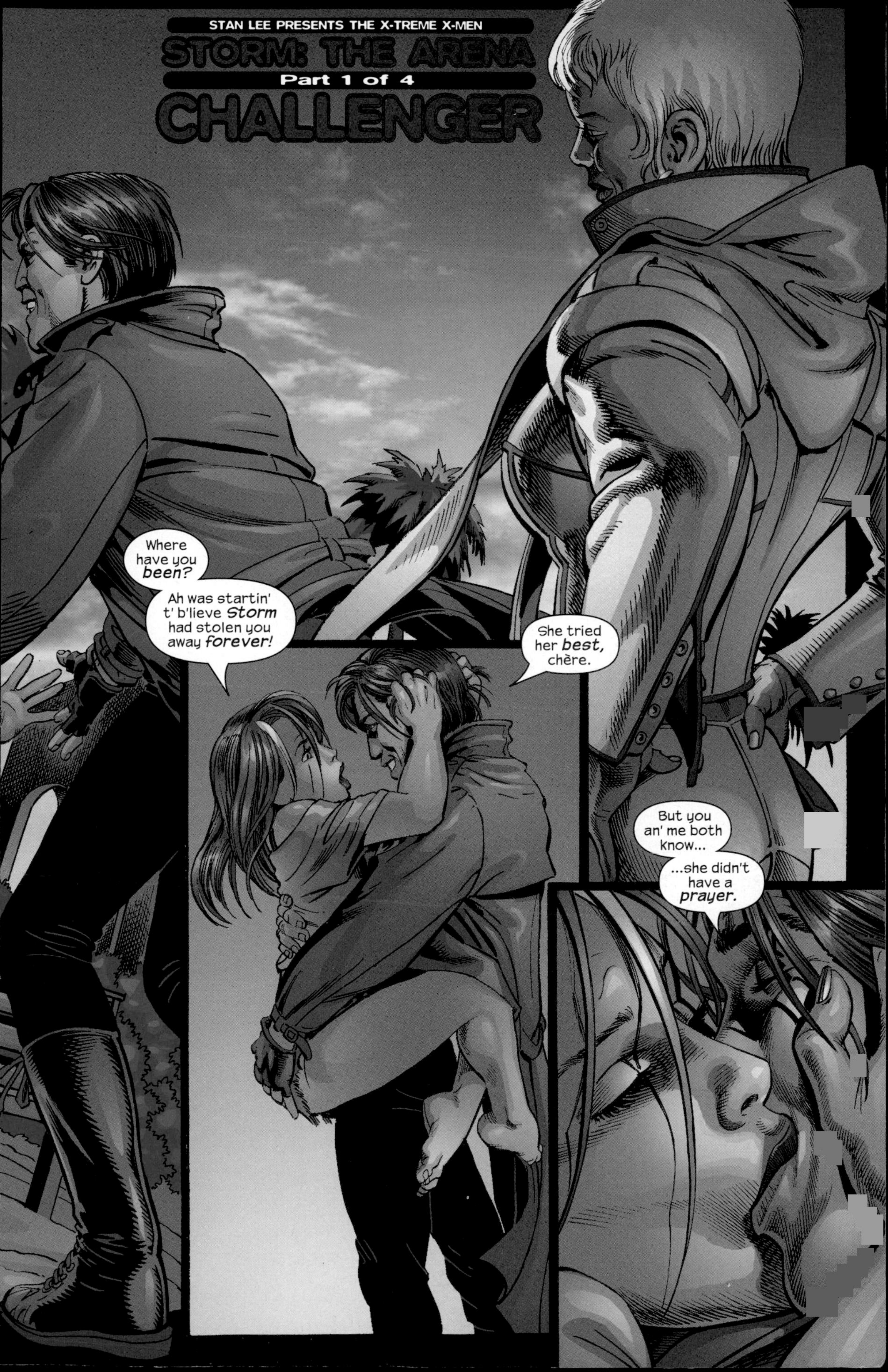
STAN LEE PRESENTS THE X-TREME X-MEN
STORM: THE ARENA
Part 1 of 4
CHALLENGER
Where have you been?
Ah was startin' t' b'lieve Storm had stolen you away forever!
She tried her best, chère.
But you an' me both know...
...she didn't have a prayer.

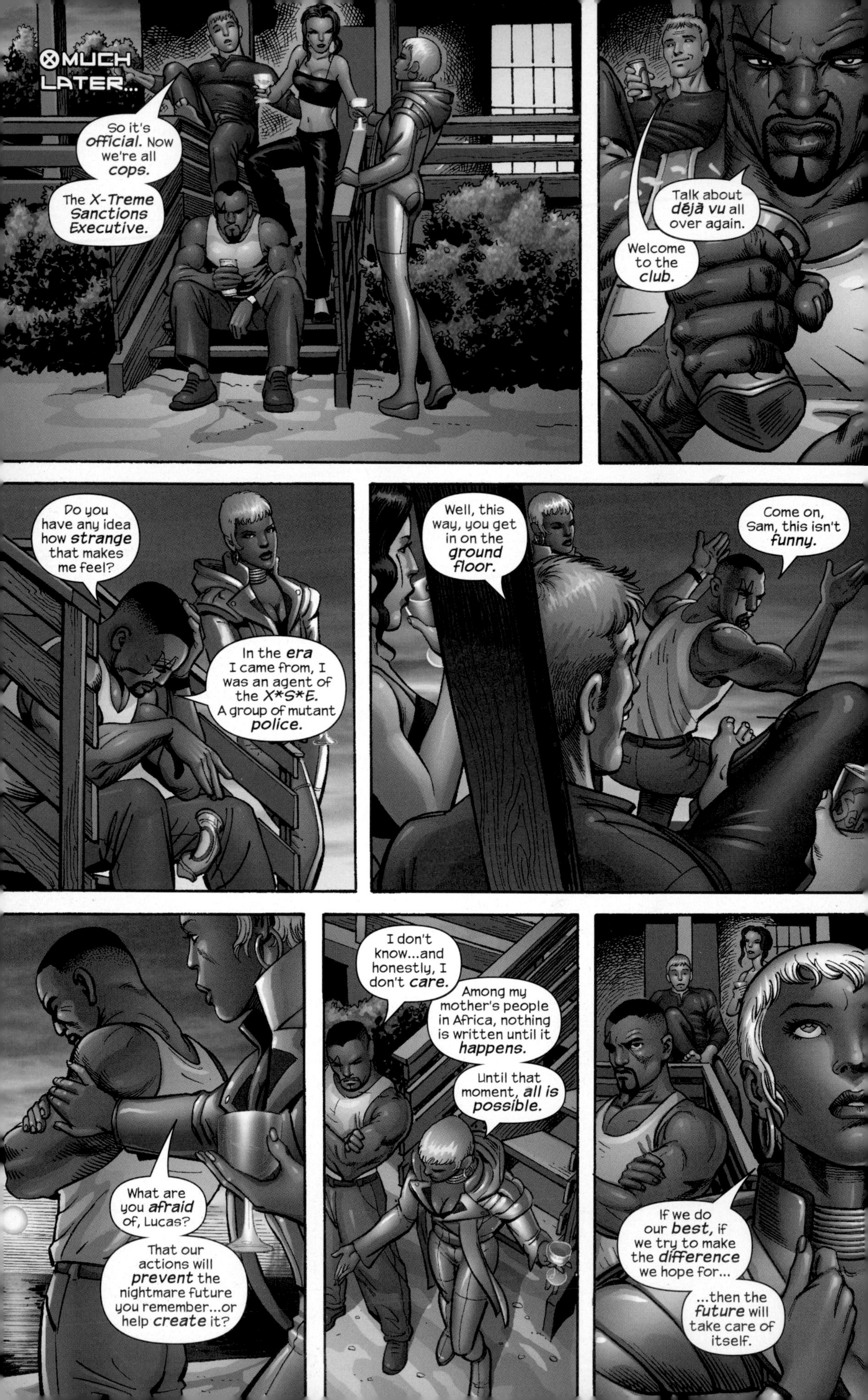
MUCH LATER...
So it's official. Now we're all cops.
The X-Treme Sanctions Executive.
Talk about déjà vu all over again.
Welcome to the club.
Do you have any idea how strange that makes me feel?
In the era I came from, I was an agent of the X*S*E. A group of mutant police.
Well, this way, you get in on the ground floor.
Come on, Sam, this isn't funny.
What are you afraid of, Lucas?
That our actions will prevent the nightmare future you remember...or help create it?
I don't know...and honestly, I don't care.
Among my mother's people in Africa, nothing is written until it happens.
Until that moment, all is possible.
If we do our best, if we try to make the difference we hope for...
...then the future will take care of itself.

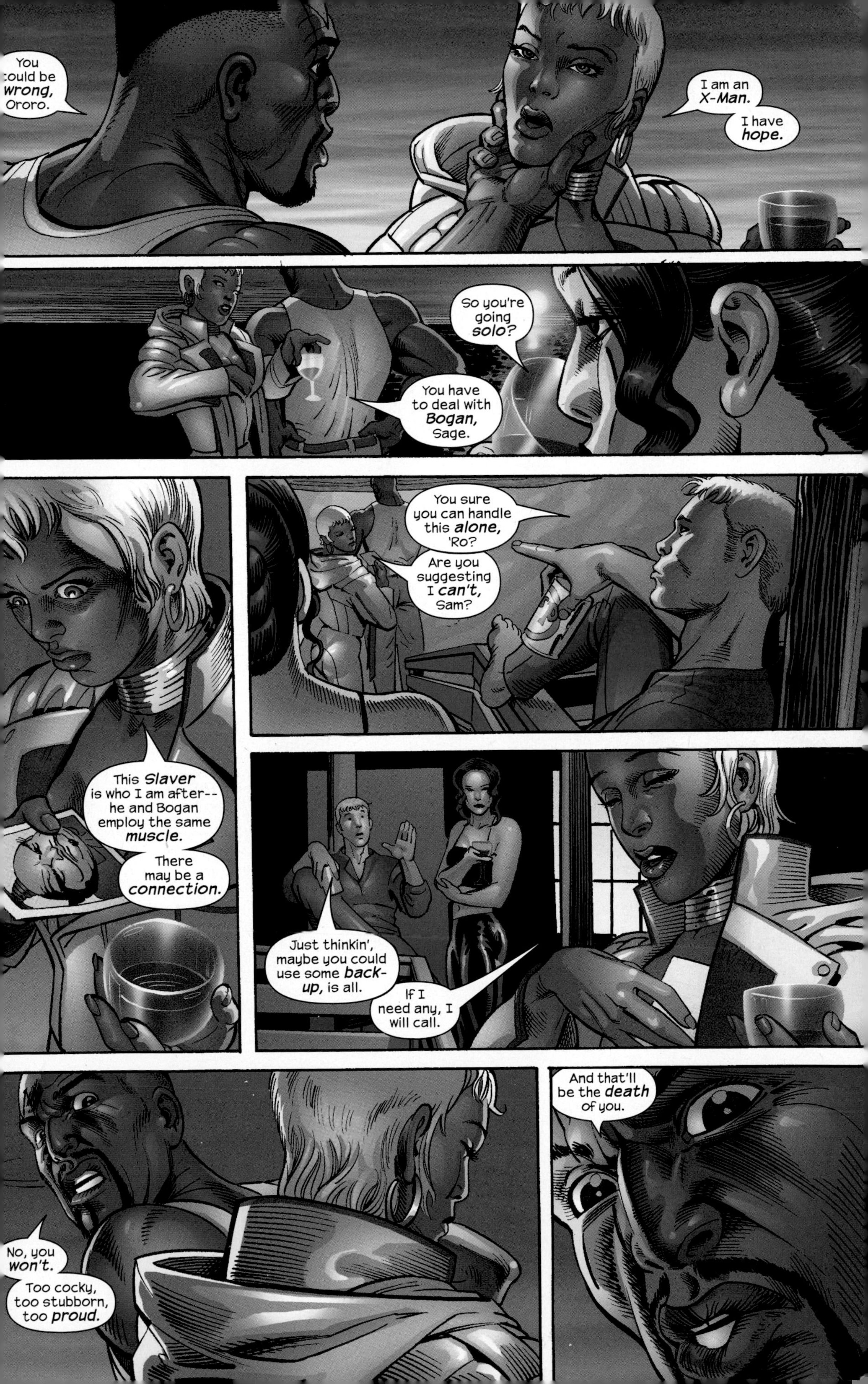
You could be wrong, Ororo.
I am an X-Man.
I have hope.
So you're going solo?
You have to deal with Bogan, Sage.
You sure you can handle this alone, 'Ro?
Are you suggesting I can't, Sam?
This Slaver is who I am after-- he and Bogan employ the same muscle.
There may be a connection.
Just thinkin', maybe you could use some back-up, is all.
If I need any, I will call.
No, you won't.
Too cocky, too stubborn, too proud.
And that'll be the death of you.

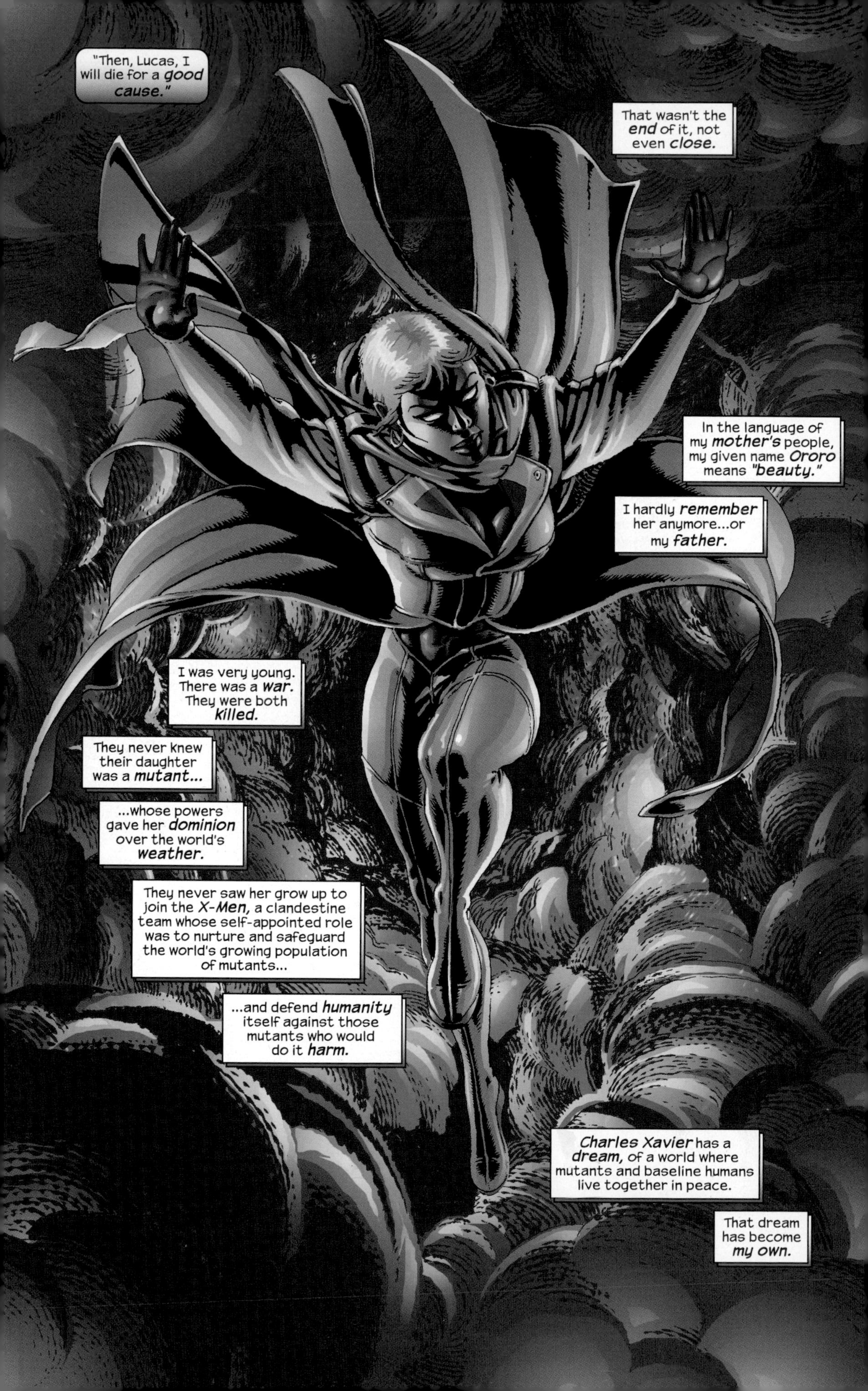
"Then, Lucas, I will die for a good cause."
That wasn't the end of it, not even close.
In the language of my mother's people, my given name Ororo means "beauty."
I hardly remember her anymore...or my father.
I was very young. There was a war. They were both killed.
They never knew their daughter was a mutant...
...whose powers gave her dominion over the world's weather.
They never saw her grow up to join the X-Men, a clandestine team whose self-appointed role was to nurture and safeguard the world's growing population of mutants...
...and defend humanity itself against those mutants who would do it harm.
Charles Xavier has a dream, of a world where mutants and baseline humans live together in peace.
That dream has become my own.

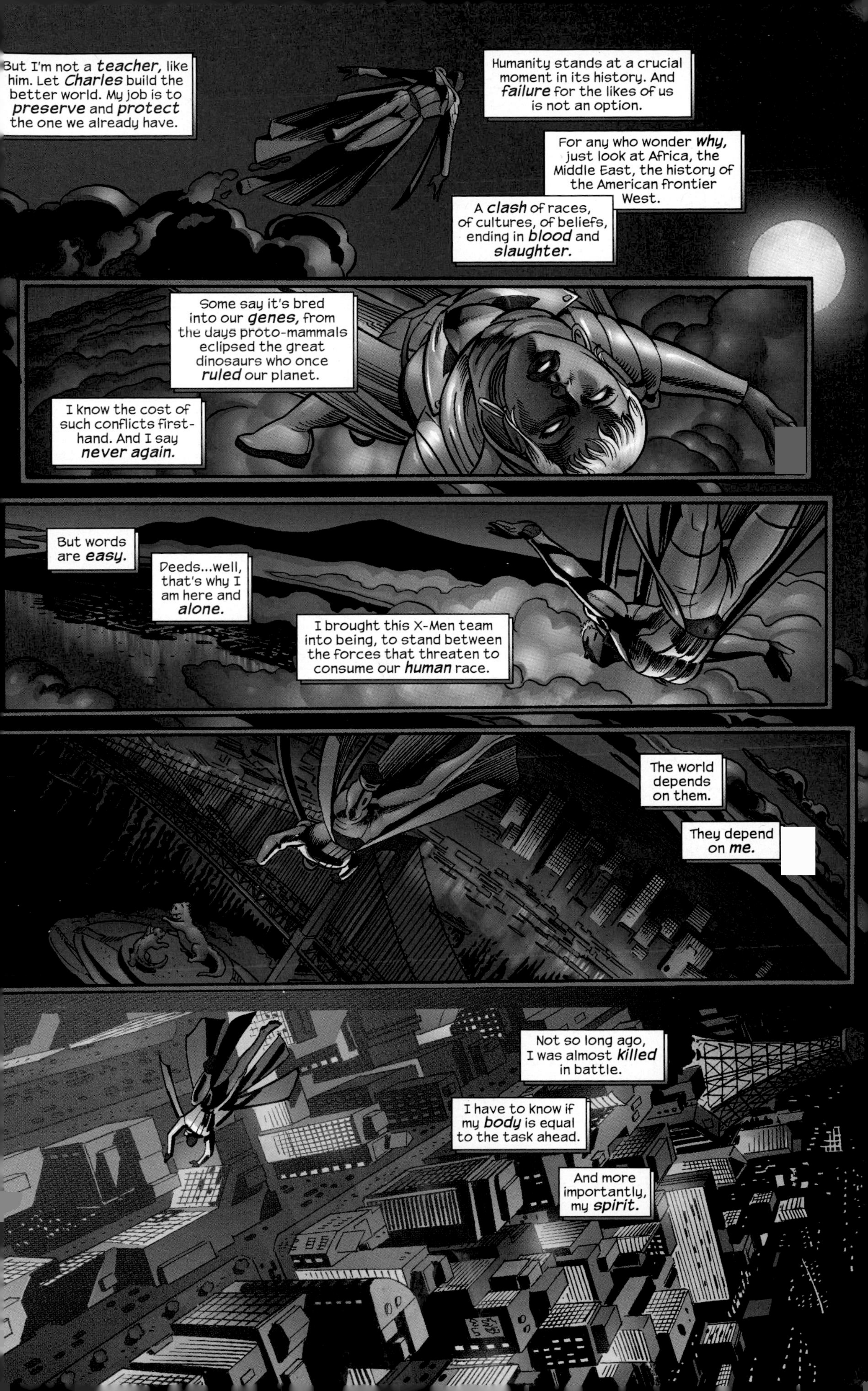
But I'm not a teacher, like him. Let Charles build the better world. My job is to preserve and protect the one we already have.
Humanity stands at a crucial moment in its history. And failure for the likes of us is not an option.
For any who wonder why, just look at Africa, the Middle East, the history of the American frontier West.
A clash of races, of cultures, of beliefs, ending in blood and slaughter.
Some say it's bred into our genes, from the days proto-mammals eclipsed the great dinosaurs who once ruled our planet.
I know the cost of such conflicts first-hand. And I say never again.
But words are easy.
Deeds...well, that's why I am here and alone.
I brought this X-Men team into being, to stand between the forces that threaten to consume our human race.
The world depends on them.
They depend on me.
Not so long ago, I was almost killed in battle.
I have to know if my body is equal to the task ahead.
And more importantly, my spirit.

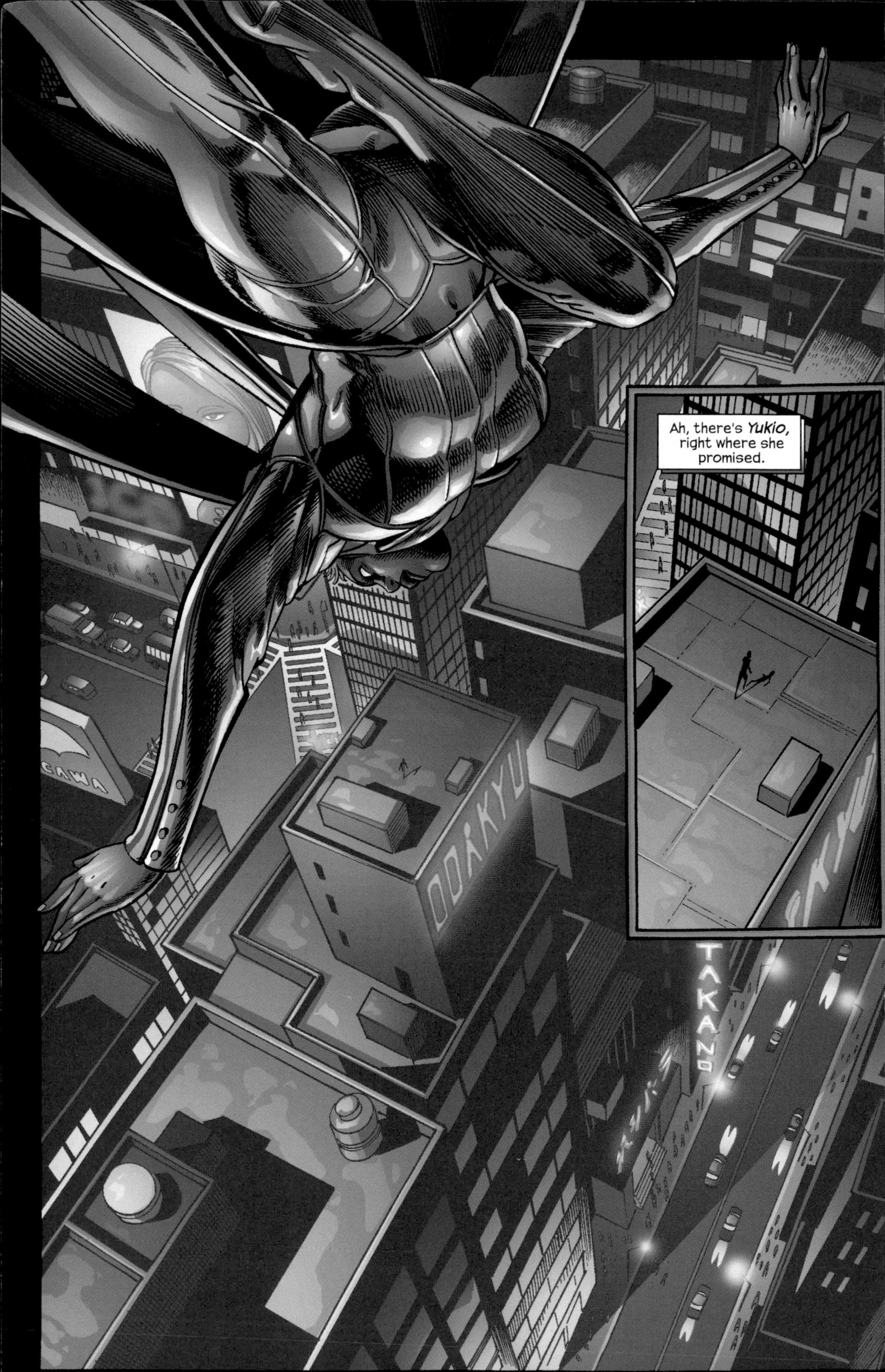
Ah, there's YUKIO, right where she promised.
ODAKYU
TAKANO

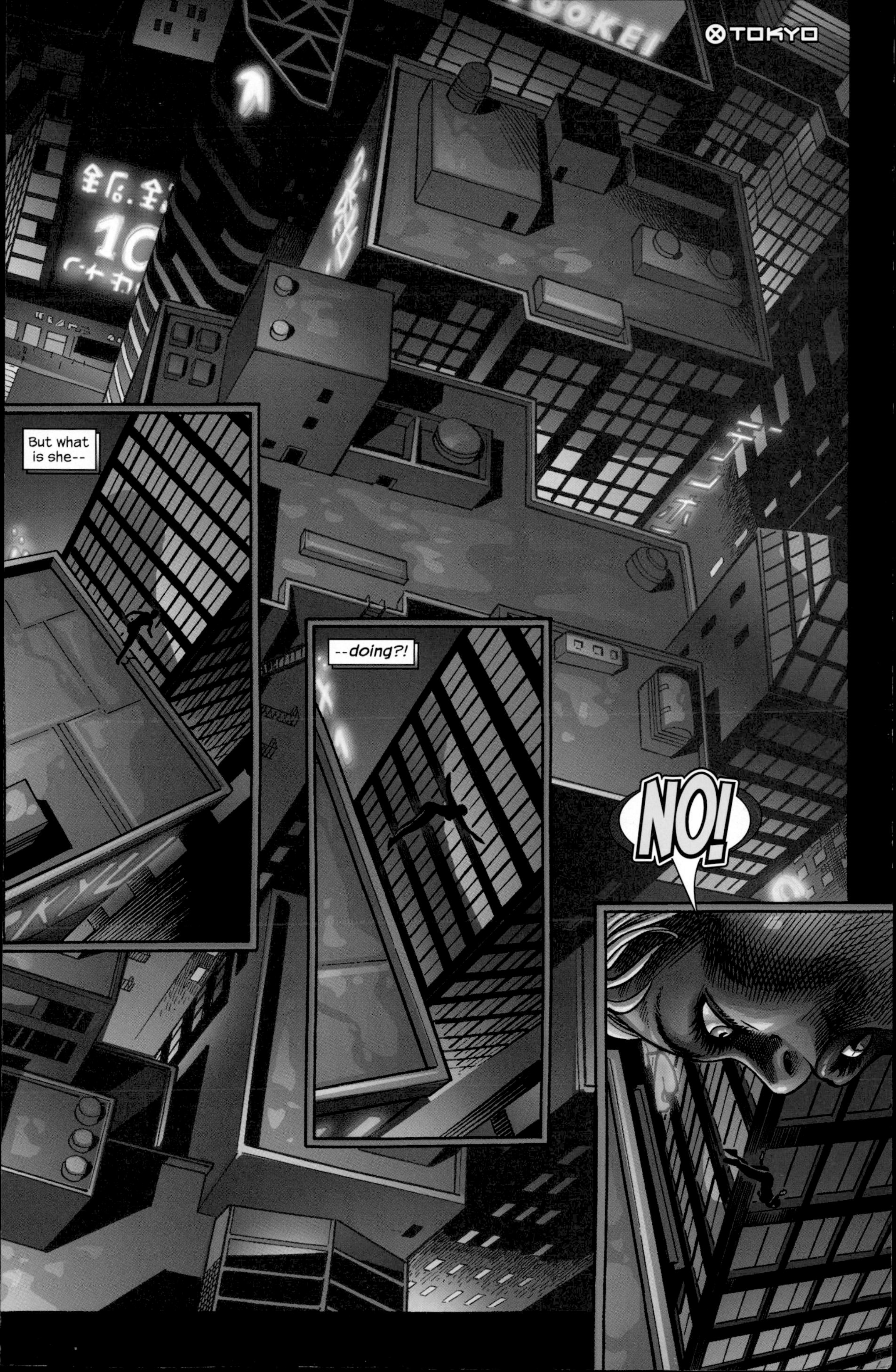
TOKYO
But what is she--
--doing?!
NO!

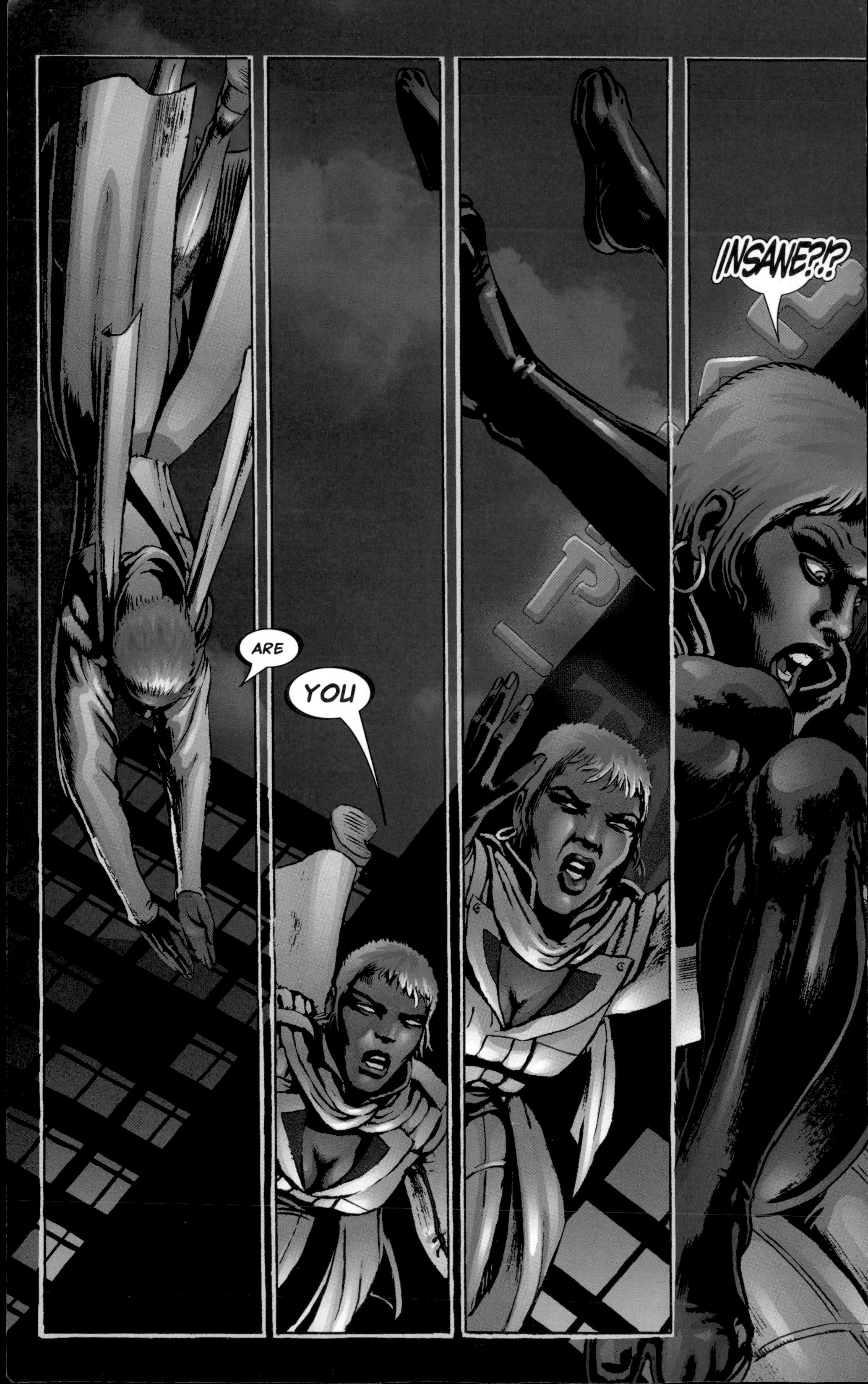
ARE
YOU
INSANE?!?

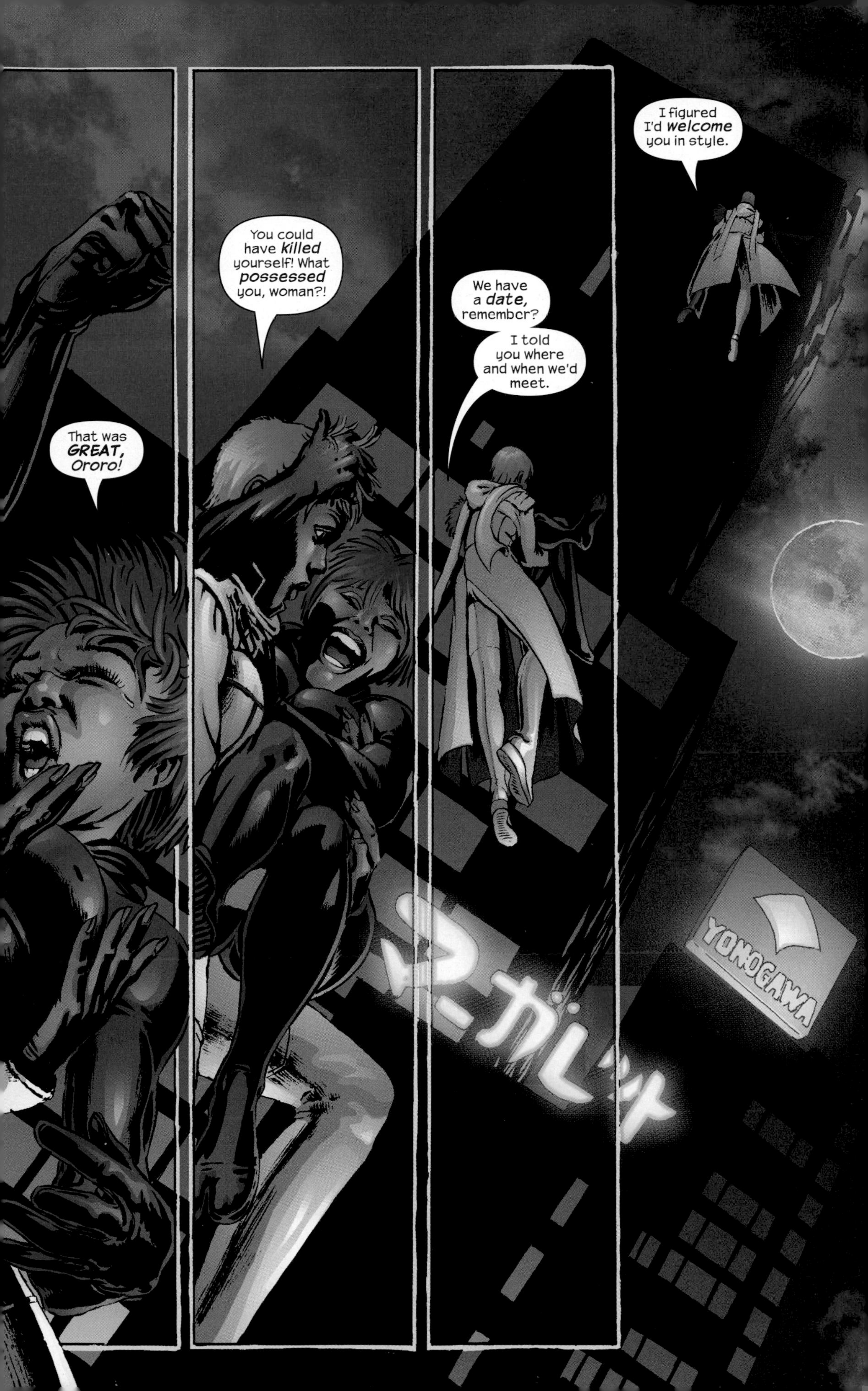

That was **GREAT,** *Ororo!*
You could have ***killed*** yourself! What ***possessed*** you, woman?!
We have a ***date,*** remember?
I told you where and when we'd meet.
I figured I'd ***welcome*** you in style.
YONOGAWA

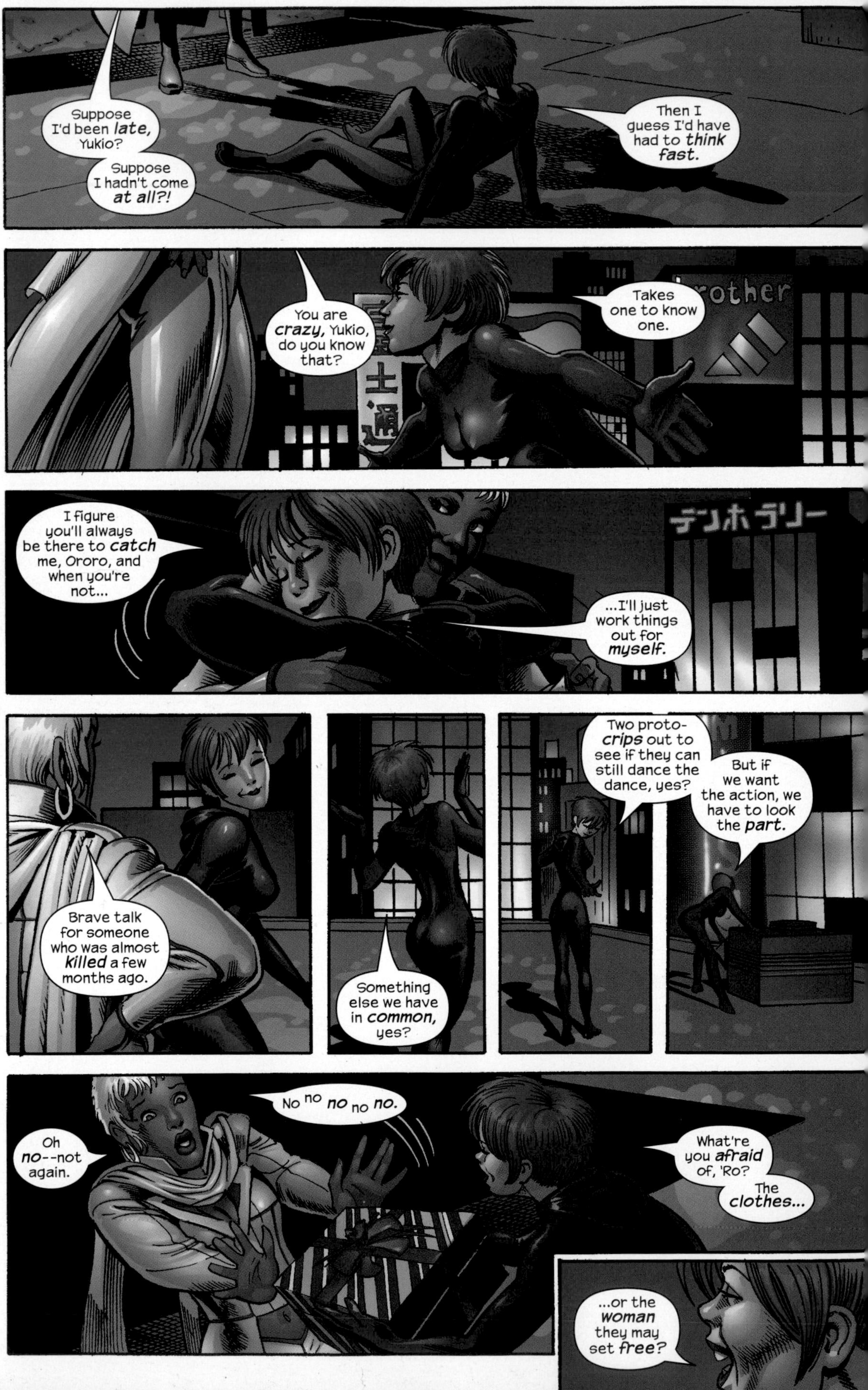
Suppose I'd been *late,* Yukio?
Suppose I hadn't come *at all?!*
Then I guess I'd have had to *think fast.*
You are *crazy,* Yukio, do you know that?
Takes one to know one.
富士通
I figure you'll always be there to *catch* me, Ororo, and when you're not...
...I'll just work things out for *myself.*
Brave talk for someone who was almost *killed* a few months ago.
Something else we have in *common,* yes?
Two proto-*crips* out to see if they can still dance the dance, yes?
But if we want the action, we have to look the *part.*
No no *no* no *no.*
Oh *no*--not again.
What're you *afraid* of, 'Ro?
The *clothes...*
...or the *woman* they may set *free?*

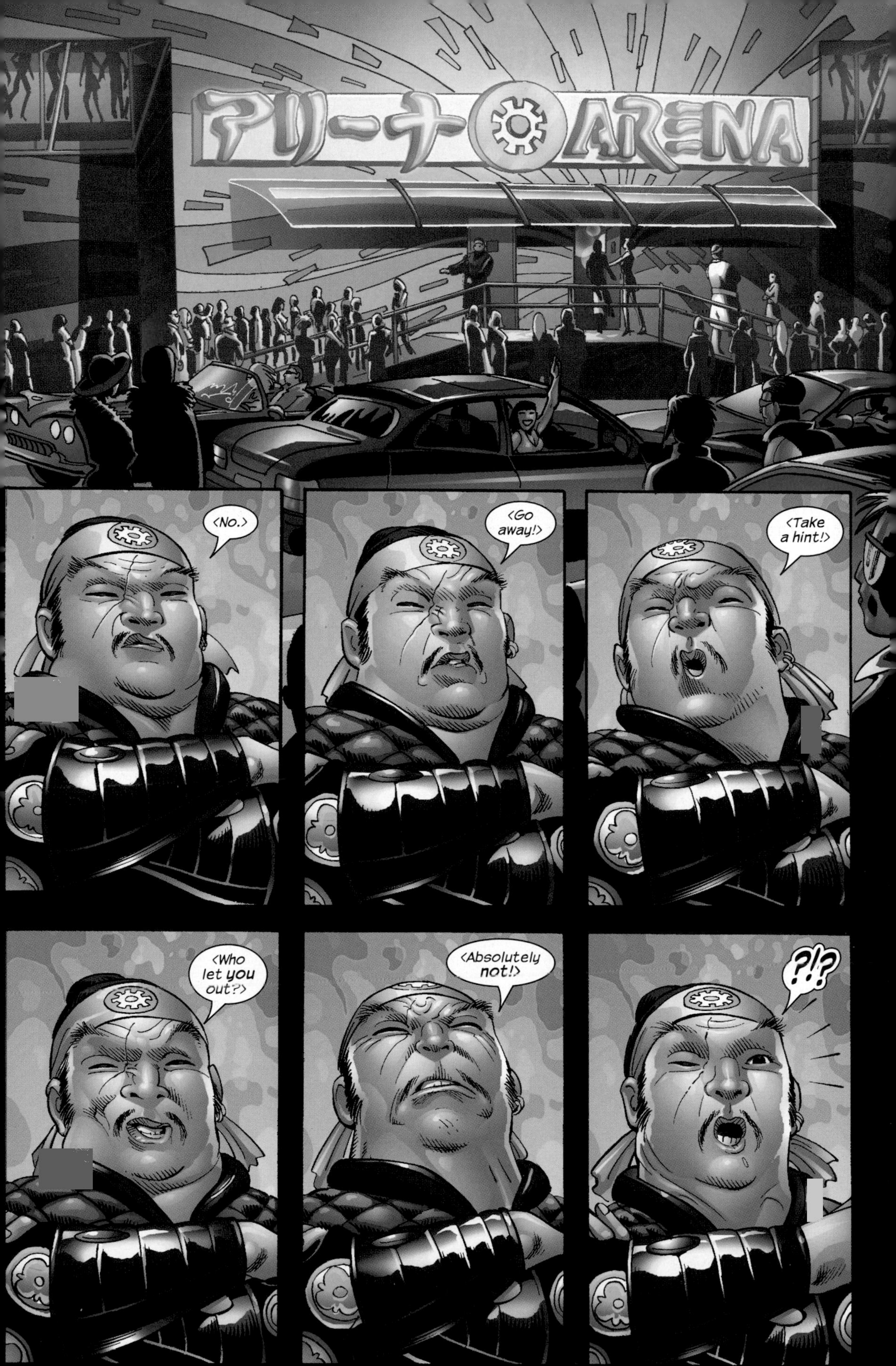

アリーナ ARENA
<No.>
<Go away!>
<Take a hint!>
<Who let you out?>
<Absolutely not!>
?!?

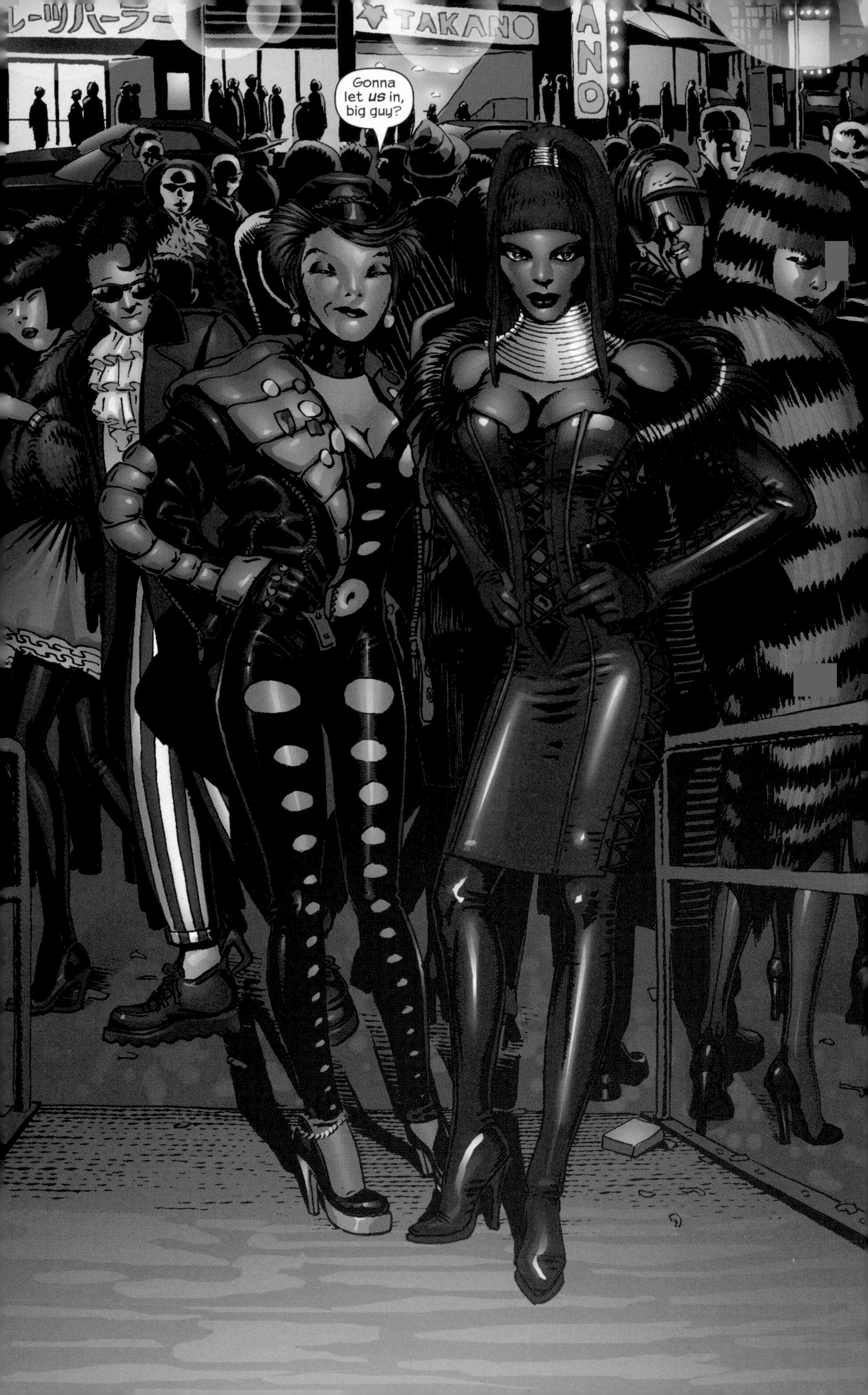
TAKANO
Gonna let *us* in, big guy?

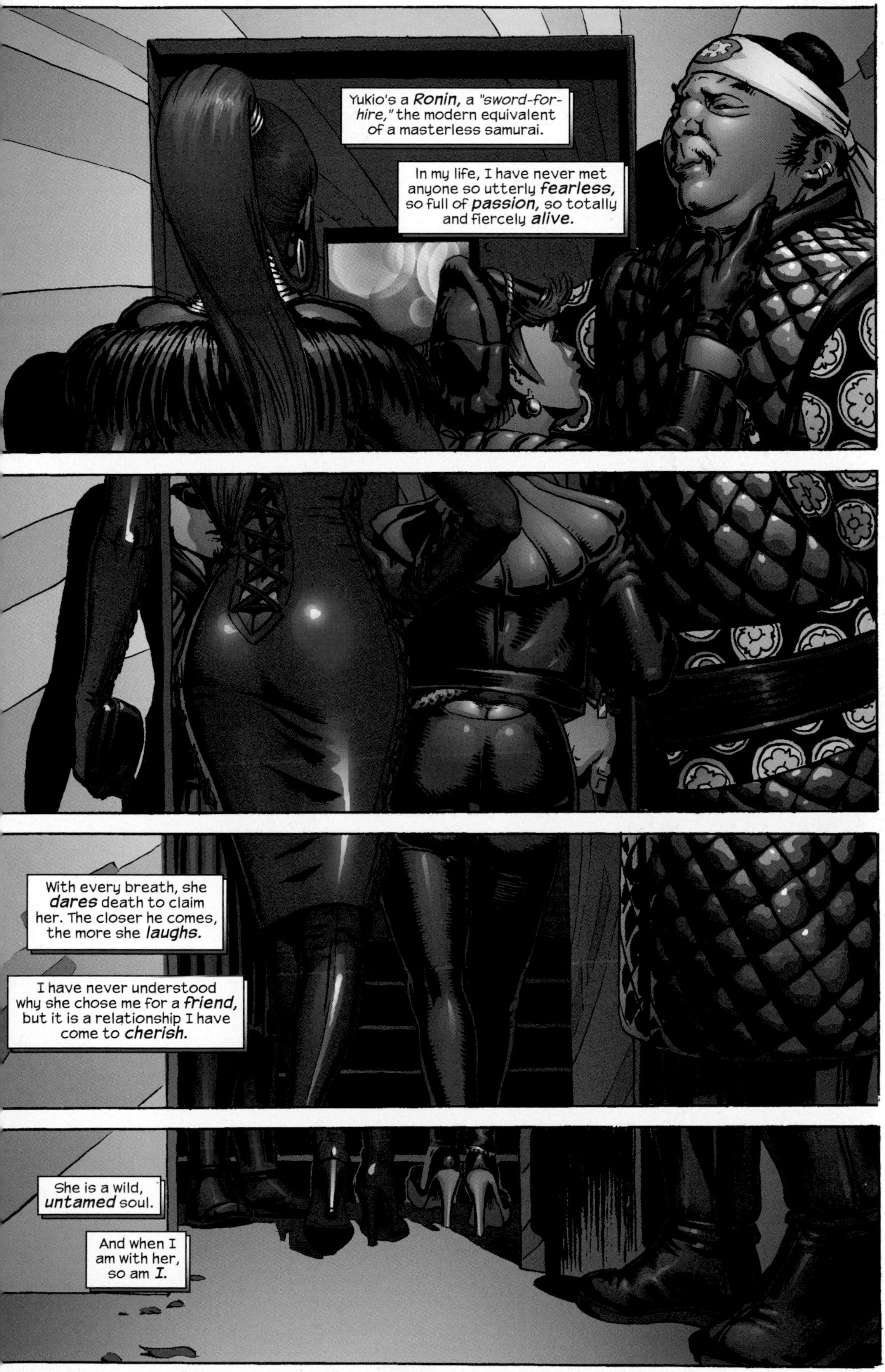

Yukio's a Ronin, a "sword-for-hire," the modern equivalent of a masterless samurai.
In my life, I have never met anyone so utterly fearless, so full of passion, so totally and fiercely alive.
With every breath, she dares death to claim her. The closer he comes, the more she laughs.
I have never understood why she chose me for a friend, but it is a relationship I have come to cherish.
She is a wild, untamed soul.
And when I am with her, so am I.

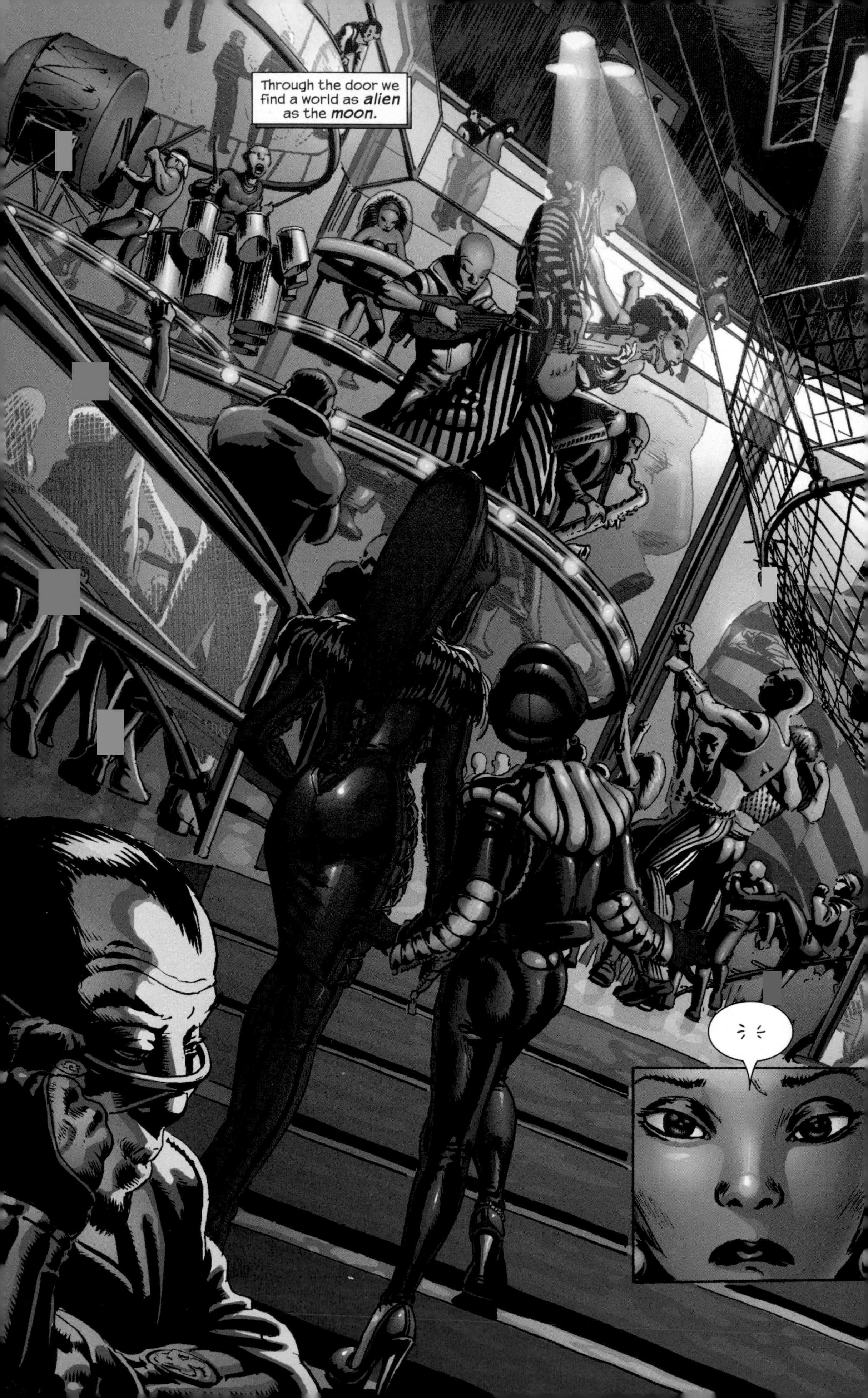
Through the door we find a world as alien as the moon.
!

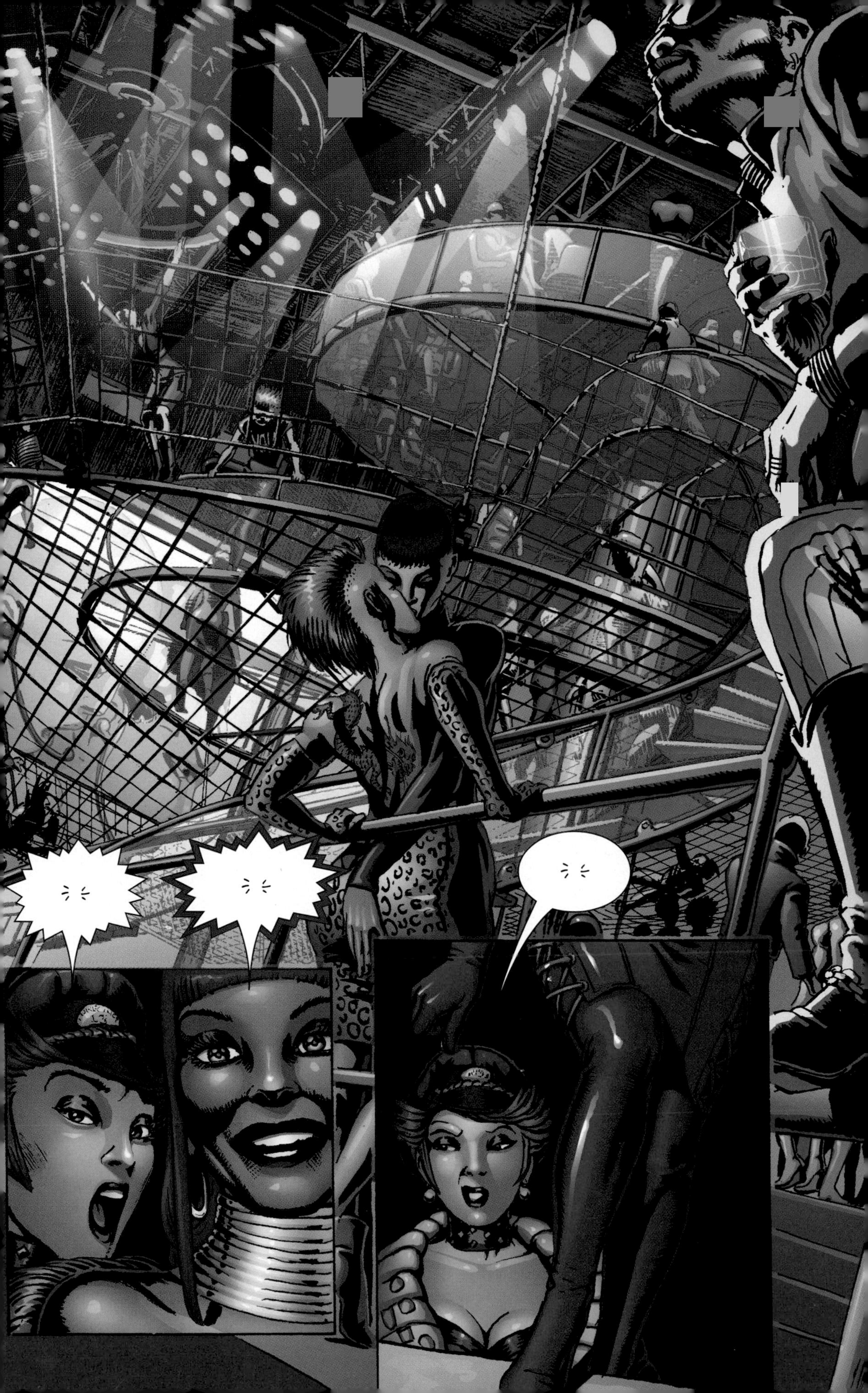

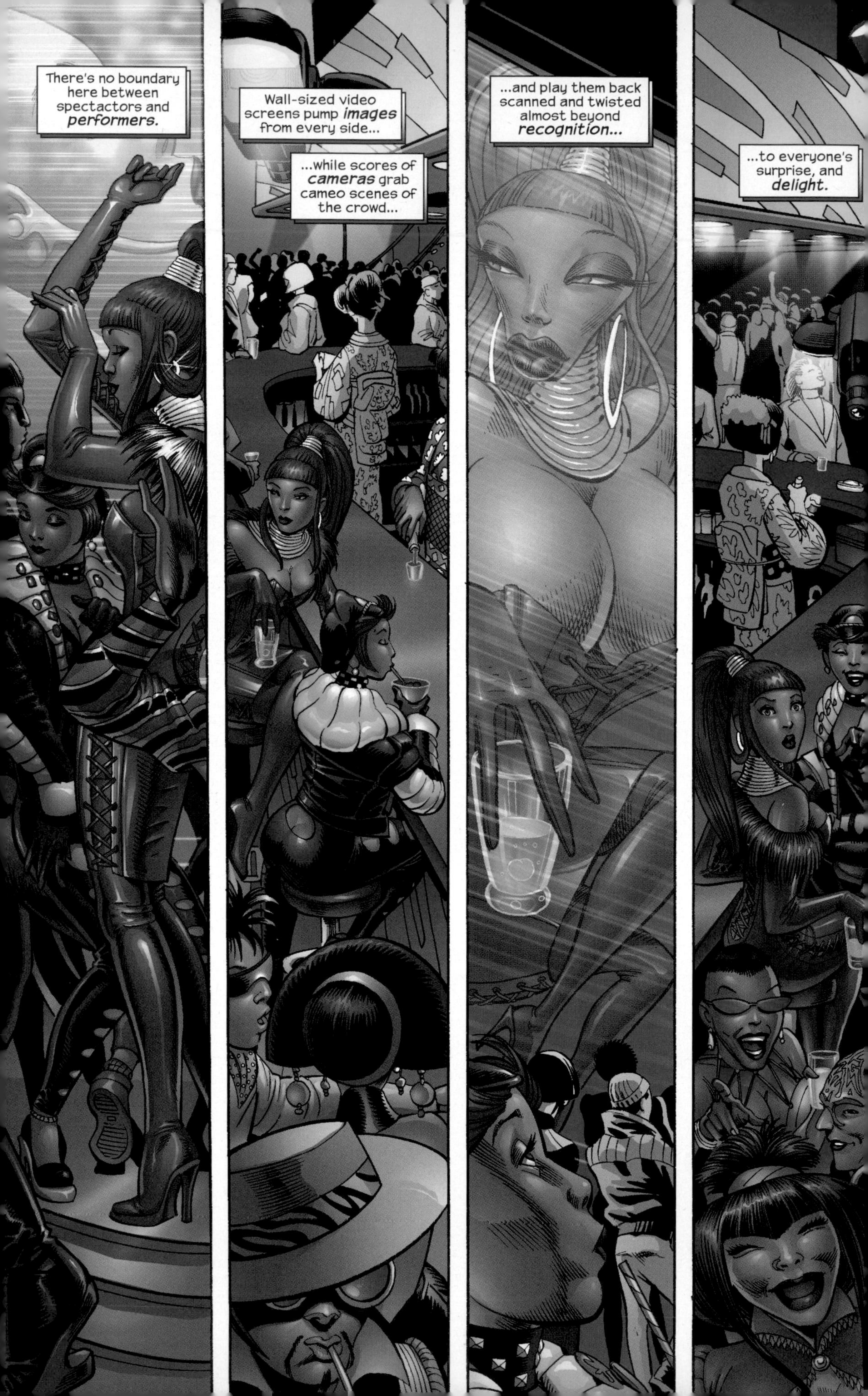
There's no boundary here between spectactors and *performers.*
Wall-sized video screens pump *images* from every side...
...while scores of *cameras* grab cameo scenes of the crowd...
...and play them back scanned and twisted almost beyond *recognition...*
...to everyone's surprise, and *delight.*

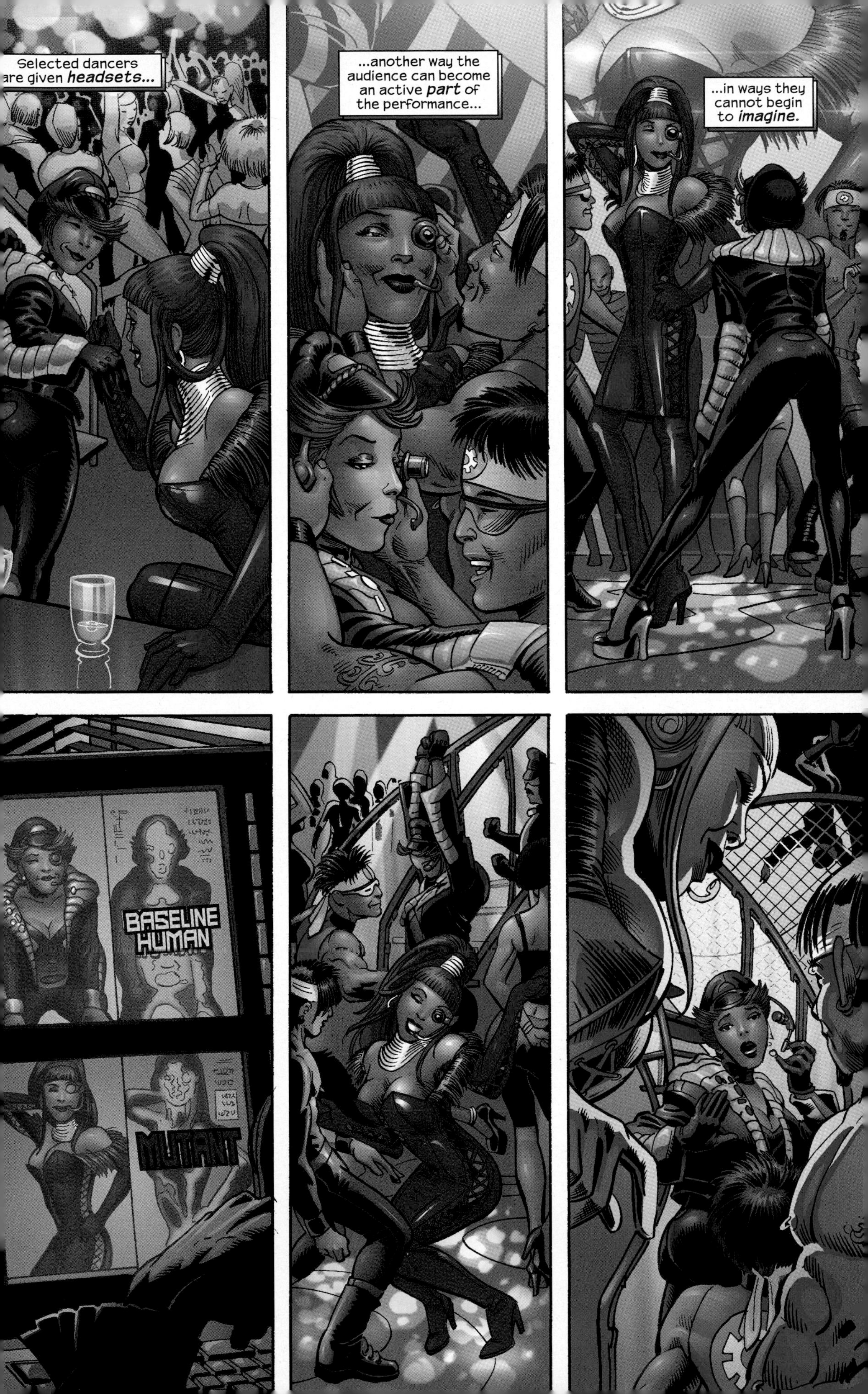
Selected dancers are given headsets...
...another way the audience can become an active part of the performance...
...in ways they cannot begin to imagine.
BASELINE HUMAN
MUTANT

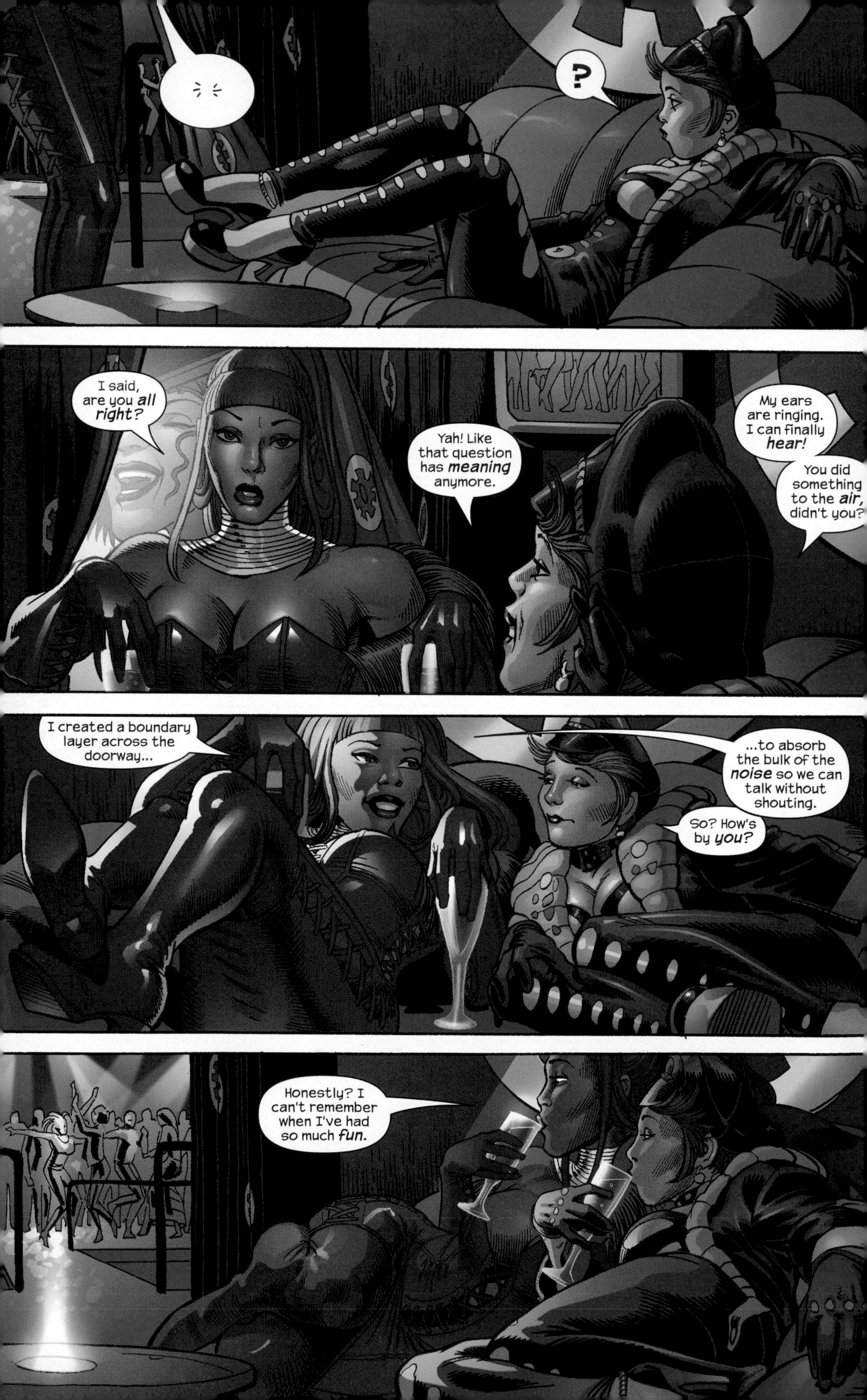
?
I said, are you *all right?*
Yah! Like that question has *meaning* anymore.
My ears are ringing. I can finally *hear!*
You did something to the *air,* didn't you?
I created a boundary layer across the doorway...
...to absorb the bulk of the *noise* so we can talk without shouting.
So? How's by *you?*
Honestly? I can't remember when I've had so much *fun.*

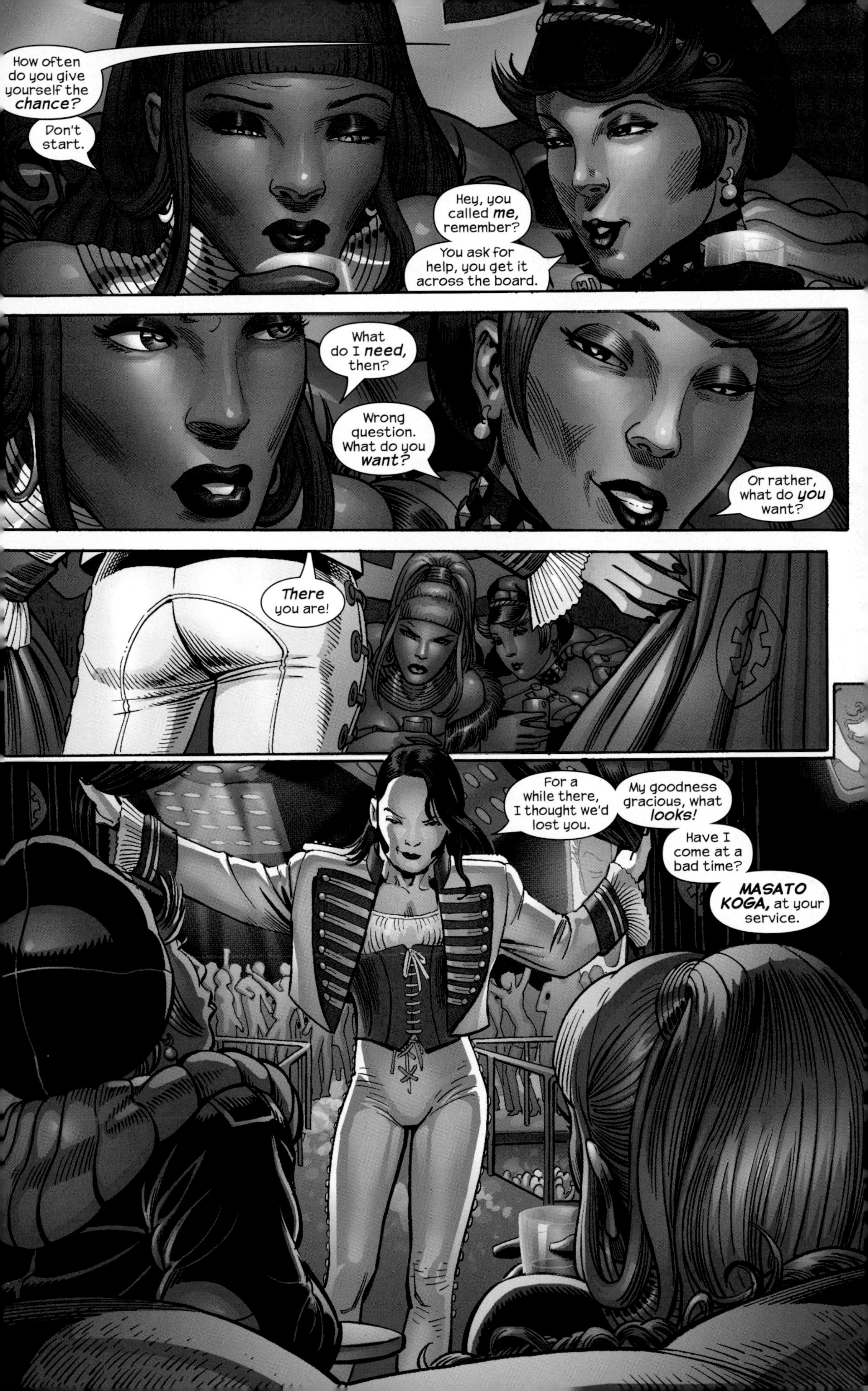
How often do you give yourself the *chance?*
Don't start.
Hey, you called *me,* remember?
You ask for help, you get it across the board.
What do I *need,* then?
Wrong question. What do you *want?*
Or rather, what do *you* want?
There you are!
For a while there, I thought we'd lost you.
My goodness gracious, what *looks!*
Have I come at a bad time?
MASATO KOGA, at your service.

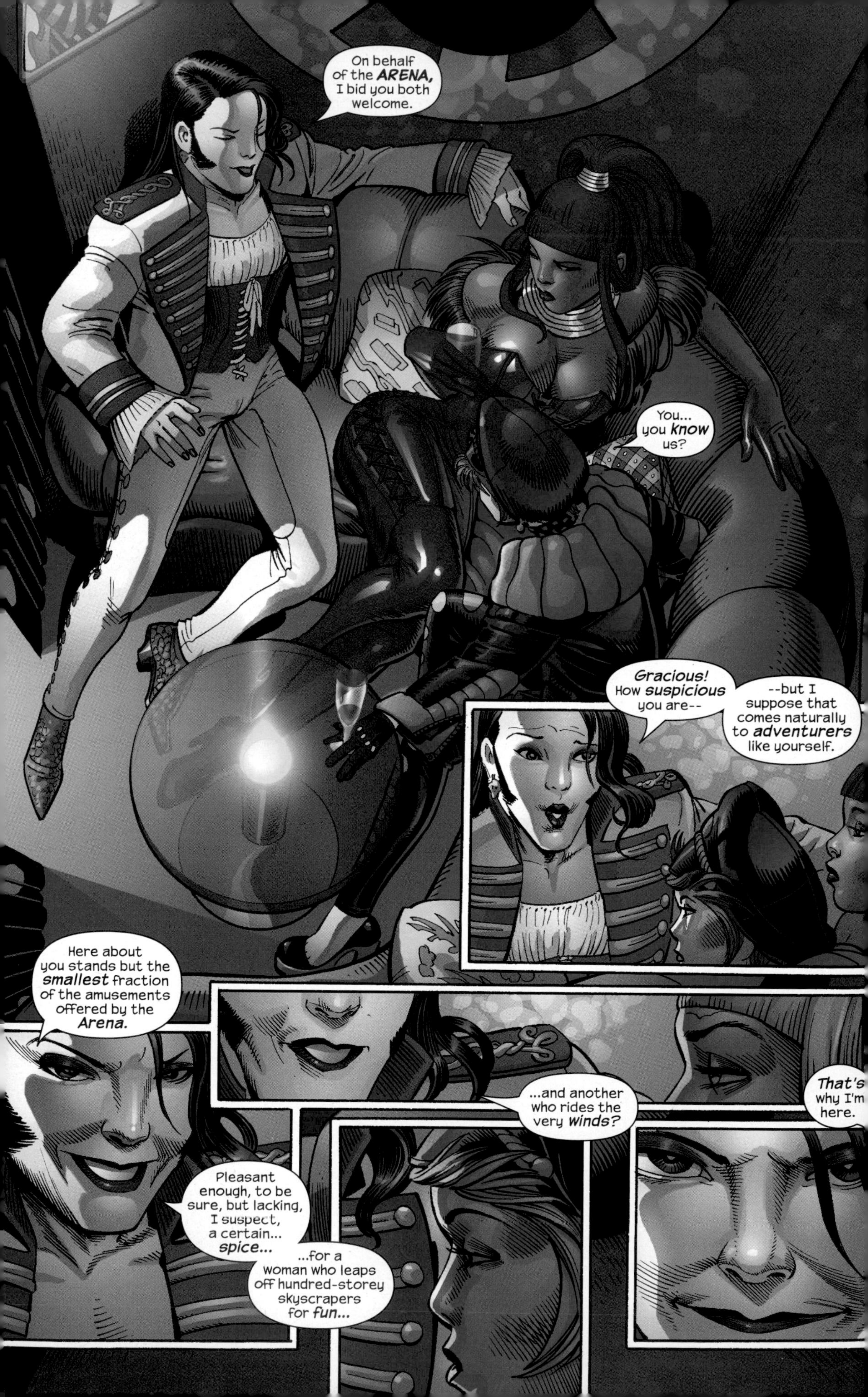
On behalf of the ARENA, I bid you both welcome.
You... you know us?
Gracious! How suspicious you are--
--but I suppose that comes naturally to adventurers like yourself.
Here about you stands but the smallest fraction of the amusements offered by the Arena.
Pleasant enough, to be sure, but lacking, I suspect, a certain... spice...
...for a woman who leaps off hundred-storey skyscrapers for fun...
...and another who rides the very winds?
That's why I'm here.

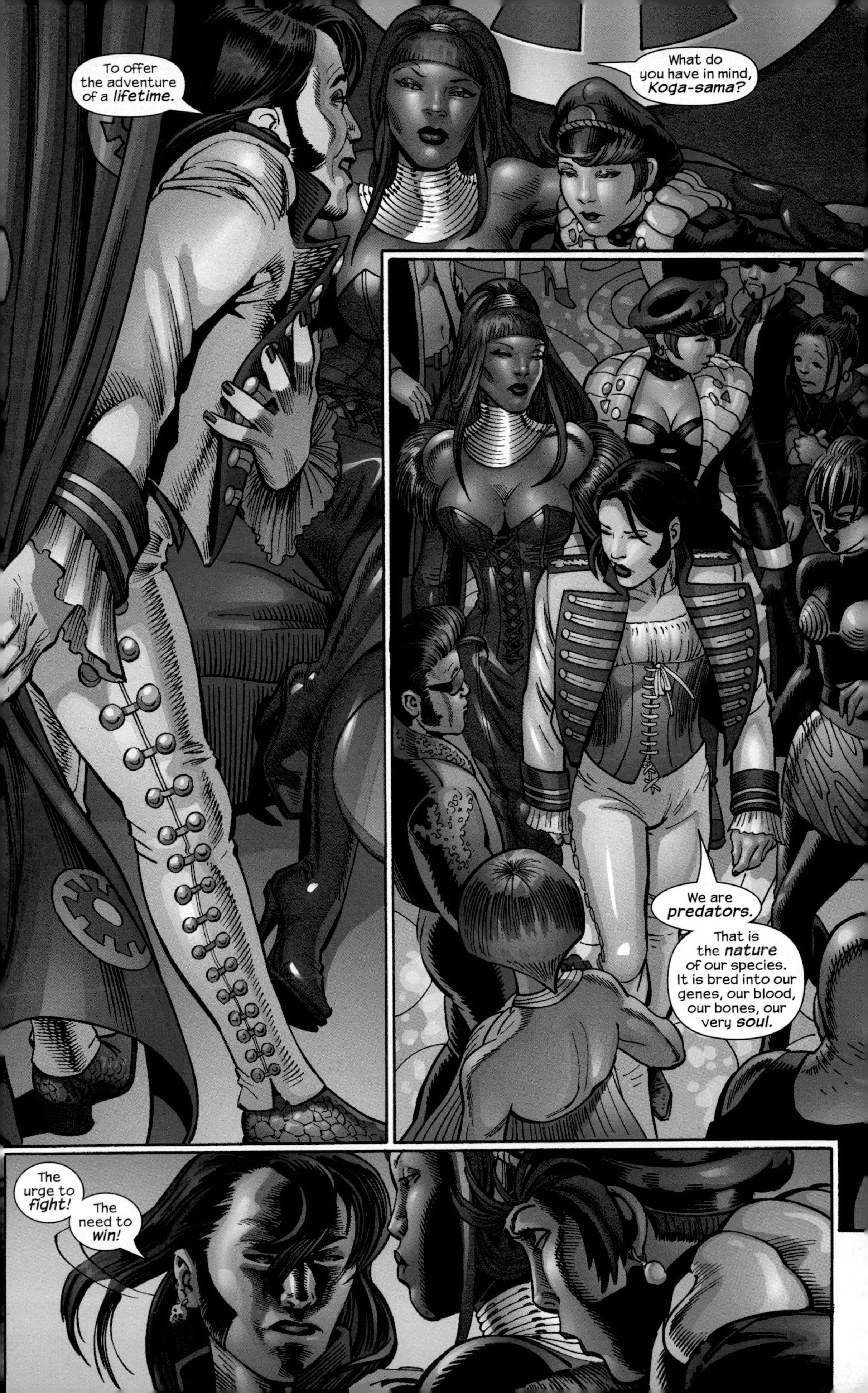
To offer the adventure of a *lifetime.*
What do you have in mind, *Koga-sama?*
We are *predators.*
That is the *nature* of our species. It is bred into our genes, our blood, our bones, our very *soul.*
The urge to *fight!*
The need to *win!*

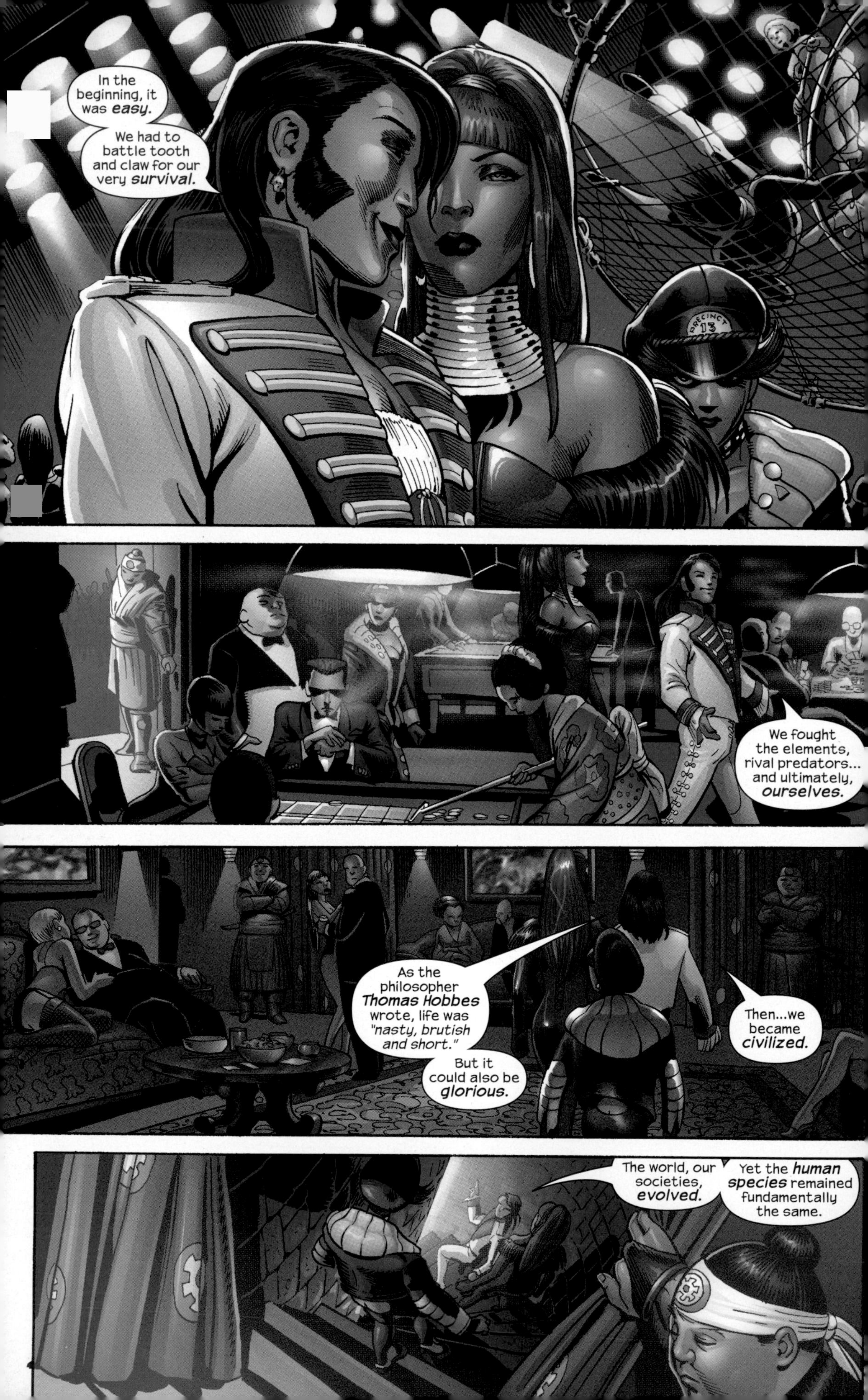

In the beginning, it was *easy.*
We had to battle tooth and claw for our very *survival.*
PRECINCT 13
We fought the elements, rival predators... and ultimately, *ourselves.*
As the philosopher **Thomas Hobbes** wrote, life was *"nasty, brutish and short."*
But it could also be *glorious.*
Then...we became *civilized.*
The world, our societies, *evolved.*
Yet the *human species* remained fundamentally the same.

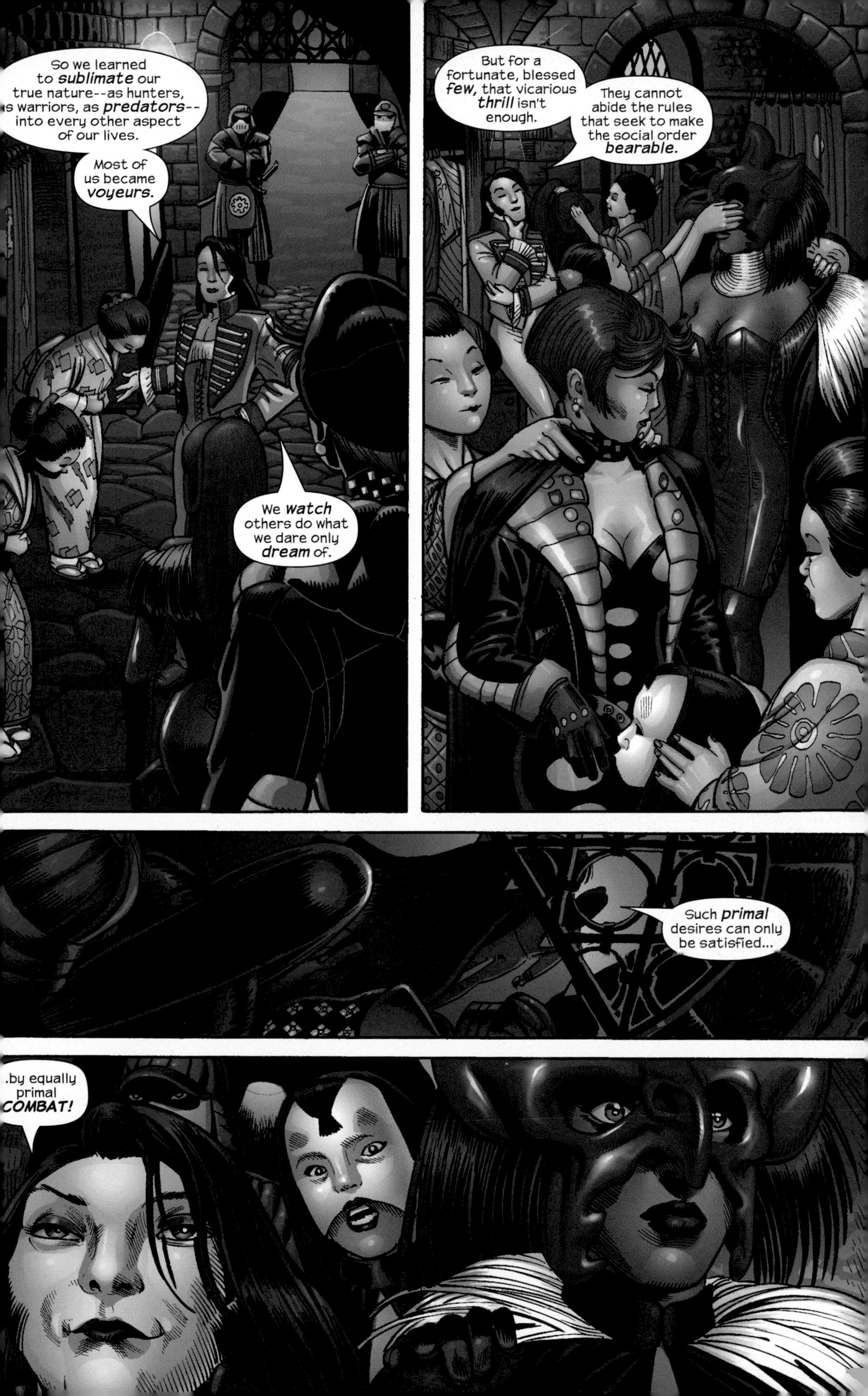
So we learned to *sublimate* our true nature--as hunters, as warriors, as *predators*--into every other aspect of our lives.
Most of us became *voyeurs.*
We *watch* others do what we dare only *dream* of.
But for a fortunate, blessed *few,* that vicarious *thrill* isn't enough.
They cannot abide the rules that seek to make the social order *bearable.*
Such *primal* desires can only be satisfied...
...by equally primal *COMBAT!*

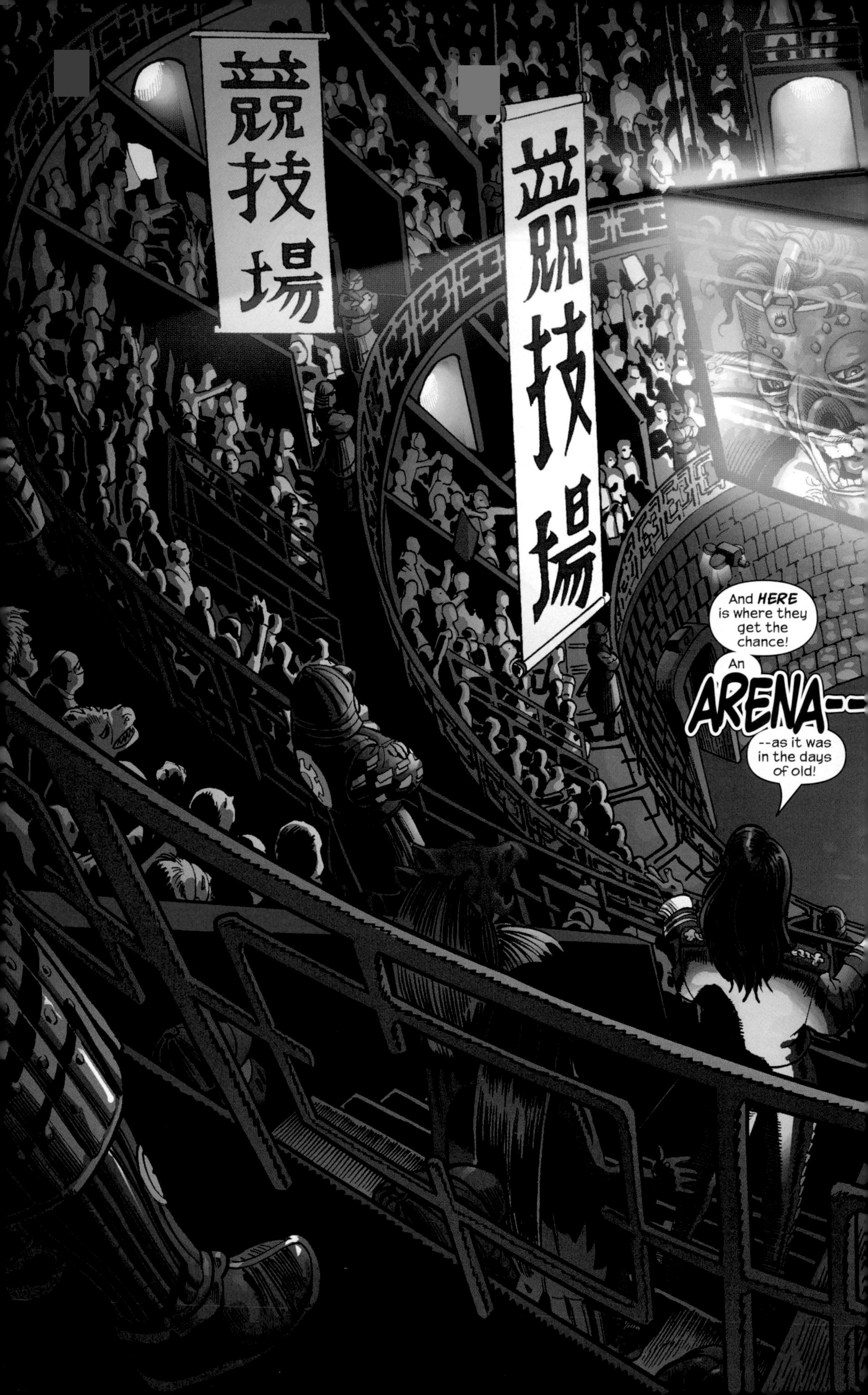
競技場
競技場
And HERE is where they get the chance!
An ARENA--
--as it was in the days of old!

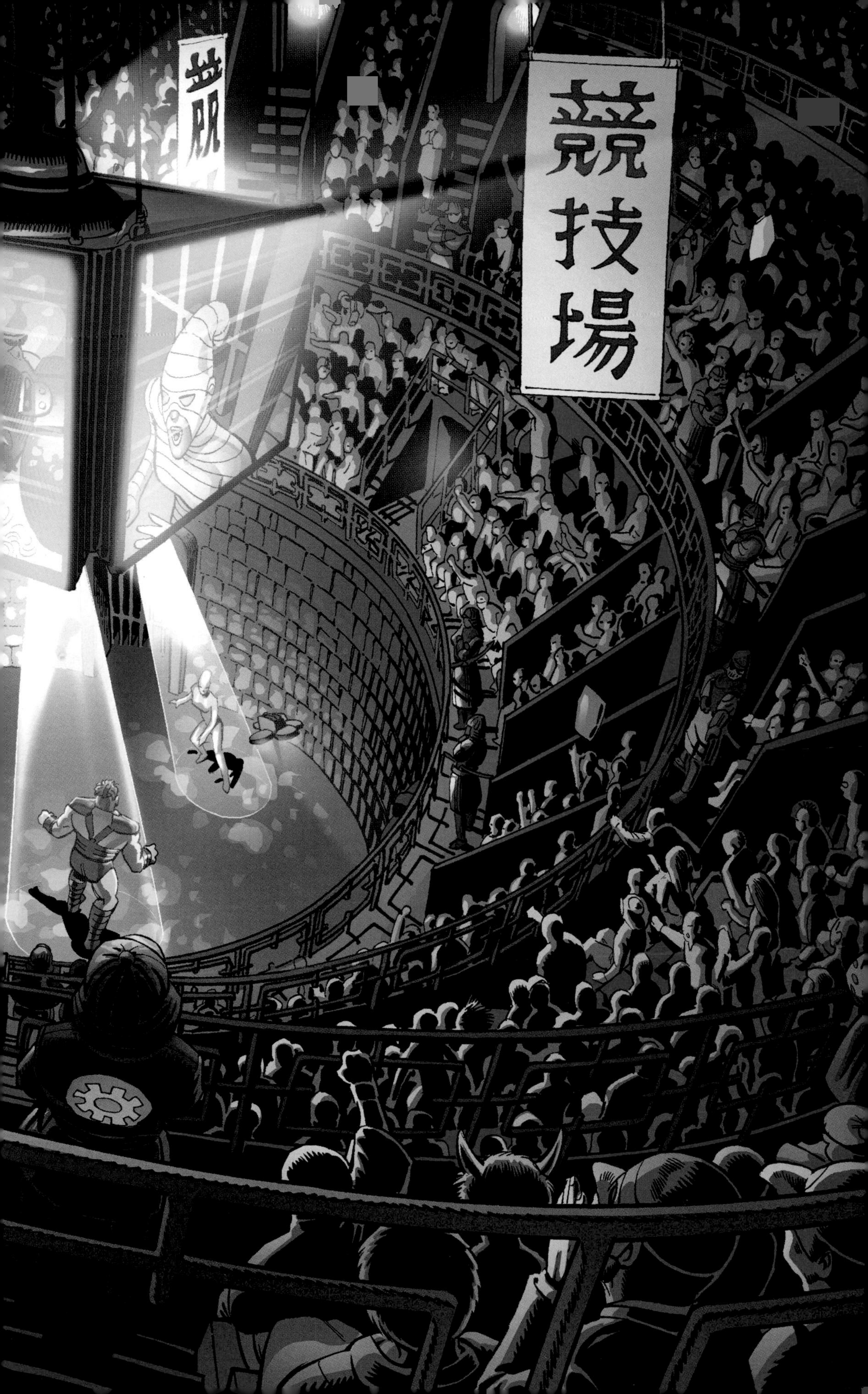
競技場

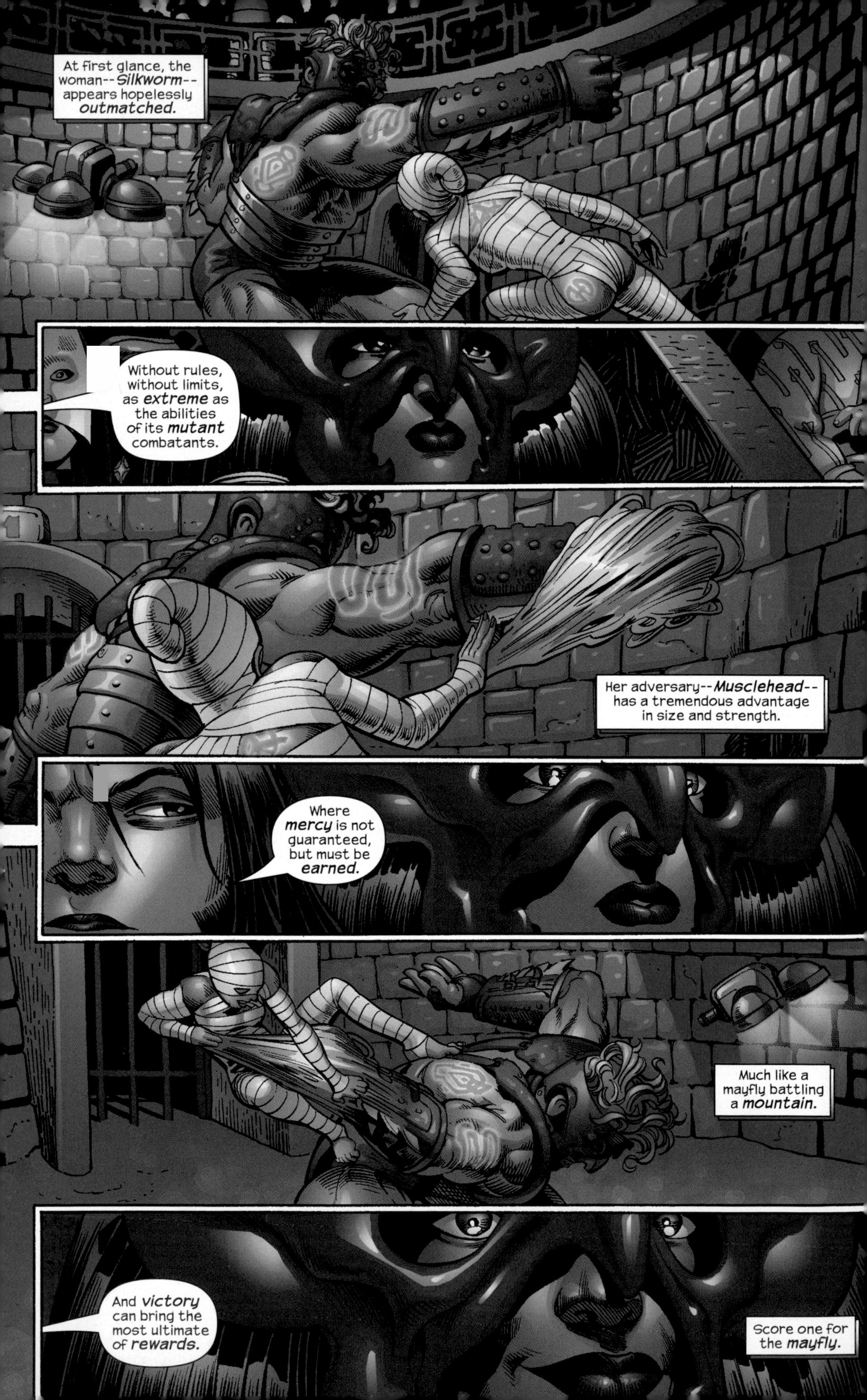
At first glance, the woman--*Silkworm*--appears hopelessly *outmatched.*
Without rules, without limits, as *extreme* as the abilities of its *mutant* combatants.
Her adversary--*Musclehead*--has a tremendous advantage in size and strength.
Where *mercy* is not guaranteed, but must be *earned.*
Much like a mayfly battling a *mountain.*
And *victory* can bring the most ultimate of *rewards.*
Score one for the *mayfly.*

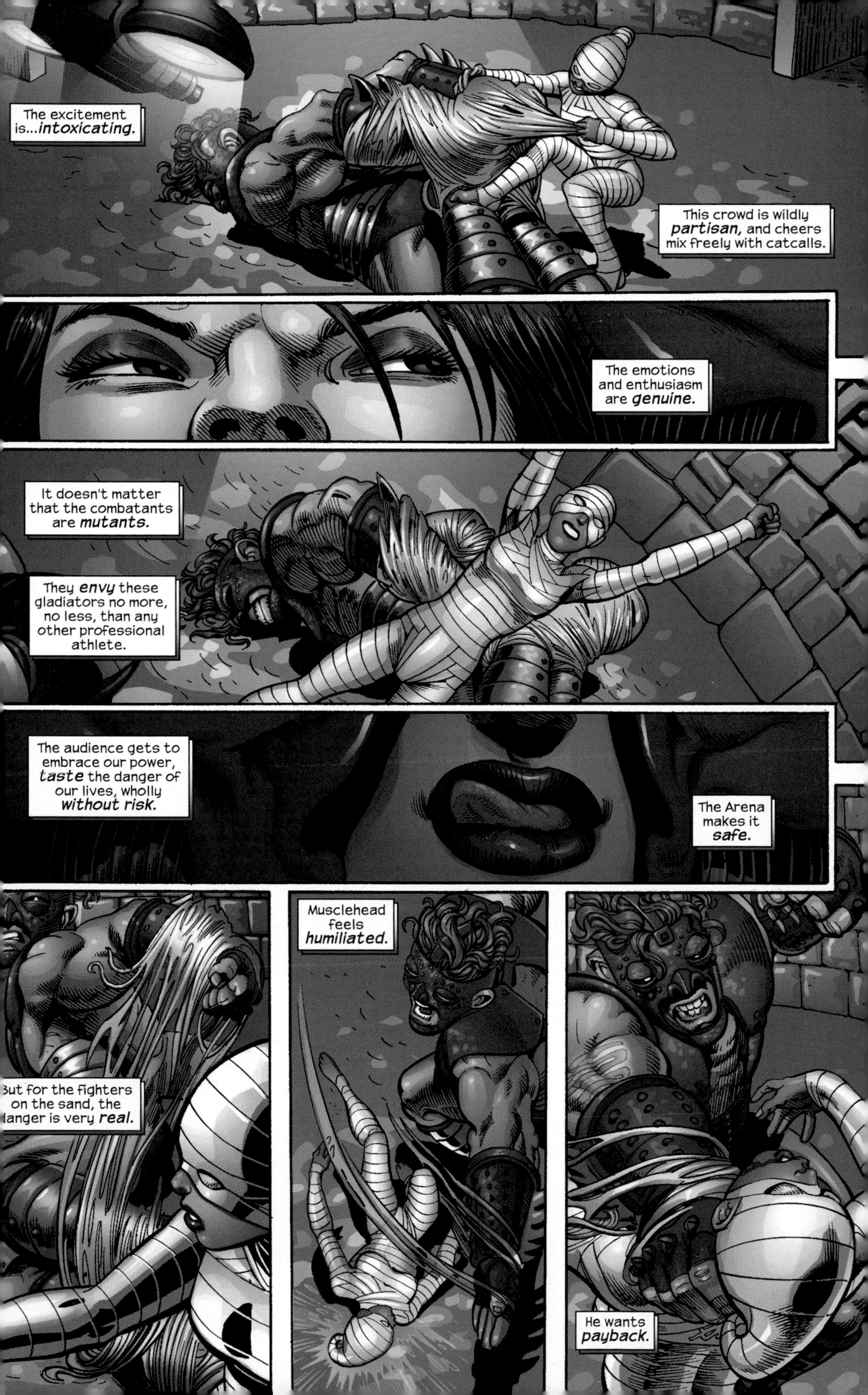
The excitement is...*intoxicating.*
This crowd is wildly *partisan,* and cheers mix freely with catcalls.
The emotions and enthusiasm are *genuine.*
It doesn't matter that the combatants are *mutants.*
They *envy* these gladiators no more, no less, than any other professional athlete.
The audience gets to embrace our power, *taste* the danger of our lives, wholly *without risk.*
The Arena makes it *safe.*
But for the fighters on the sand, the danger is very *real.*
Musclehead feels *humiliated.*
He wants *payback.*

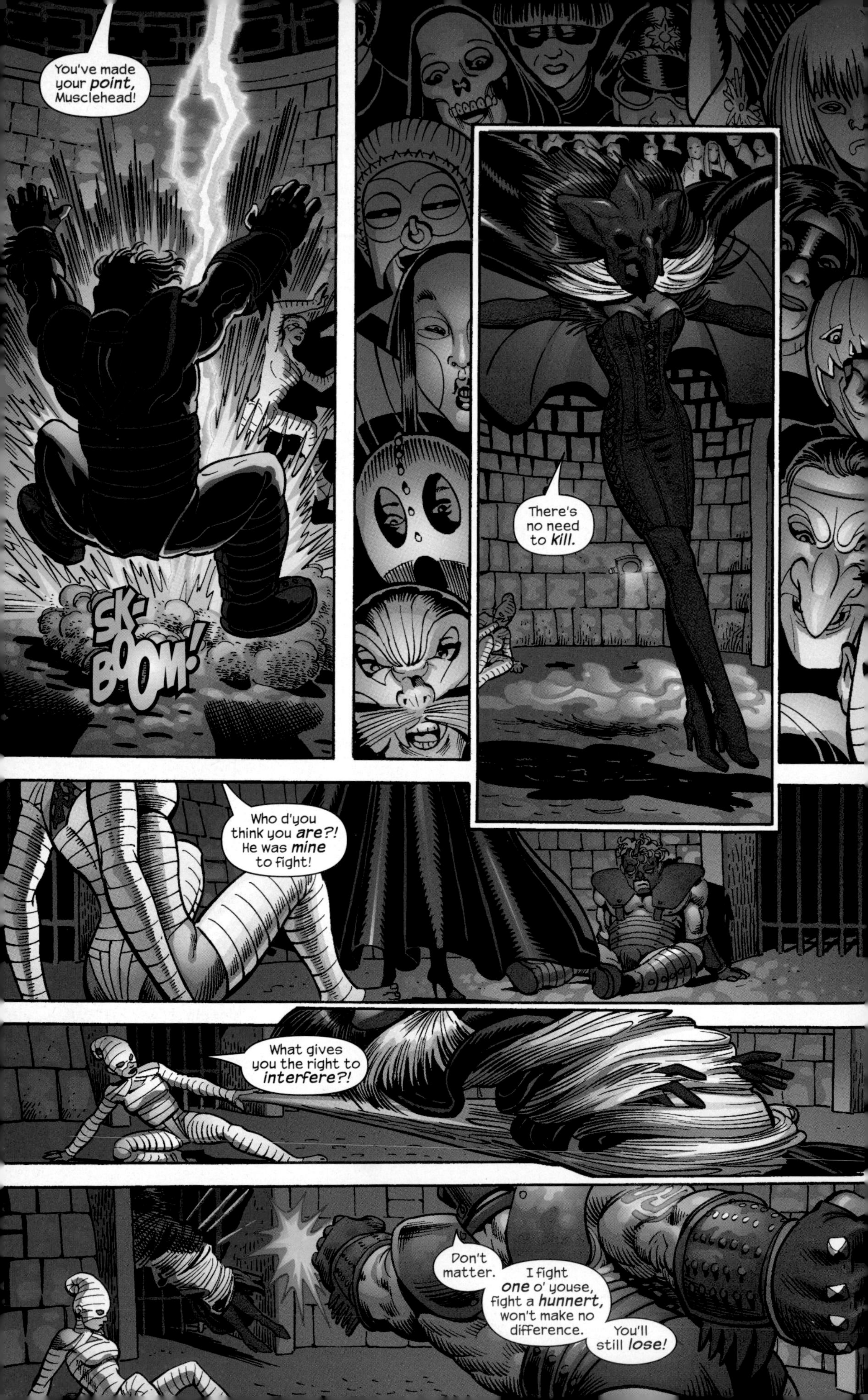

You've made your point, Musclehead!
SK-BOOM!
There's no need to kill.
Who d'you think you are?! He was mine to fight!
What gives you the right to interfere?!
Don't matter.
I fight one o' youse, fight a hunnert, won't make no difference.
You'll still lose!

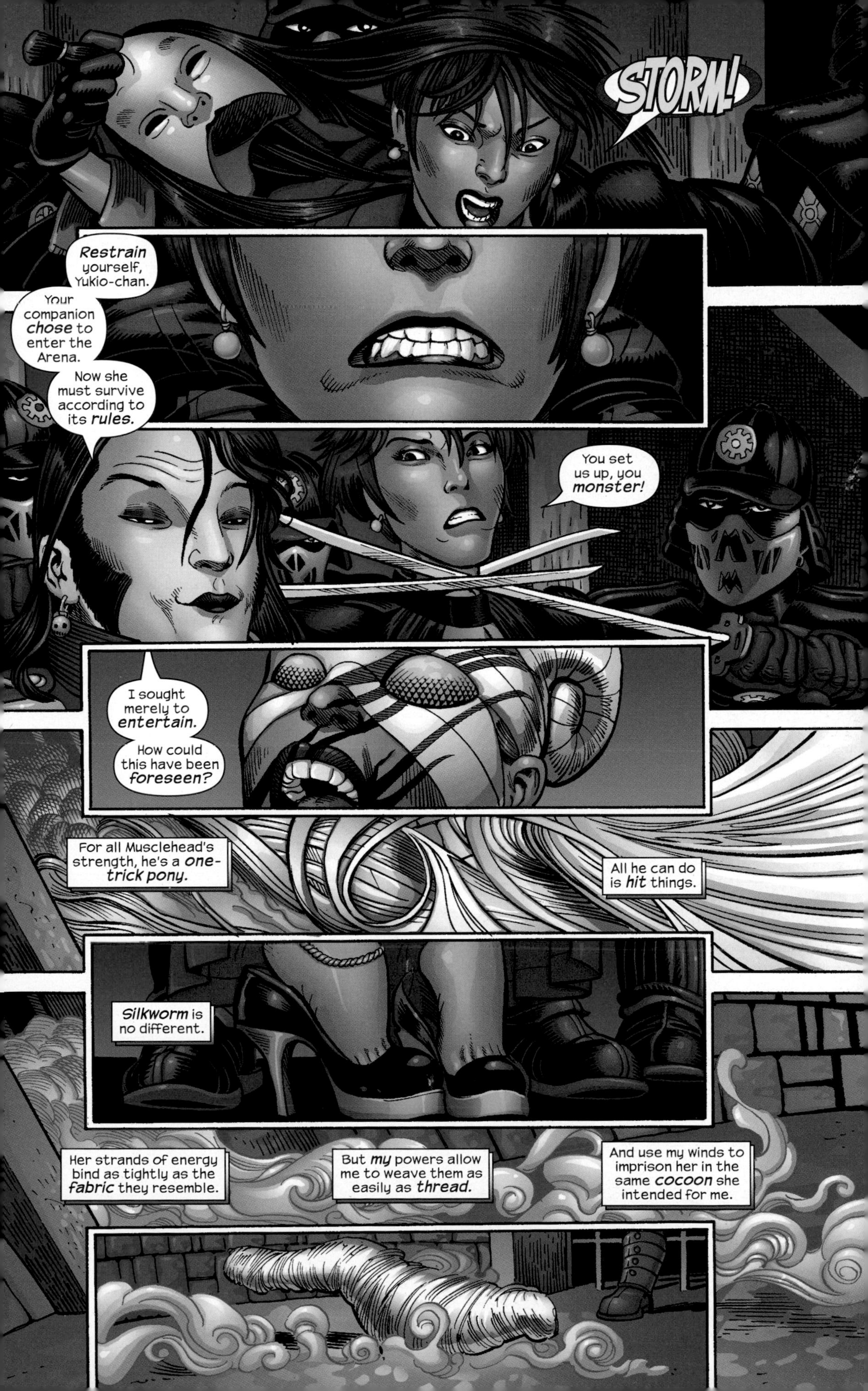
STORM!
Restrain yourself, Yukio-chan.
Your companion chose to enter the Arena.
Now she must survive according to its rules.
You set us up, you monster!
I sought merely to entertain.
How could this have been foreseen?
For all Musclehead's strength, he's a one-trick pony.
All he can do is hit things.
Silkworm is no different.
Her strands of energy bind as tightly as the fabric they resemble.
But my powers allow me to weave them as easily as thread.
And use my winds to imprison her in the same cocoon she intended for me.

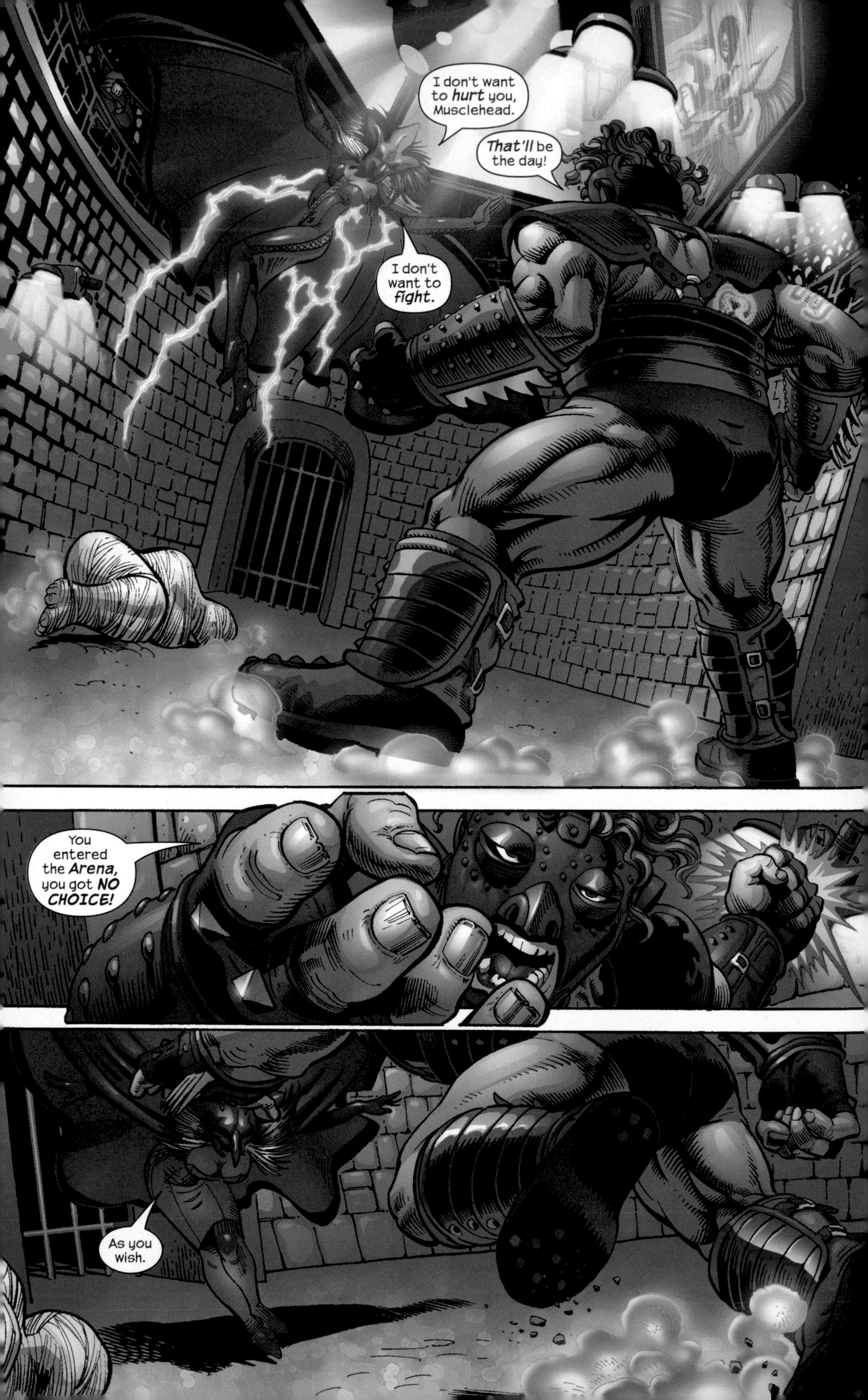
I don't want to *hurt* you, Musclehead.
That'll be the day!
I don't want to *fight*.
You entered the *Arena*, you got *NO CHOICE!*
As you wish.

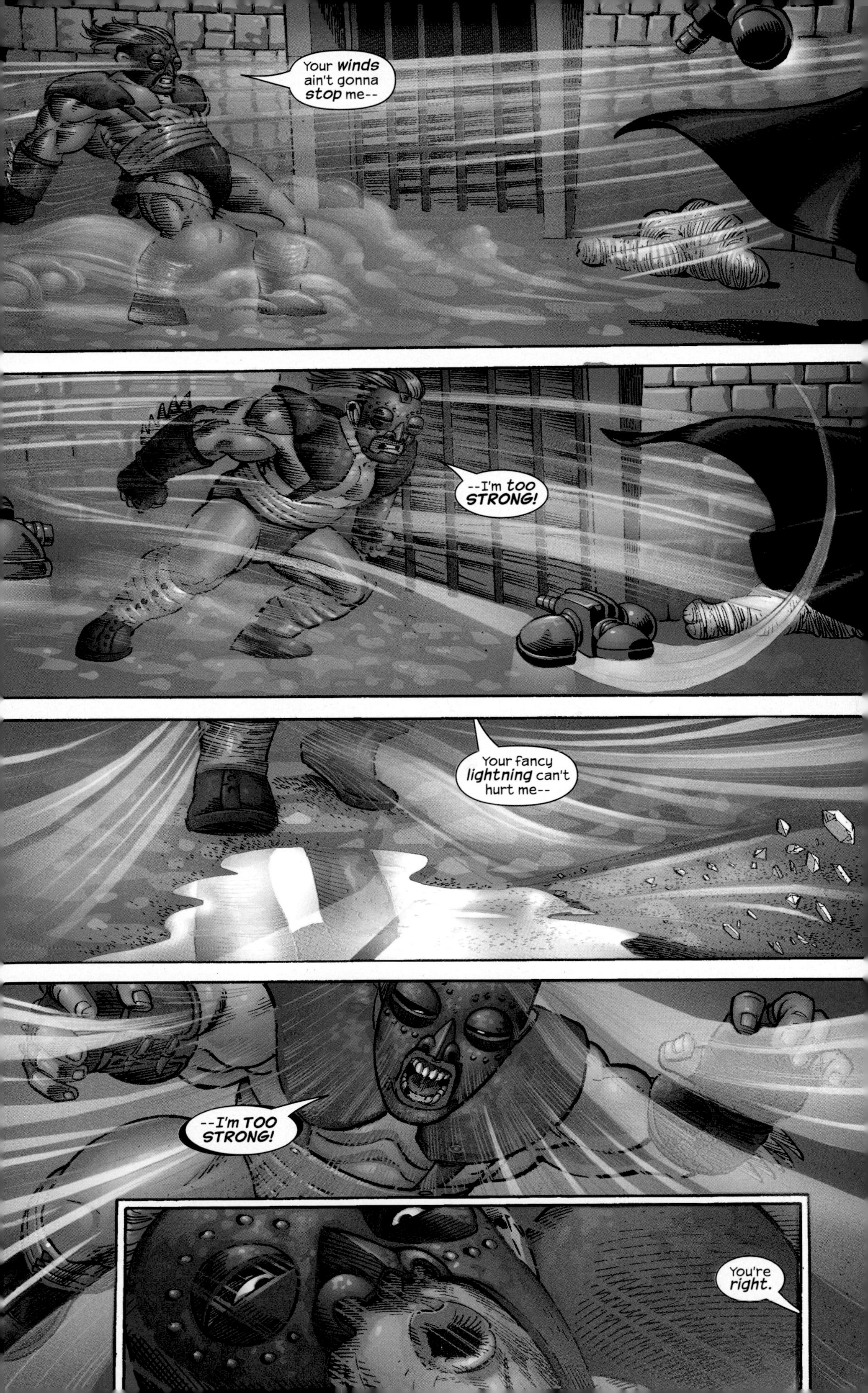
Your winds ain't gonna stop me--
--I'm too STRONG!
Your fancy lightning can't hurt me--
--I'm TOO STRONG!
You're right.

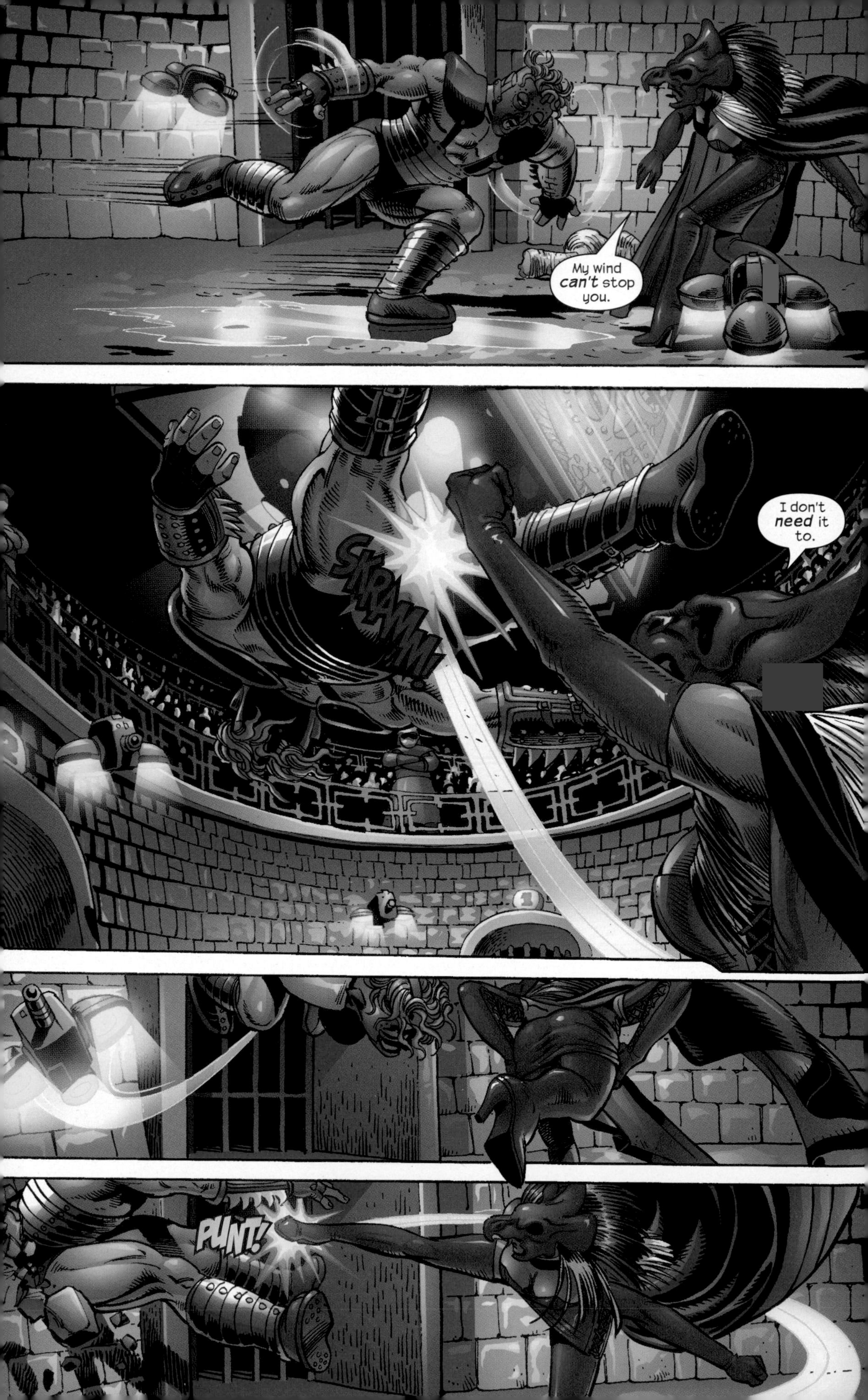
My wind *can't* stop you.
SKRAMM!
I don't *need* it to.
PUNT!

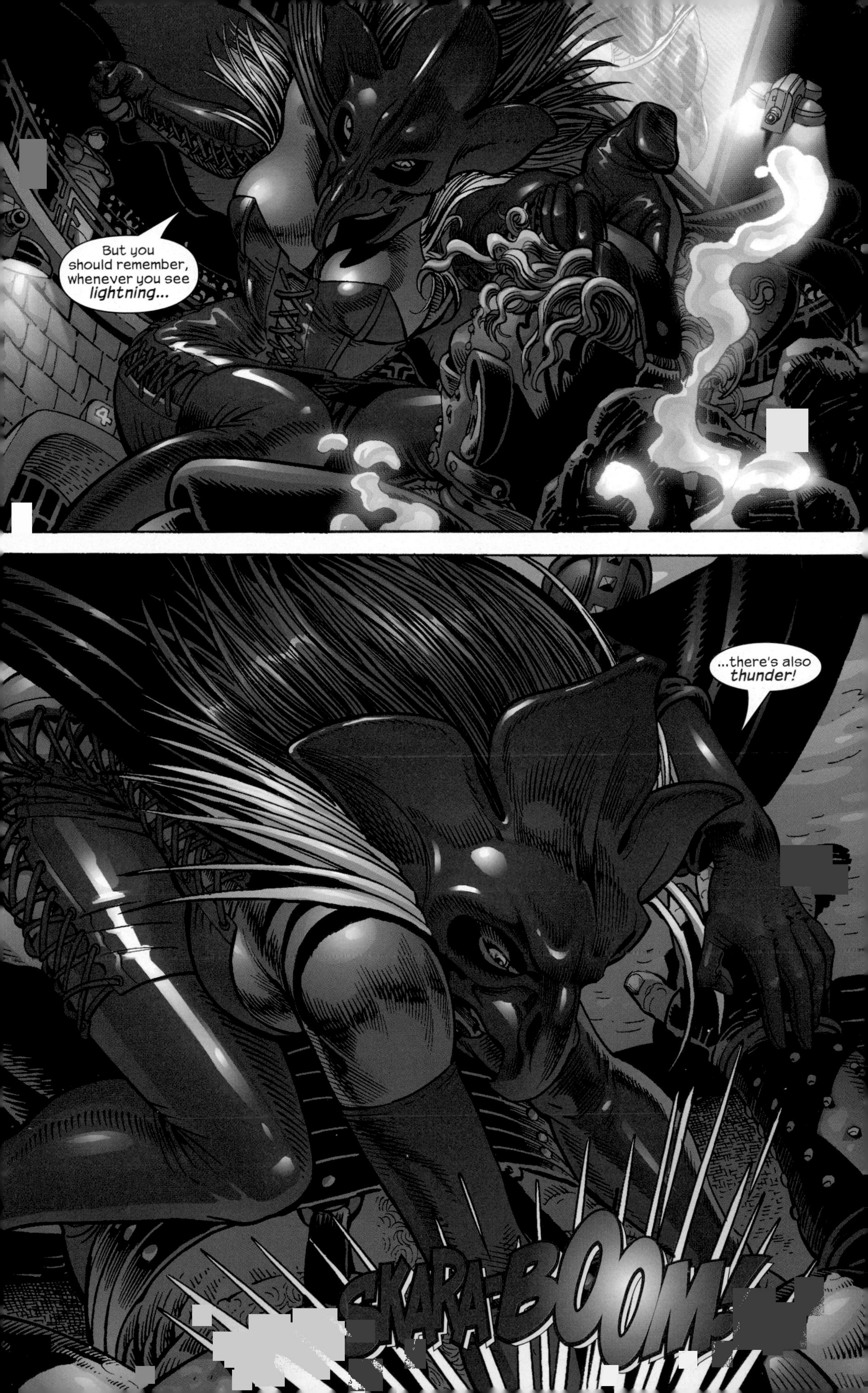
But you should remember, whenever you see *lightning*...
...there's also *thunder!*
SKARA-BOOM!

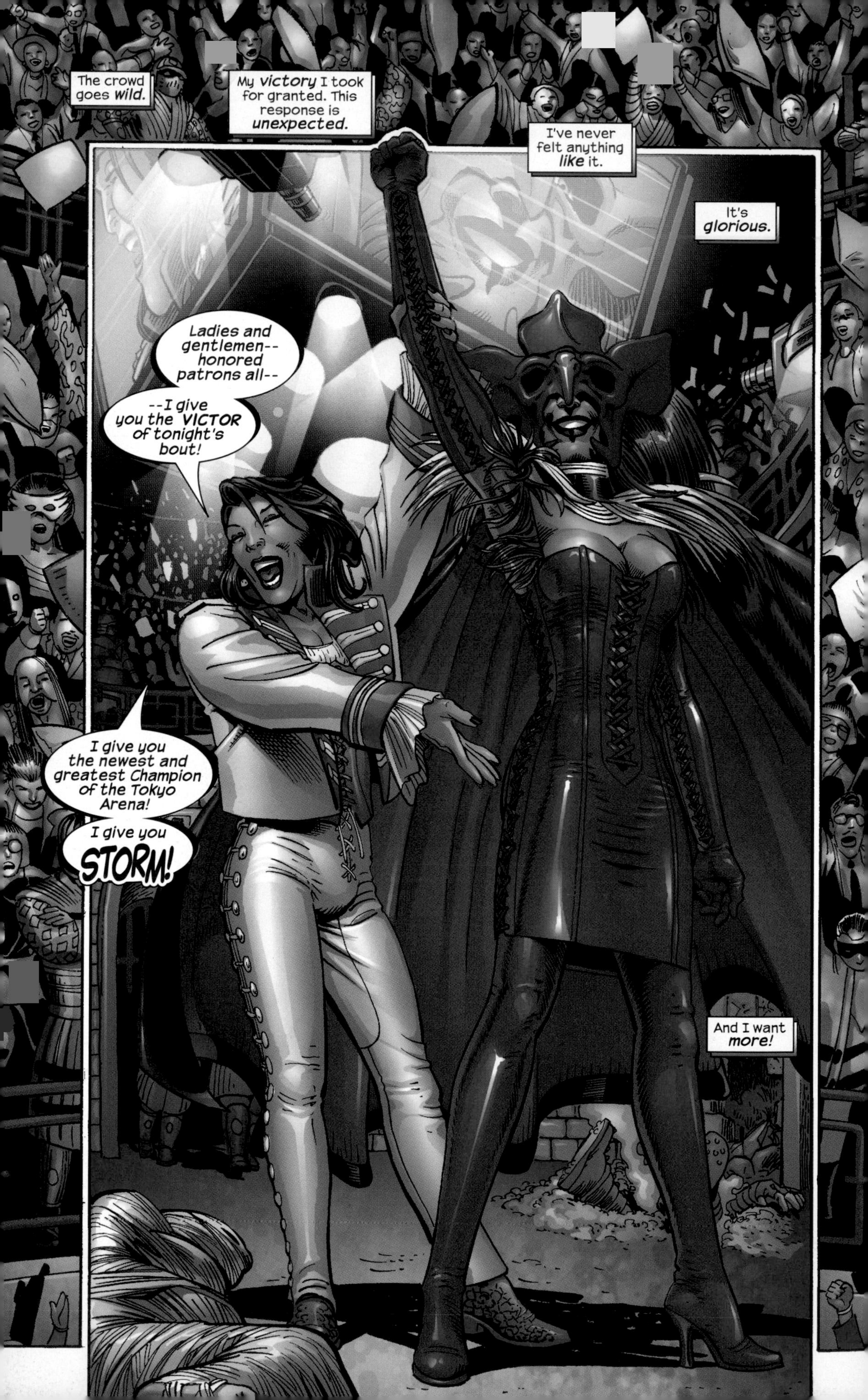
The crowd goes *wild.*
My *victory* I took for granted. This response is *unexpected.*
I've never felt anything *like* it.
It's *glorious.*
Ladies and gentlemen--honored patrons all--
--I give you the VICTOR of tonight's bout!
I give you the newest and greatest Champion of the Tokyo Arena!
I give you STORM!
And I want *more!*

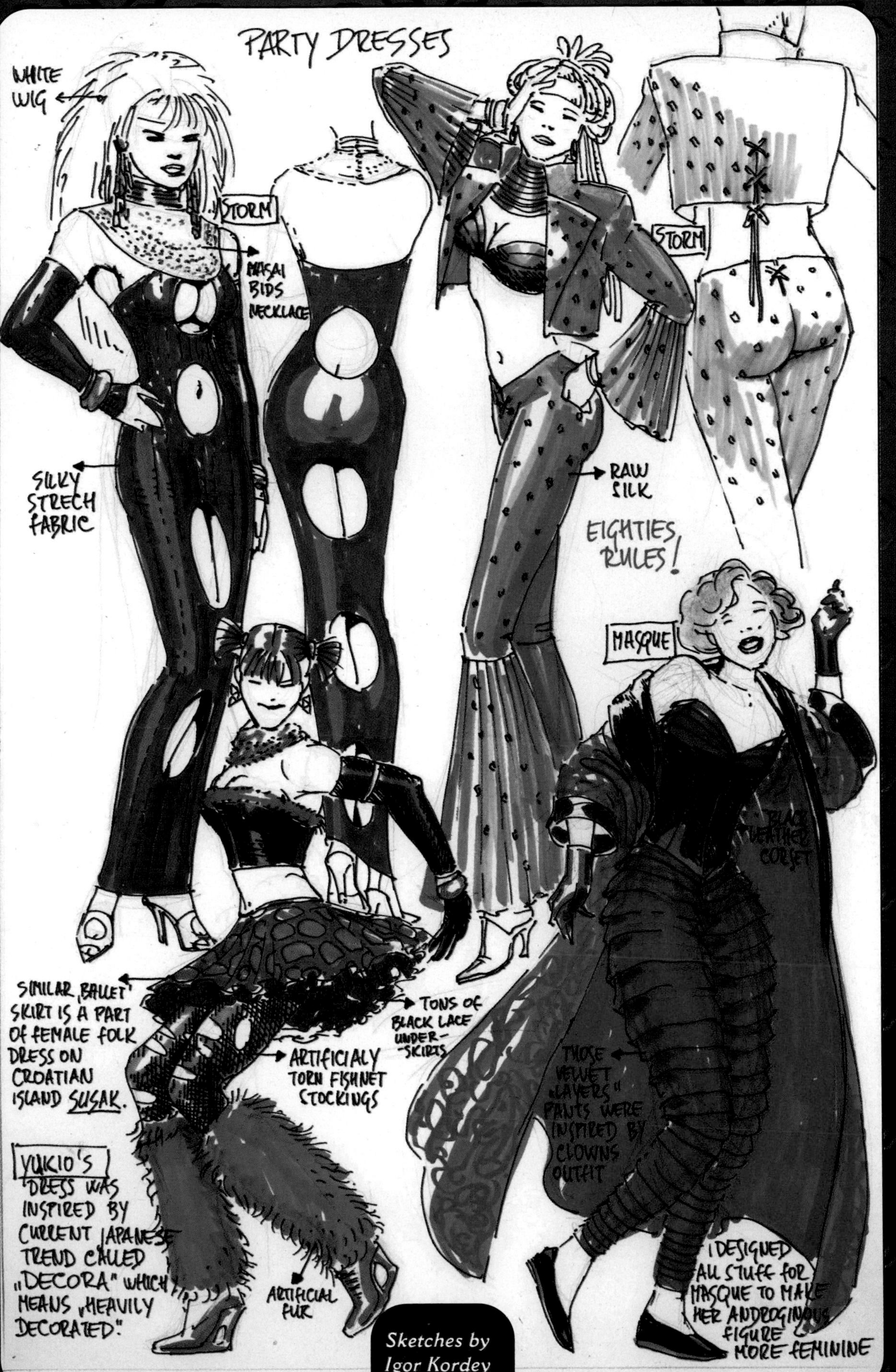
PARTY DRESSES
WHITE WIG
STORM
MASAI BIDS NECKLACE
SILKY STRECH FABRIC
STORM
RAW SILK
EIGHTIES RULES!
MASQUE
BLACK LEATHER CORSET
SIMILAR BALLET SKIRT IS A PART OF FEMALE FOLK DRESS ON CROATIAN ISLAND SUSAK.
TONS OF BLACK LACE UNDER-SKIRTS
ARTIFICIALY TORN FISHNET STOCKINGS
THOSE VELVET "LAYERS" PANTS WERE INSPIRED BY CLOWNS OUTFIT
YUKIO'S
DRESS WAS INSPIRED BY CURRENT JAPANESE TREND CALLED "DECORA" WHICH MEANS "HEAVILY DECORATED."
ARTIFICIAL FUR
I DESIGNED ALL STUFF FOR MASQUE TO MAKE HER ANDROGINOUS FIGURE MORE FEMININE

Sketches by Igor Kordey

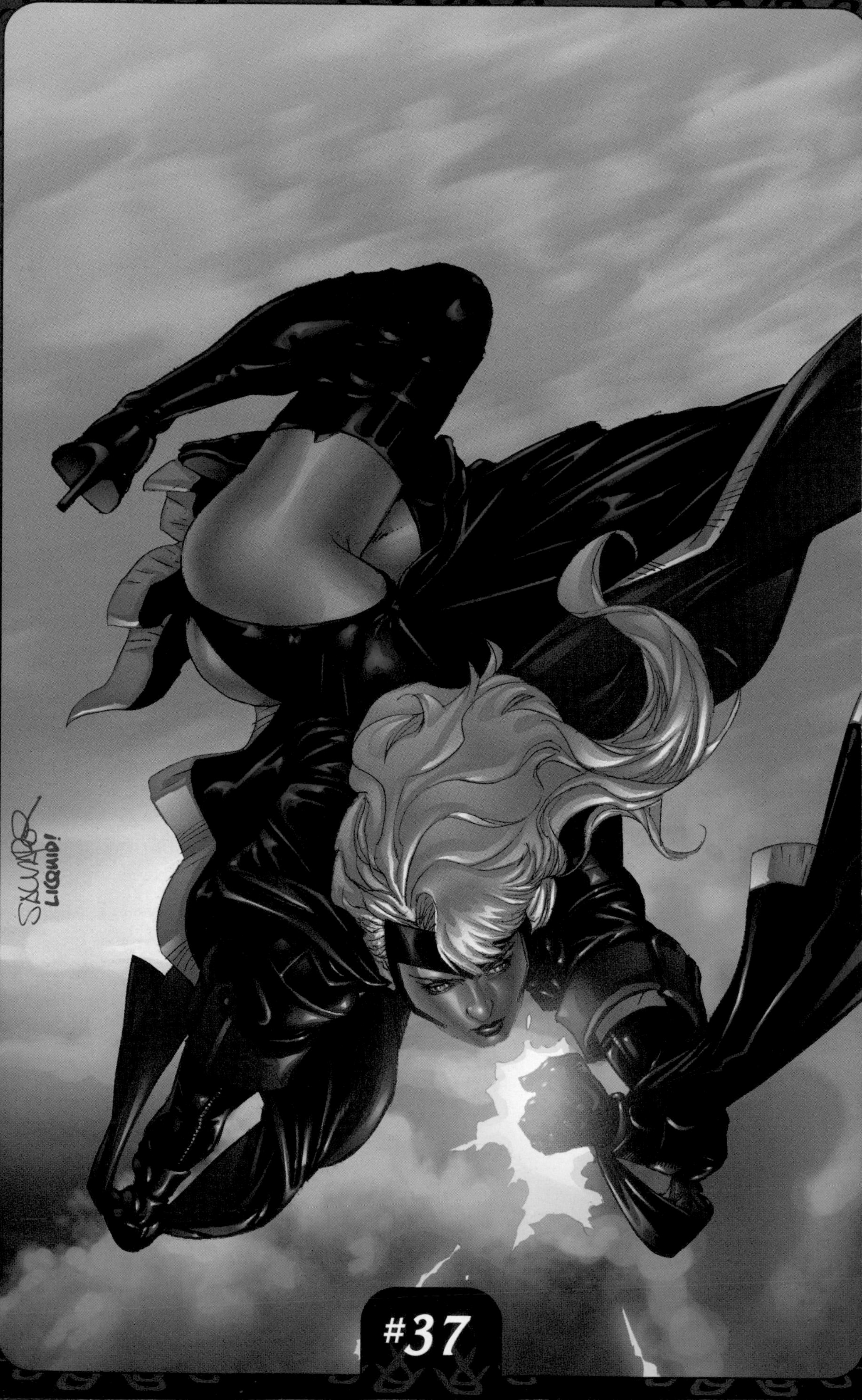
LIQUID!

#37

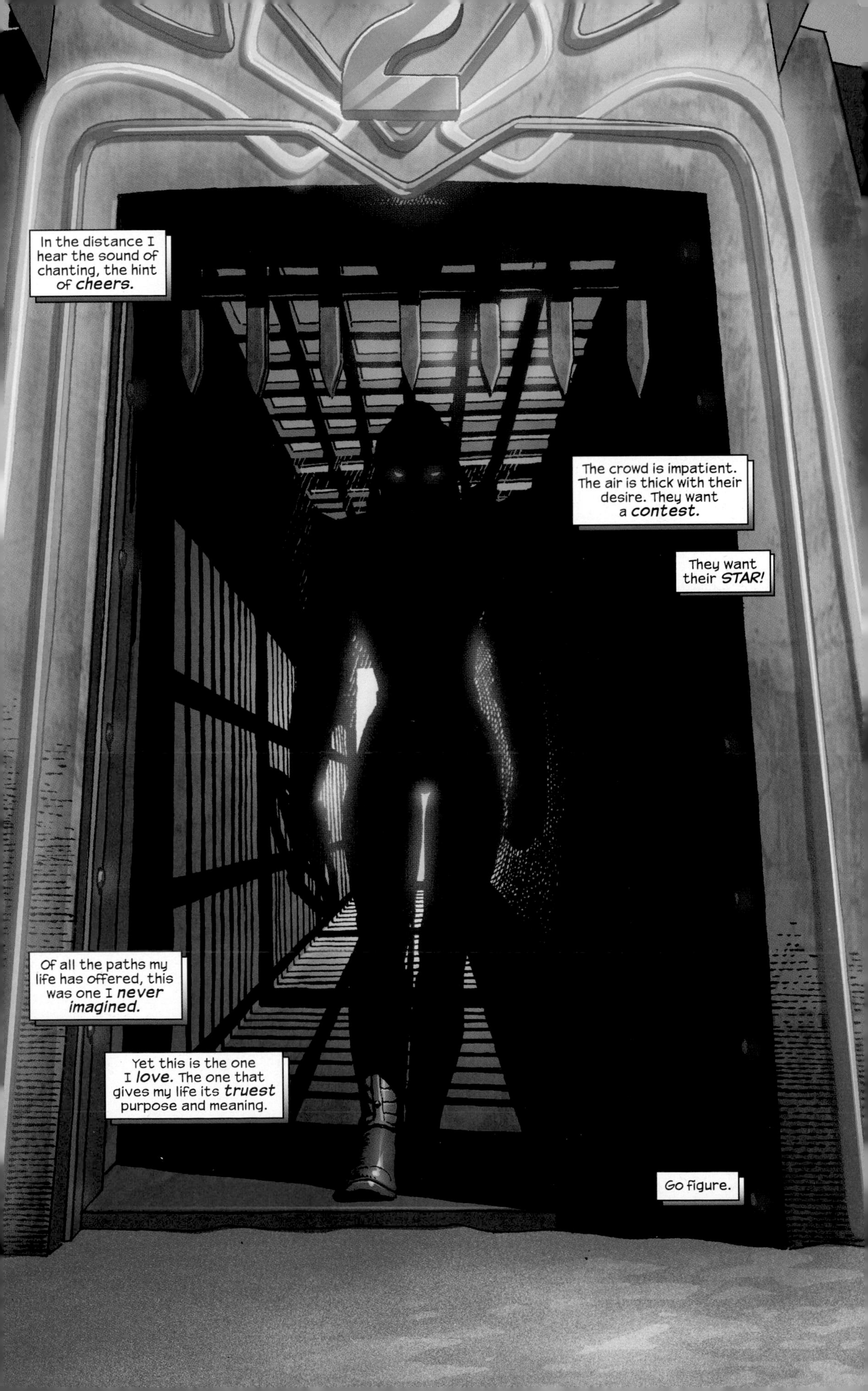
In the distance I hear the sound of chanting, the hint of *cheers.*
The crowd is impatient. The air is thick with their desire. They want a *contest.*
They want their *STAR!*
Of all the paths my life has offered, this was one I *never imagined.*
Yet this is the one I *love.* The one that gives my life its *truest* purpose and meaning.
Go figure.

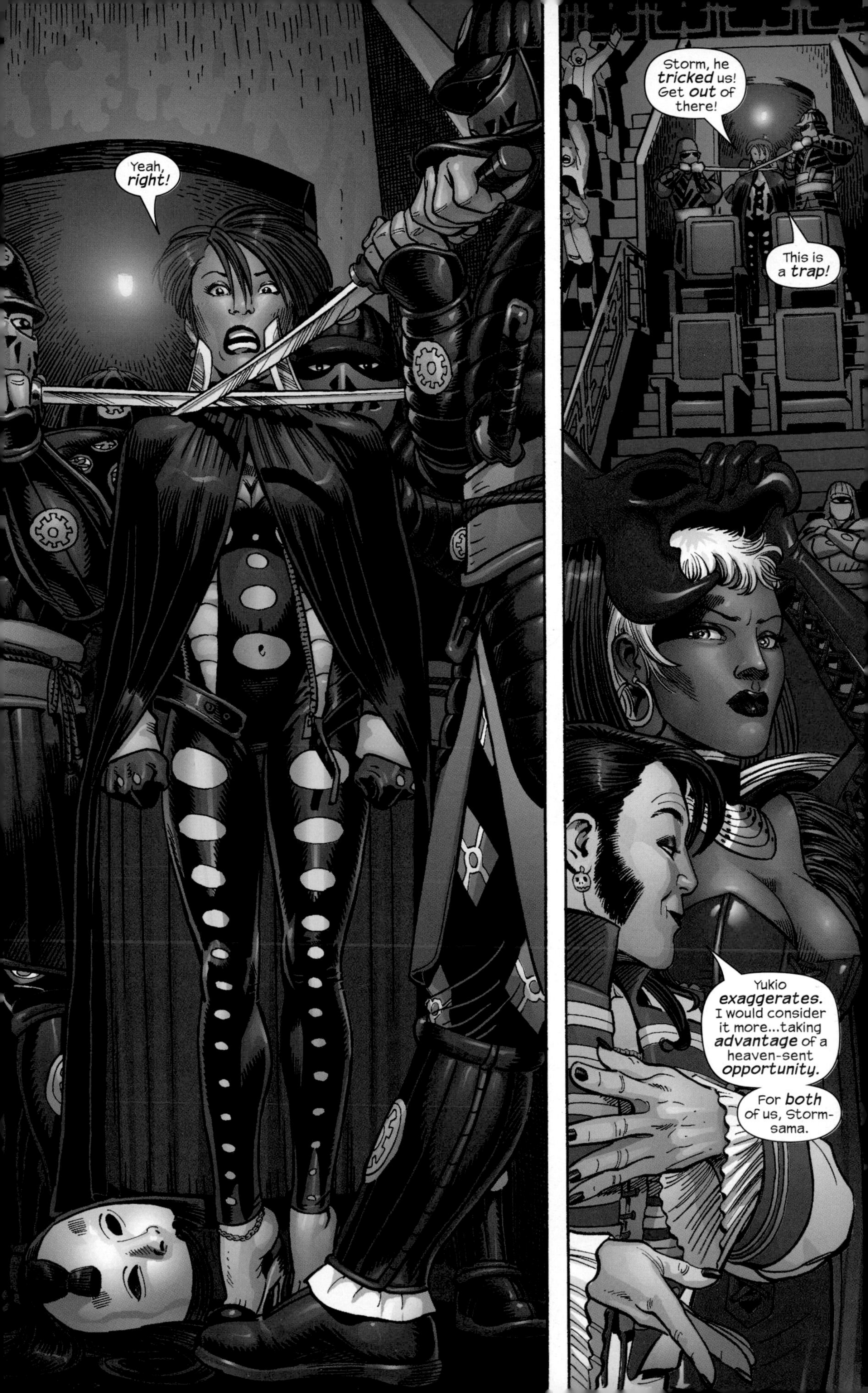
Yeah, *right!*
Storm, he *tricked* us! Get *out* of there!
This is a *trap!*
Yukio *exaggerates.* I would consider it more...taking *advantage* of a heaven-sent *opportunity.*
For *both* of us, Storm-sama.

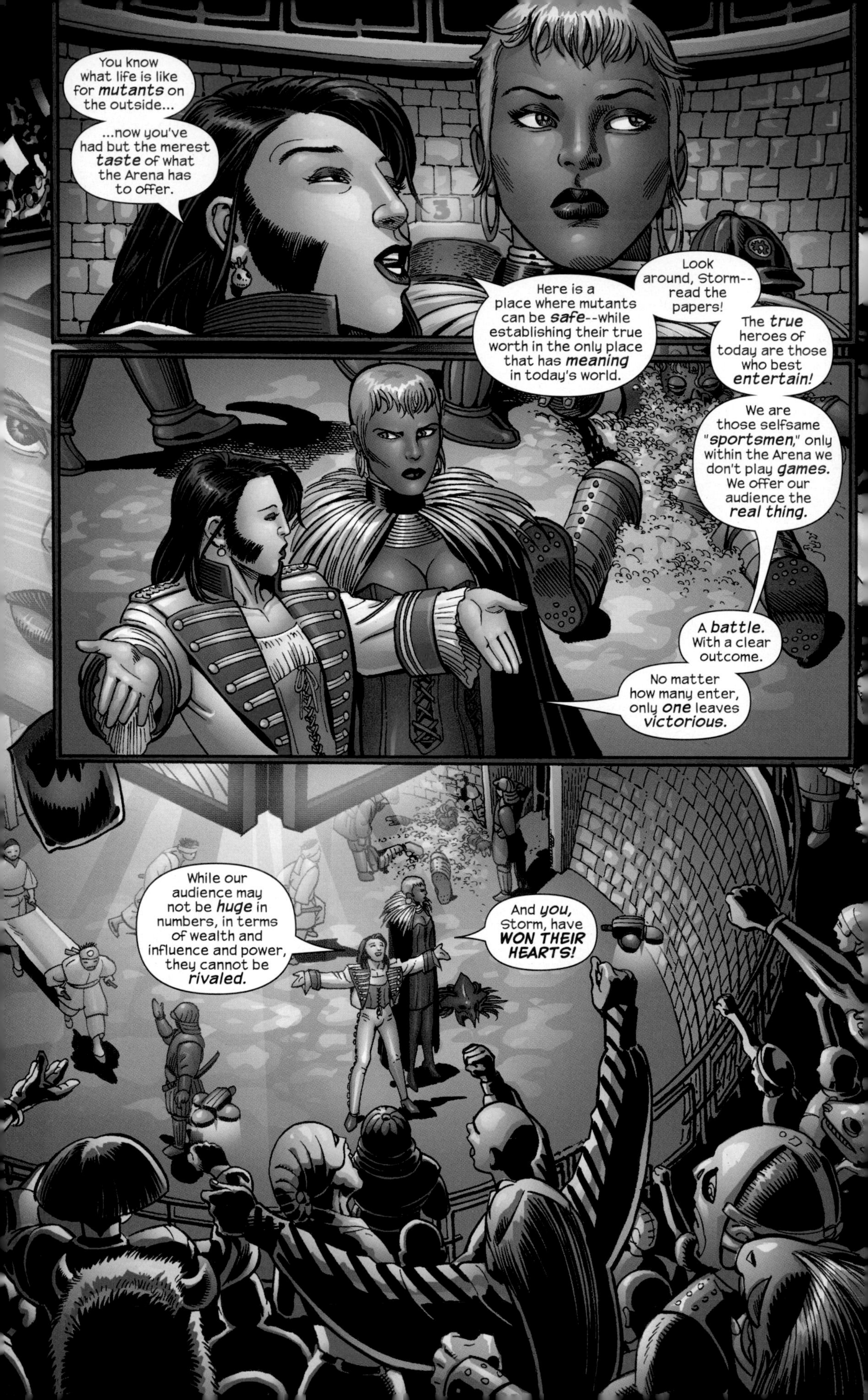
You know what life is like for mutants on the outside...
...now you've had but the merest taste of what the Arena has to offer.
Here is a place where mutants can be safe--while establishing their true worth in the only place that has meaning in today's world.
Look around, Storm--read the papers!
The true heroes of today are those who best entertain!
We are those selfsame "sportsmen," only within the Arena we don't play games. We offer our audience the real thing.
A battle. With a clear outcome.
No matter how many enter, only one leaves victorious.
While our audience may not be huge in numbers, in terms of wealth and influence and power, they cannot be rivaled.
And you, Storm, have WON THEIR HEARTS!

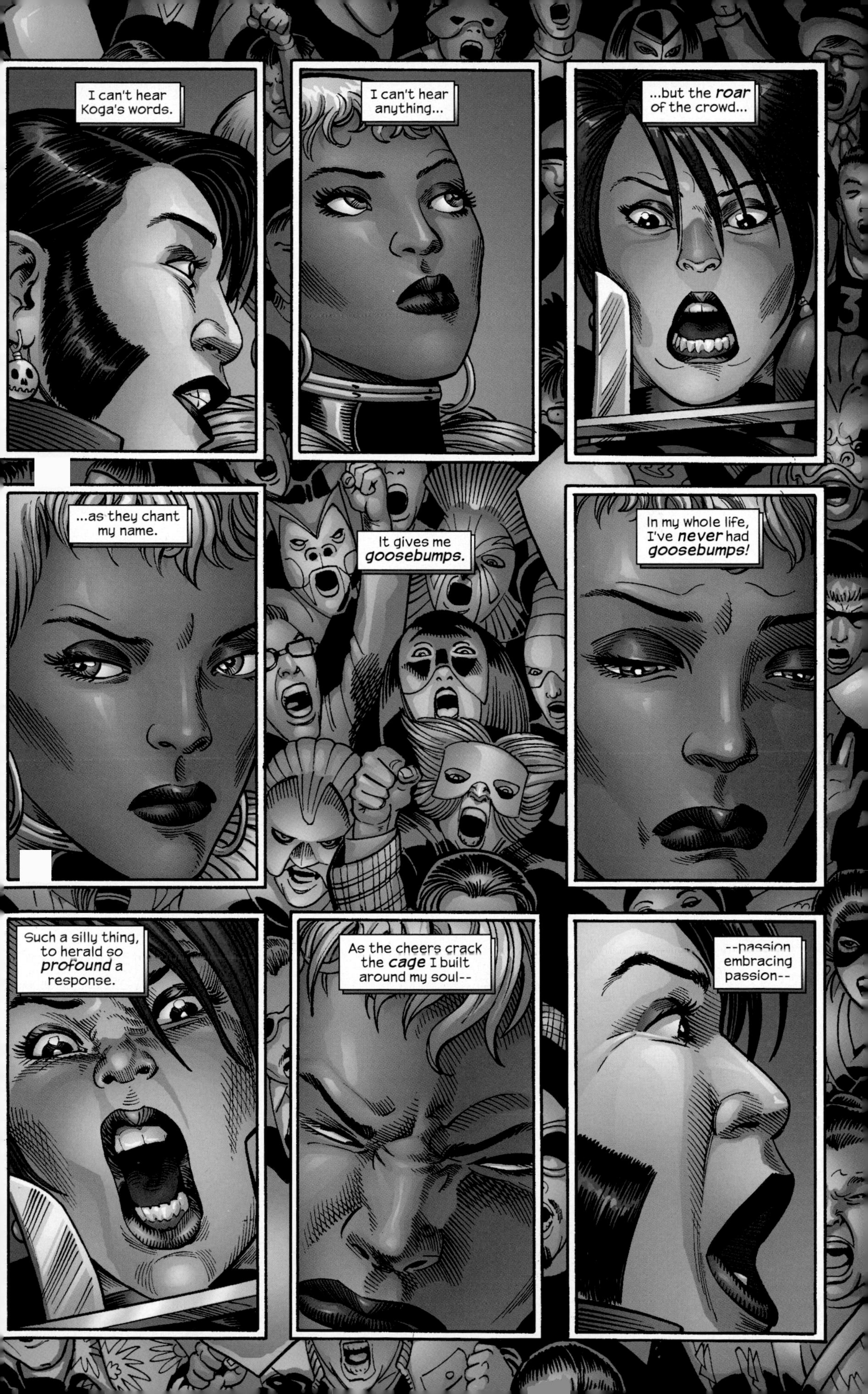
I can't hear Koga's words.
I can't hear anything...
...but the roar of the crowd...
...as they chant my name.
It gives me goosebumps.
In my whole life, I've never had goosebumps!
Such a silly thing, to herald so profound a response.
As the cheers crack the cage I built around my soul--
--passion embracing passion--

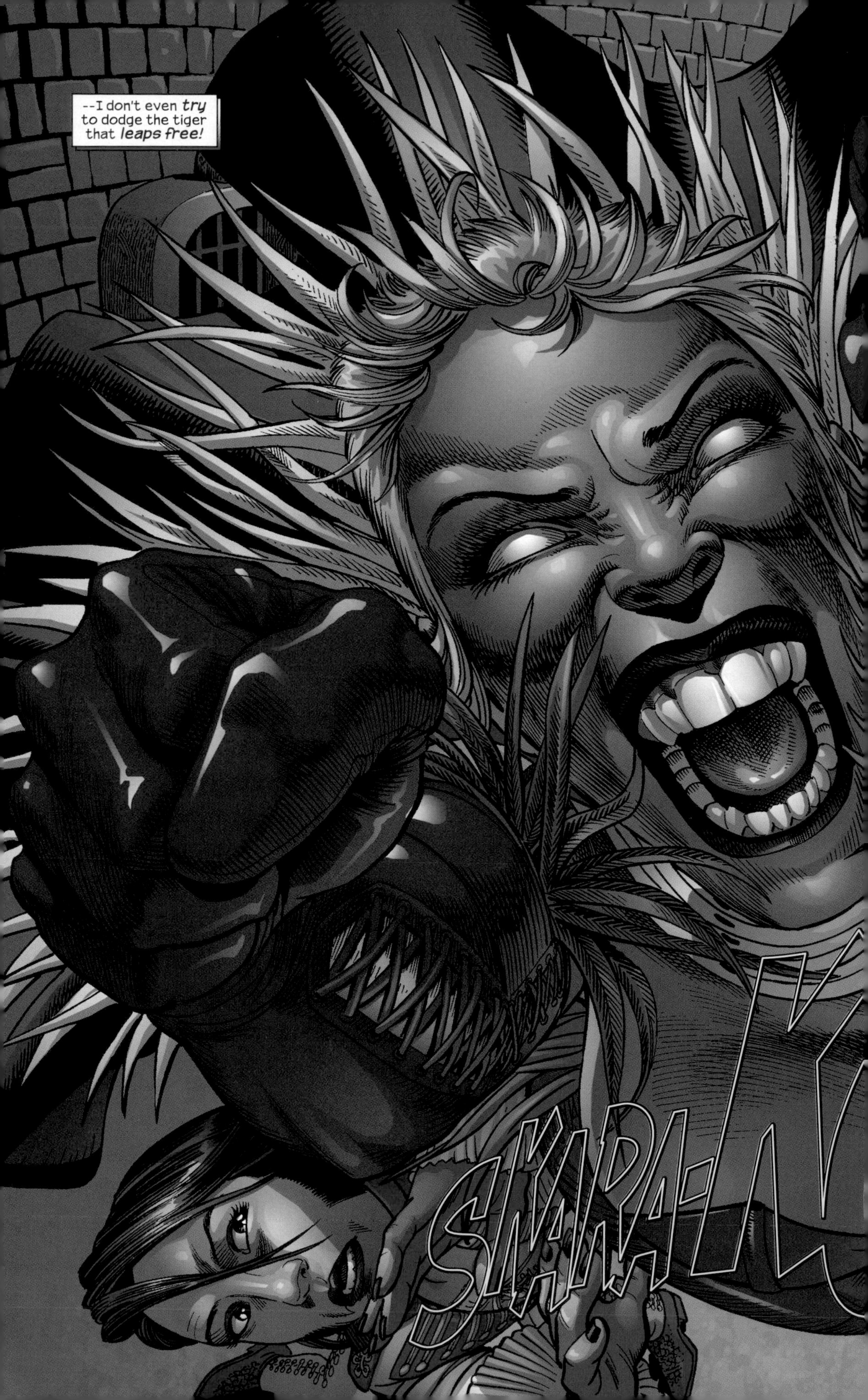
--I don't even *try* to dodge the tiger that *leaps free!*
SKRAPAKAAK

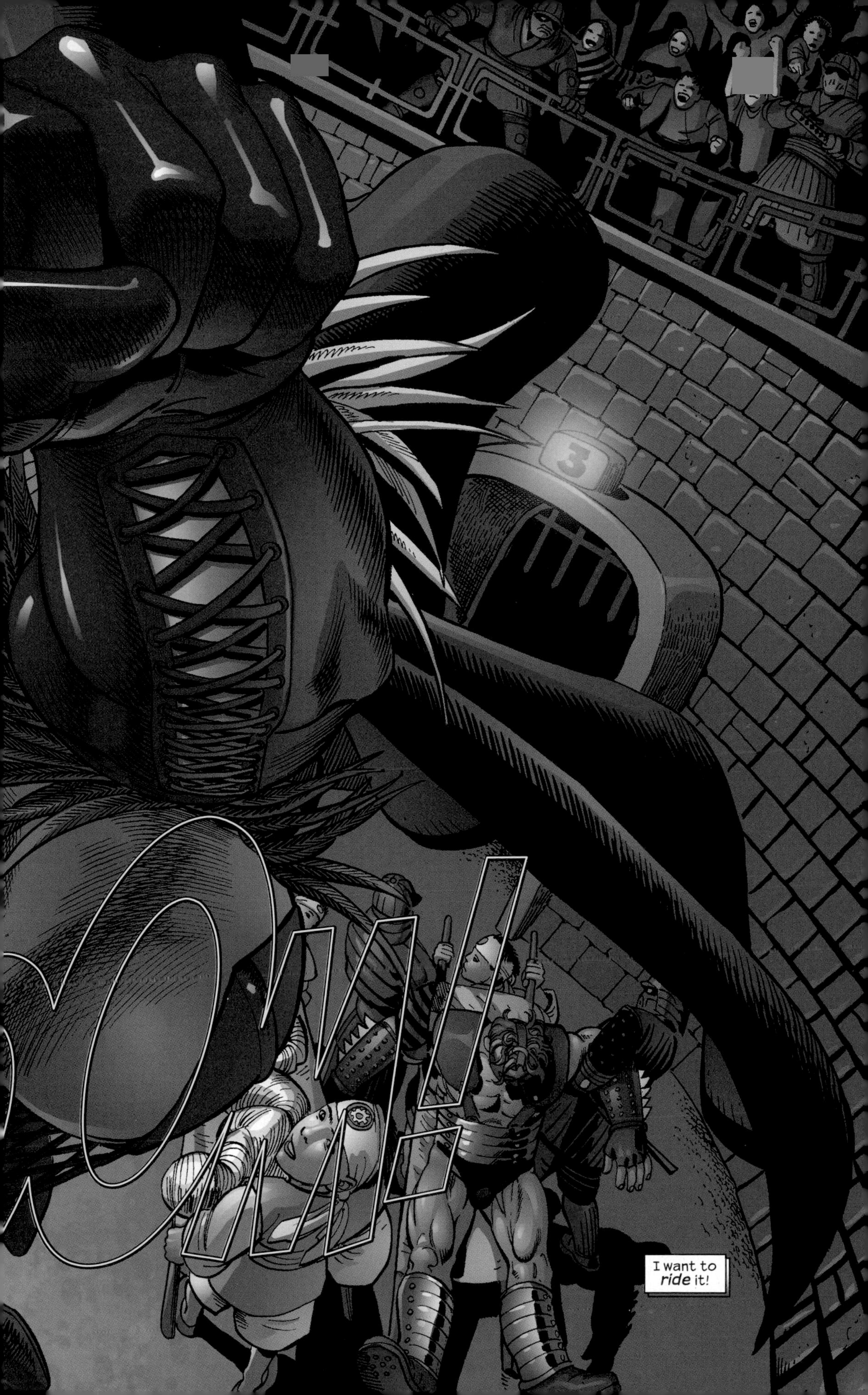
I want to *ride* it!

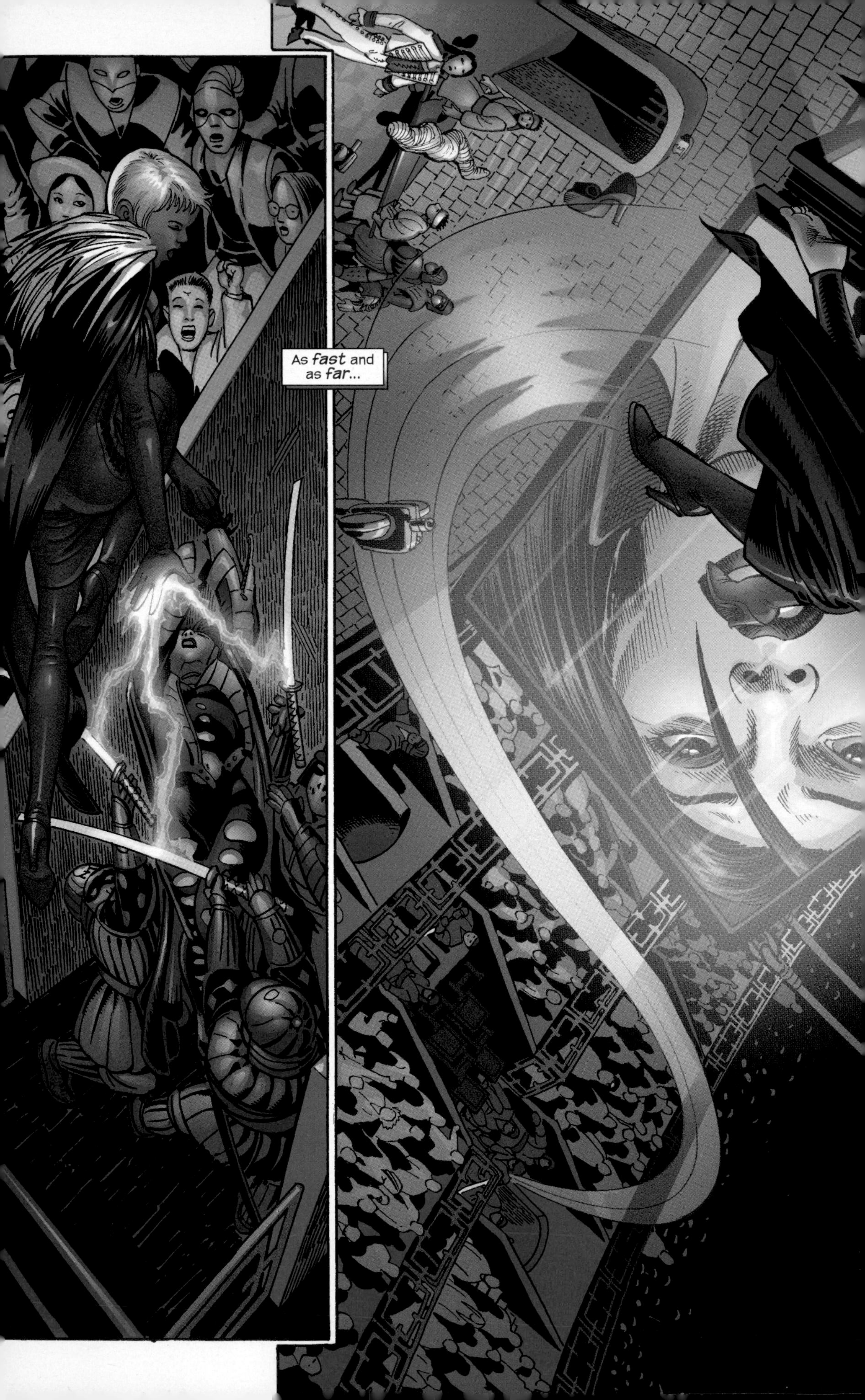
As *fast* and as *far*...

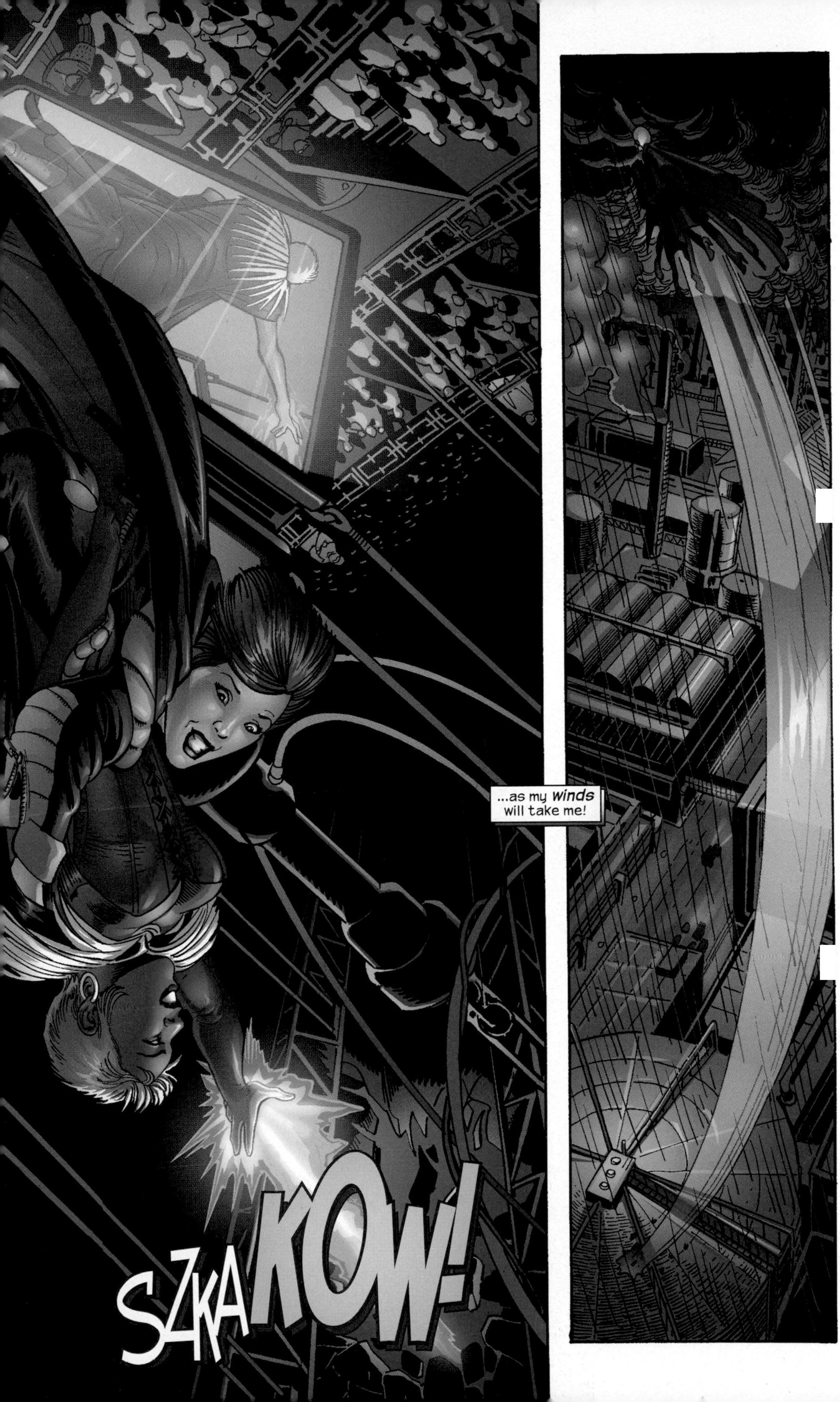
...as my *winds* will take me!
SZKAKOW!

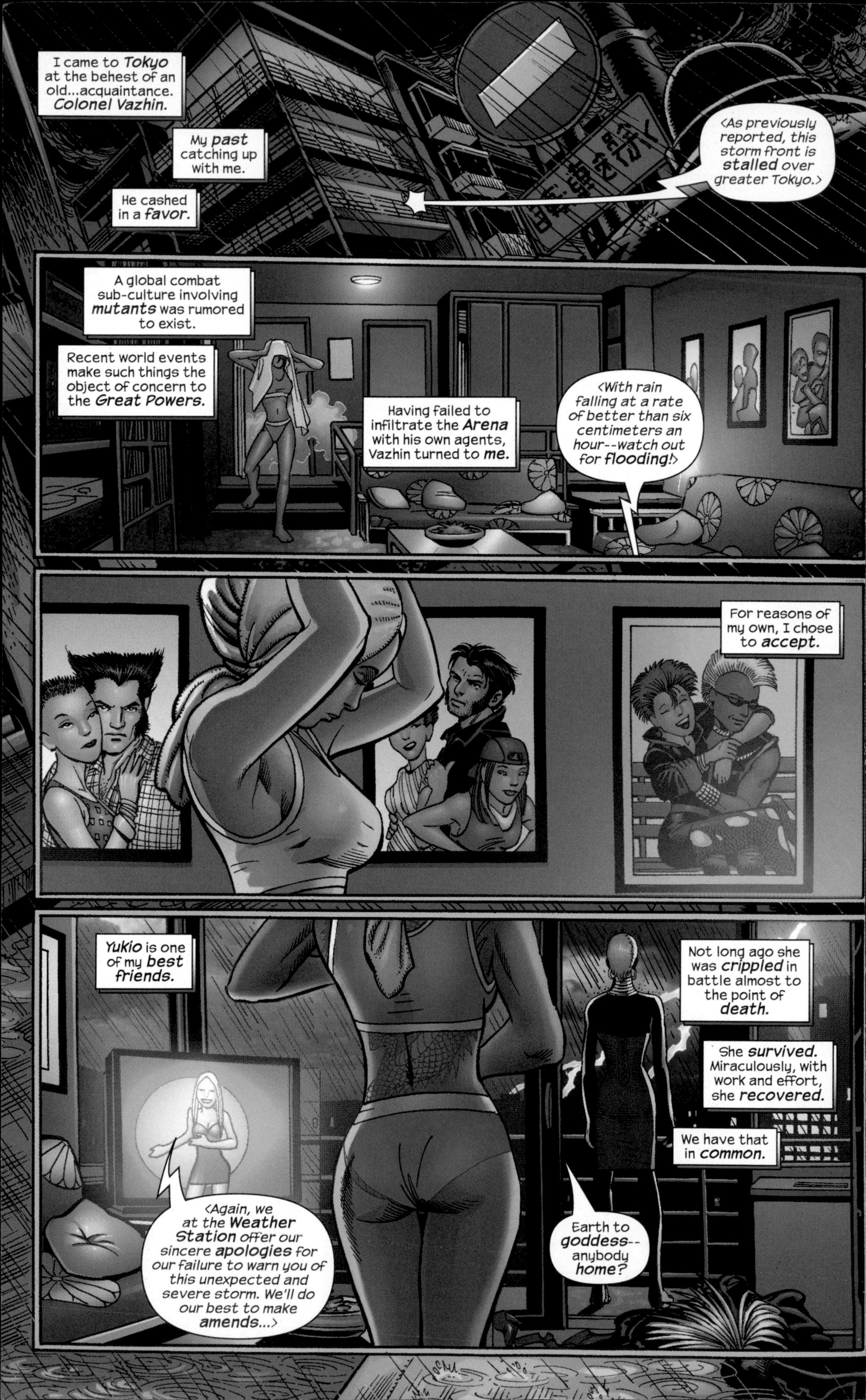
I came to Tokyo at the behest of an old...acquaintance. Colonel Vazhin.
My past catching up with me.
He cashed in a favor.
<As previously reported, this storm front is stalled over greater Tokyo.>
A global combat sub-culture involving mutants was rumored to exist.
Recent world events make such things the object of concern to the Great Powers.
Having failed to infiltrate the Arena with his own agents, Vazhin turned to me.
<With rain falling at a rate of better than six centimeters an hour--watch out for flooding!>
For reasons of my own, I chose to accept.
Yukio is one of my best friends.
Not long ago she was crippled in battle almost to the point of death.
She survived. Miraculously, with work and effort, she recovered.
We have that in common.
<Again, we at the Weather Station offer our sincere apologies for our failure to warn you of this unexpected and severe storm. We'll do our best to make amends...>
Earth to goddess-- anybody home?

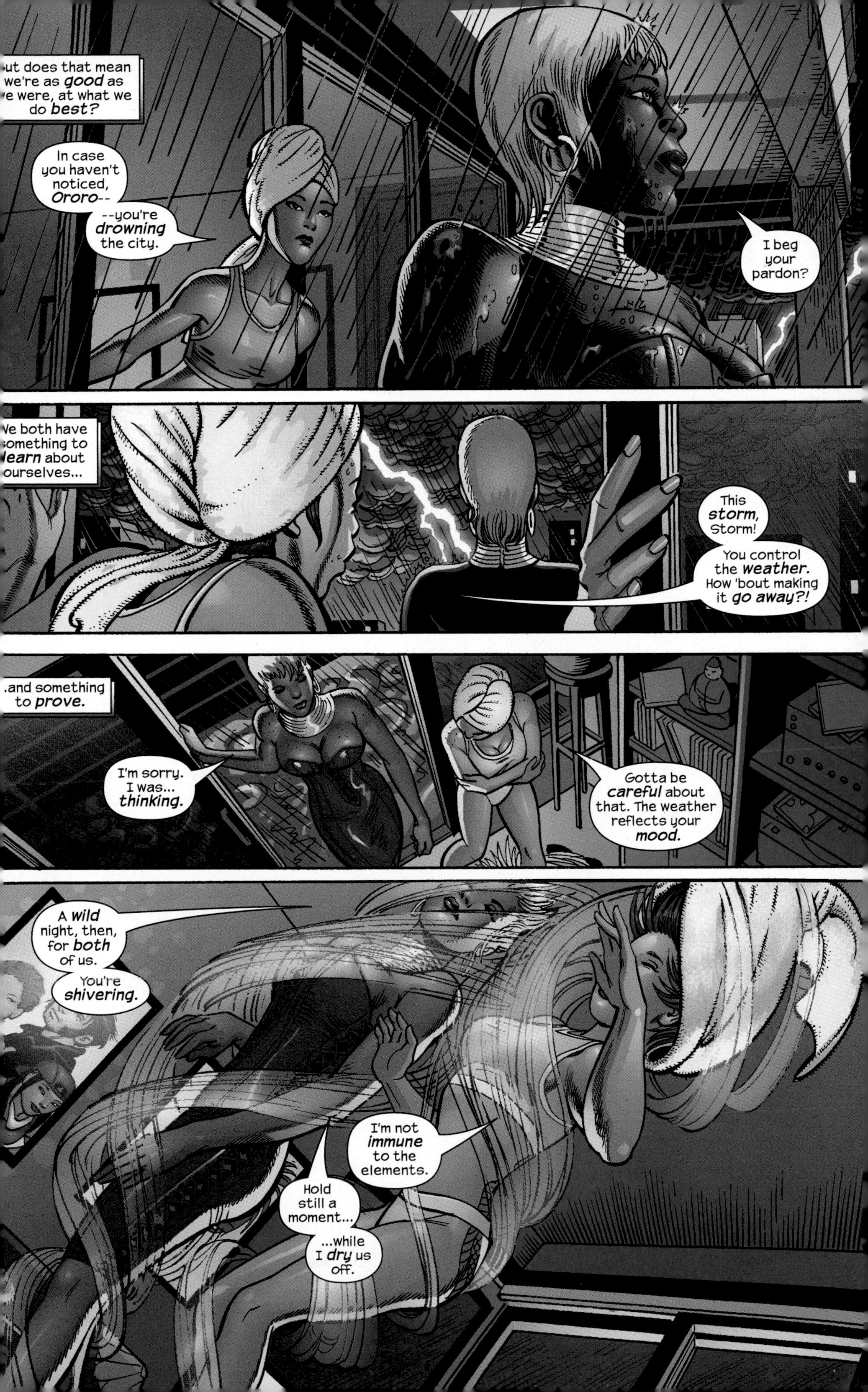
ut does that mean we're as good as e were, at what we do best?
In case you haven't noticed, Ororo--
--you're drowning the city.
I beg your pardon?
Ve both have something to learn about ourselves...
This storm, Storm!
You control the weather. How 'bout making it go away?!
.and something to prove.
I'm sorry. I was... thinking.
Gotta be careful about that. The weather reflects your mood.
A wild night, then, for both of us.
You're shivering.
I'm not immune to the elements.
Hold still a moment...
...while I dry us off.

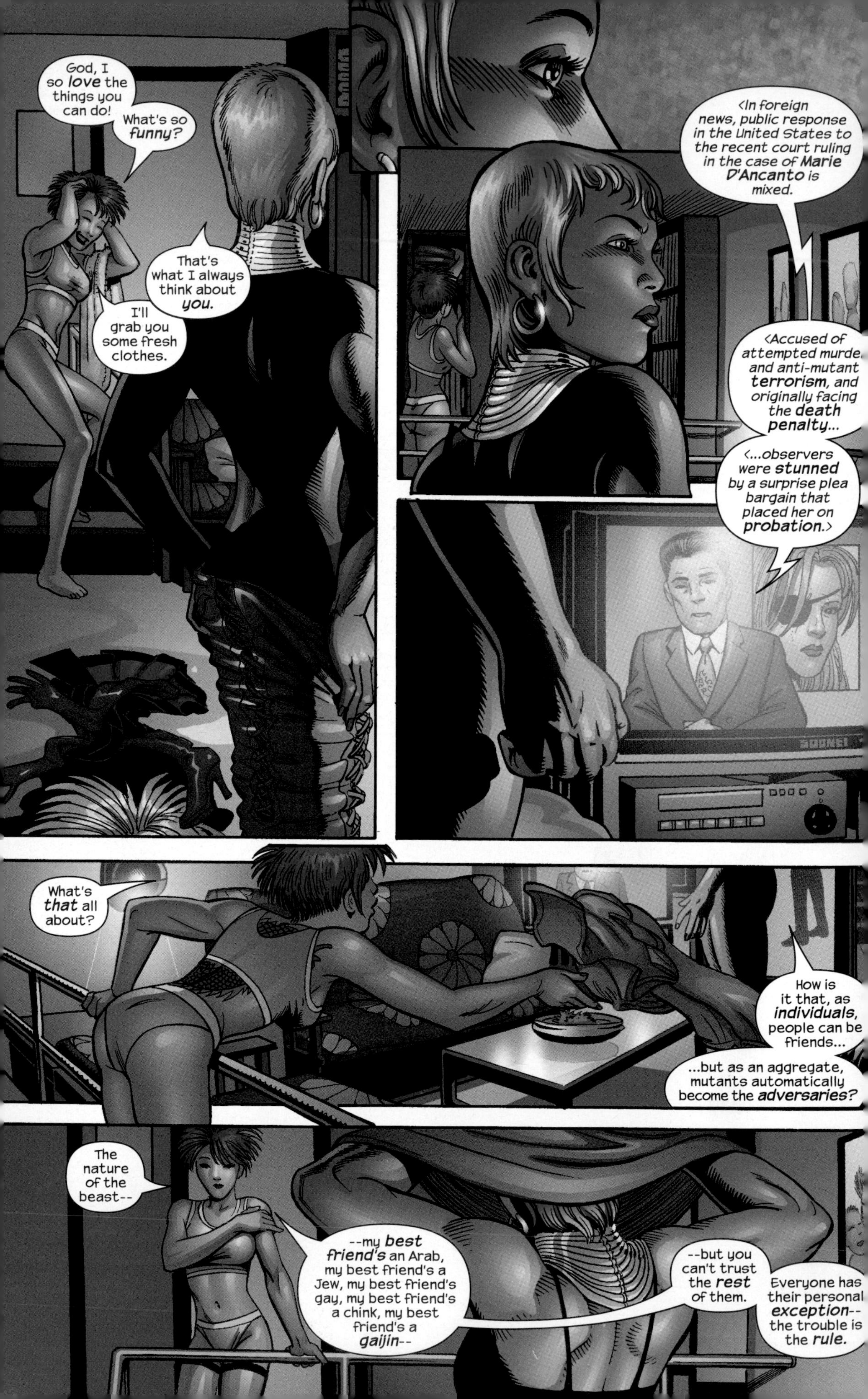

God, I so *love* the things you can do!
What's so *funny*?
That's what I always think about *you.*
I'll grab you some fresh clothes.
<In foreign news, public response in the United States to the recent court ruling in the case of **Marie D'Ancanto** is mixed.
<Accused of attempted murder and anti-mutant **terrorism**, and originally facing the **death penalty**...
<...observers were **stunned** by a surprise plea bargain that placed her on **probation.**>
What's *that* all about?
How is it that, as *individuals*, people can be friends...
...but as an aggregate, mutants automatically become the *adversaries*?
The nature of the beast--
--my *best friend's* an Arab, my best friend's a Jew, my best friend's gay, my best friend's a chink, my best friend's a *gaijin*--
--but you can't trust the *rest* of them.
Everyone has their personal *exception*--the trouble is the *rule*.

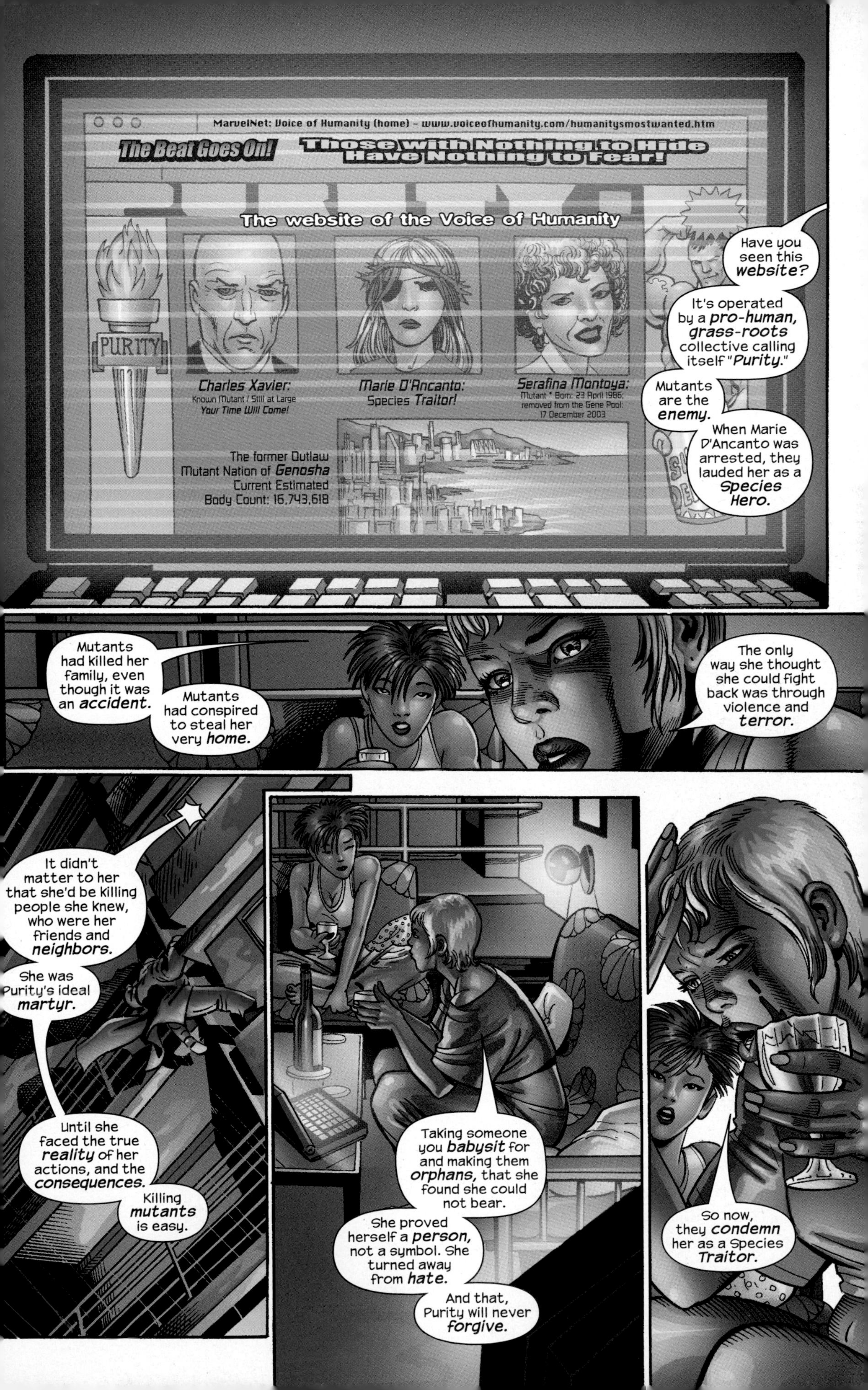
MarvelNet: Voice of Humanity (home) ~ www.voiceofhumanity.com/humanitysmostwanted.htm
The Beat Goes On!
Those with Nothing to Hide Have Nothing to Fear!
The website of the Voice of Humanity
PURITY
Charles Xavier:
Known Mutant / Still at Large
Your Time Will Come!
Marie D'Ancanto:
Species Traitor!
Serafina Montoya:
Mutant * Born: 23 April 1986; removed from the Gene Pool: 17 December 2003
The former Outlaw Mutant Nation of Genosha Current Estimated Body Count: 16,743,618
Have you seen this *website*?
It's operated by a *pro-human, grass-roots* collective calling itself "*Purity*."
Mutants are the *enemy*.
When Marie D'Ancanto was arrested, they lauded her as a *Species Hero*.
Mutants had killed her family, even though it was an *accident*.
Mutants had conspired to steal her very *home*.
The only way she thought she could fight back was through violence and *terror*.
It didn't matter to her that she'd be killing people she knew, who were her friends and *neighbors*.
She was Purity's ideal *martyr*.
Until she faced the true *reality* of her actions, and the *consequences*.
Killing *mutants* is easy.
Taking someone you *babysit* for and making them *orphans*, that she found she could not bear.
She proved herself a *person*, not a symbol. She turned away from *hate*.
And that, Purity will never *forgive*.
So now, they *condemn* her as a Species *Traitor*.

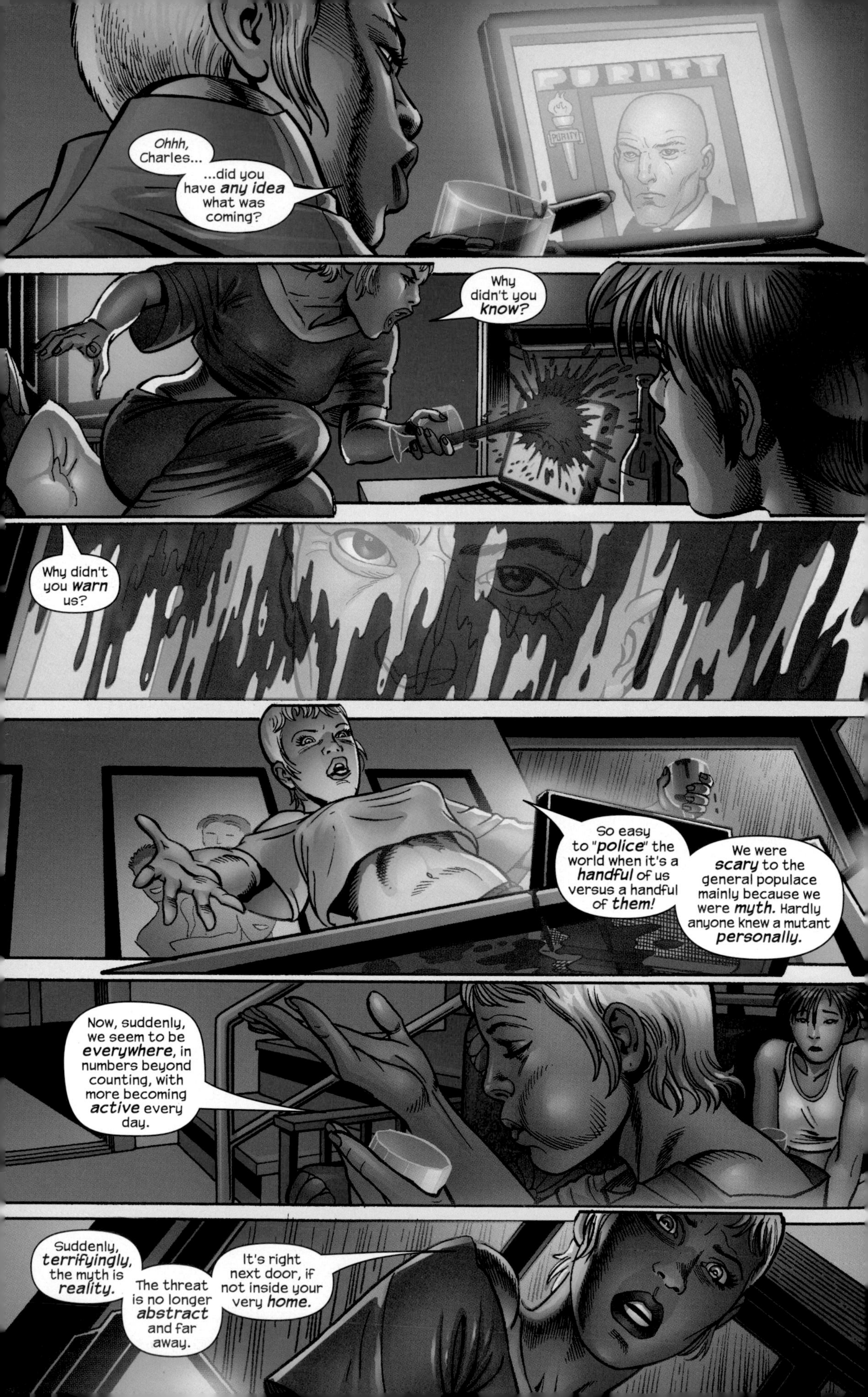
PURITY
PURITY
Ohhh, Charles...
...did you have any idea what was coming?
Why didn't you know?
Why didn't you warn us?
So easy to "police" the world when it's a handful of us versus a handful of them!
We were scary to the general populace mainly because we were myth. Hardly anyone knew a mutant personally.
Now, suddenly, we seem to be everywhere, in numbers beyond counting, with more becoming active every day.
Suddenly, terrifyingly, the myth is reality.
The threat is no longer abstract and far away.
It's right next door, if not inside your very home.

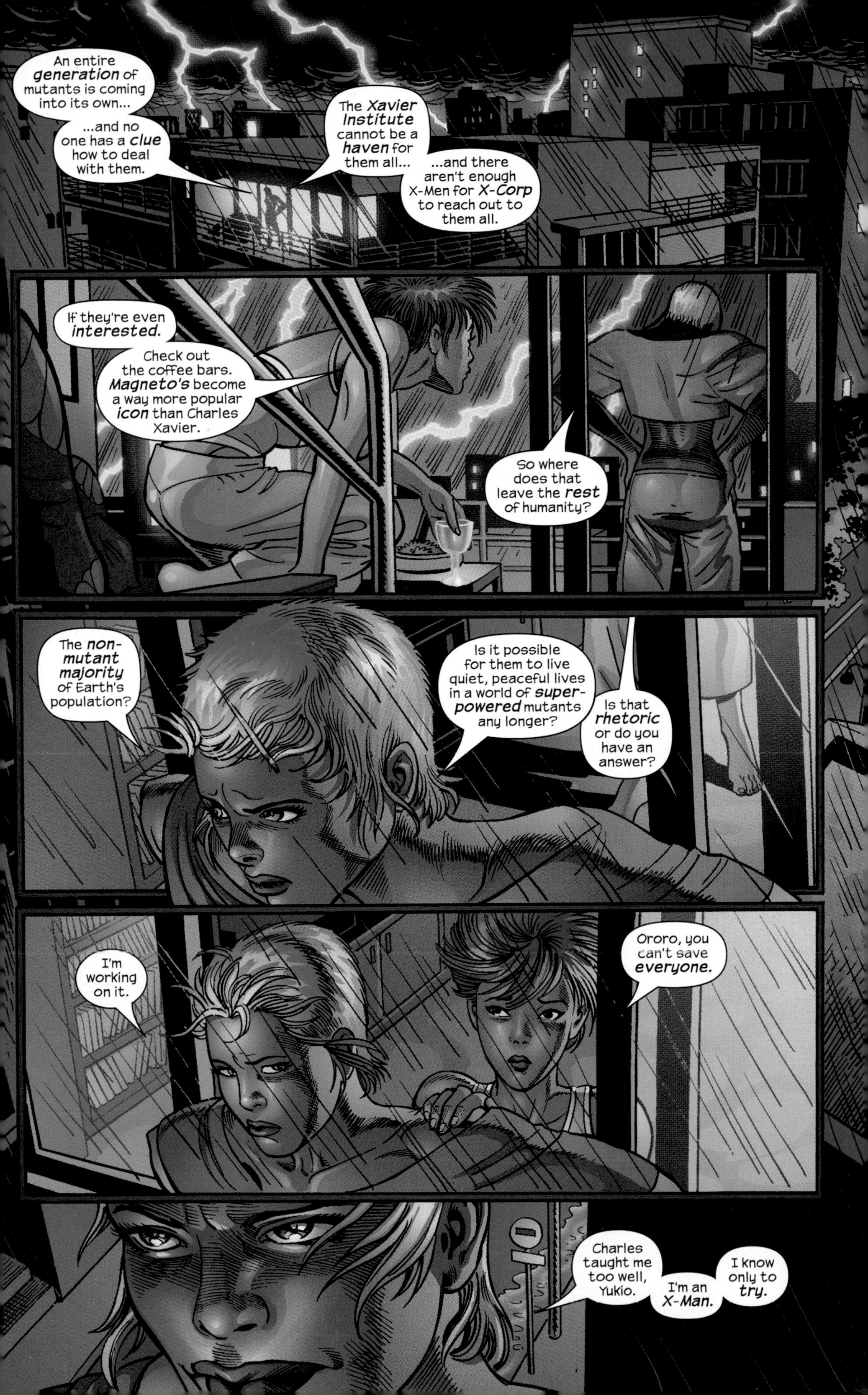

An entire *generation* of mutants is coming into its own...
...and no one has a *clue* how to deal with them.
The *Xavier Institute* cannot be a *haven* for them all...
...and there aren't enough X-Men for *X-Corp* to reach out to them all.
If they're even *interested.*
Check out the coffee bars. *Magneto's* become a way more popular *icon* than Charles Xavier.
So where does that leave the *rest* of humanity?
The *non-mutant majority* of Earth's population?
Is it possible for them to live quiet, peaceful lives in a world of *super-powered* mutants any longer?
Is that *rhetoric* or do you have an answer?
I'm working on it.
Ororo, you can't save *everyone.*
Charles taught me too well, Yukio.
I'm an *X-Man.*
I know only to *try.*

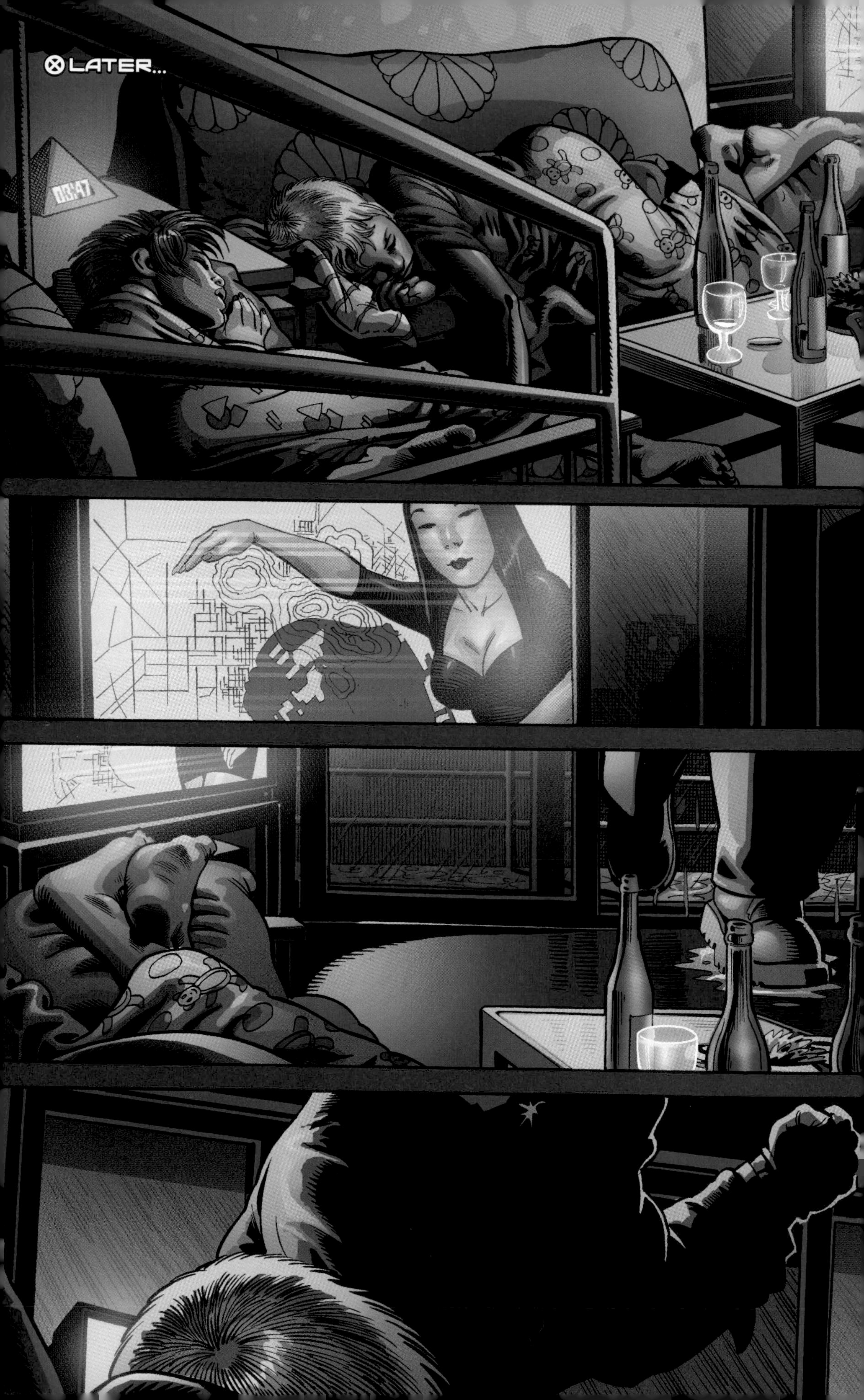
LATER...
03:47

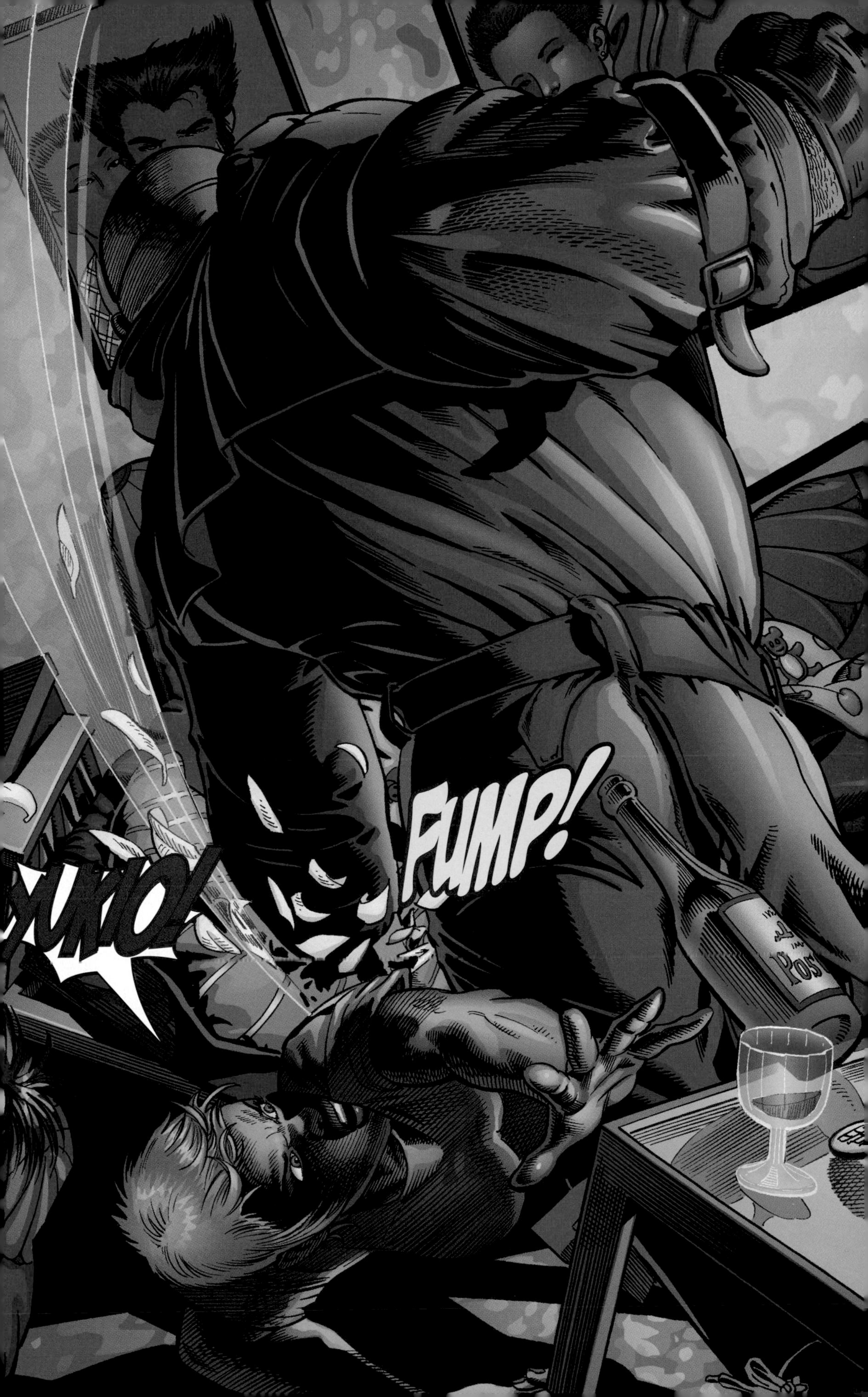
YUKIO!
FUMP!

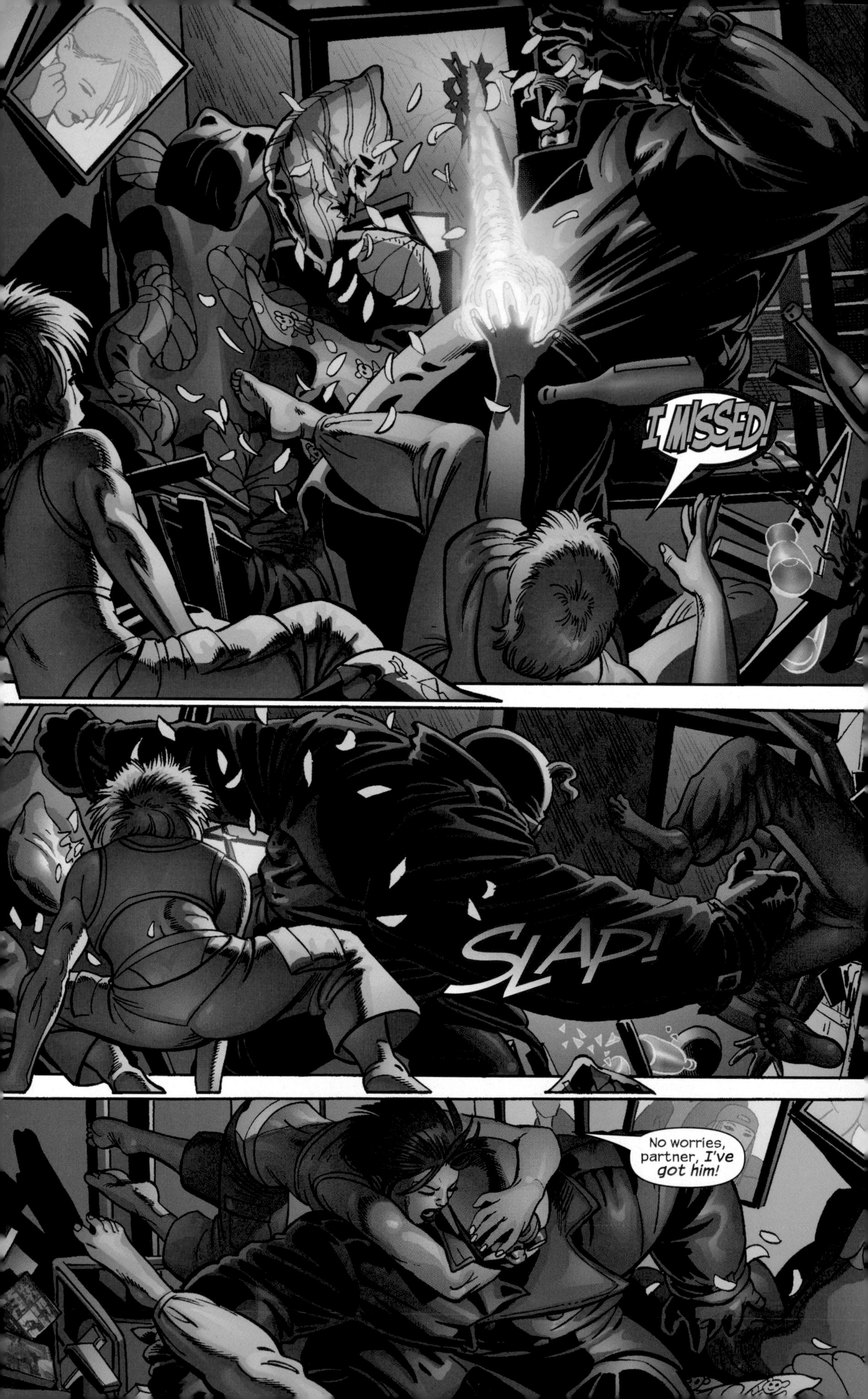
I MISSED!
SLAP!
No worries, partner, I've got him!

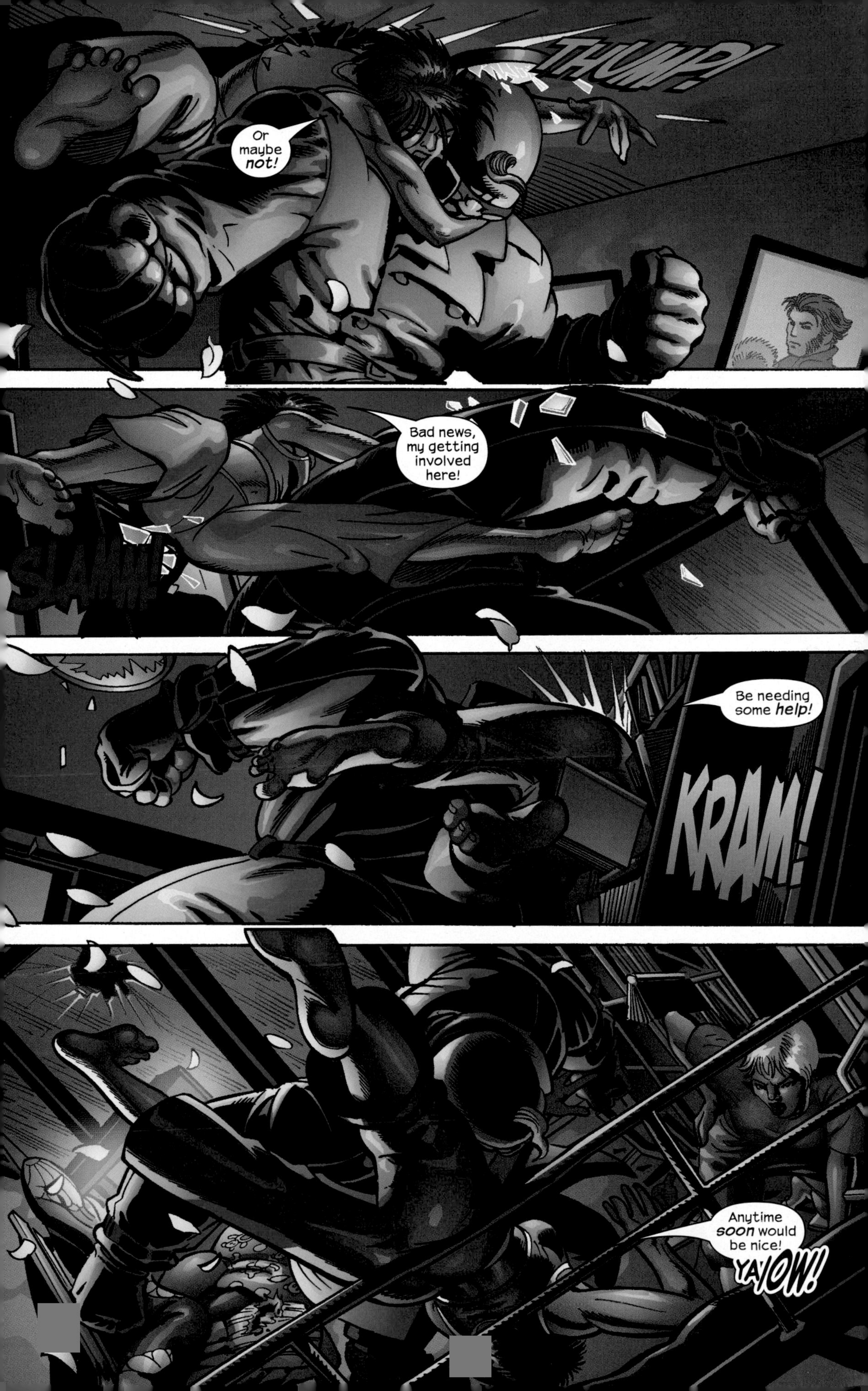
THUMP!
Or maybe not!
Bad news, my getting involved here!
SLAMM!
Be needing some help!
KRAM!
Anytime soon would be nice!
YA'OW!

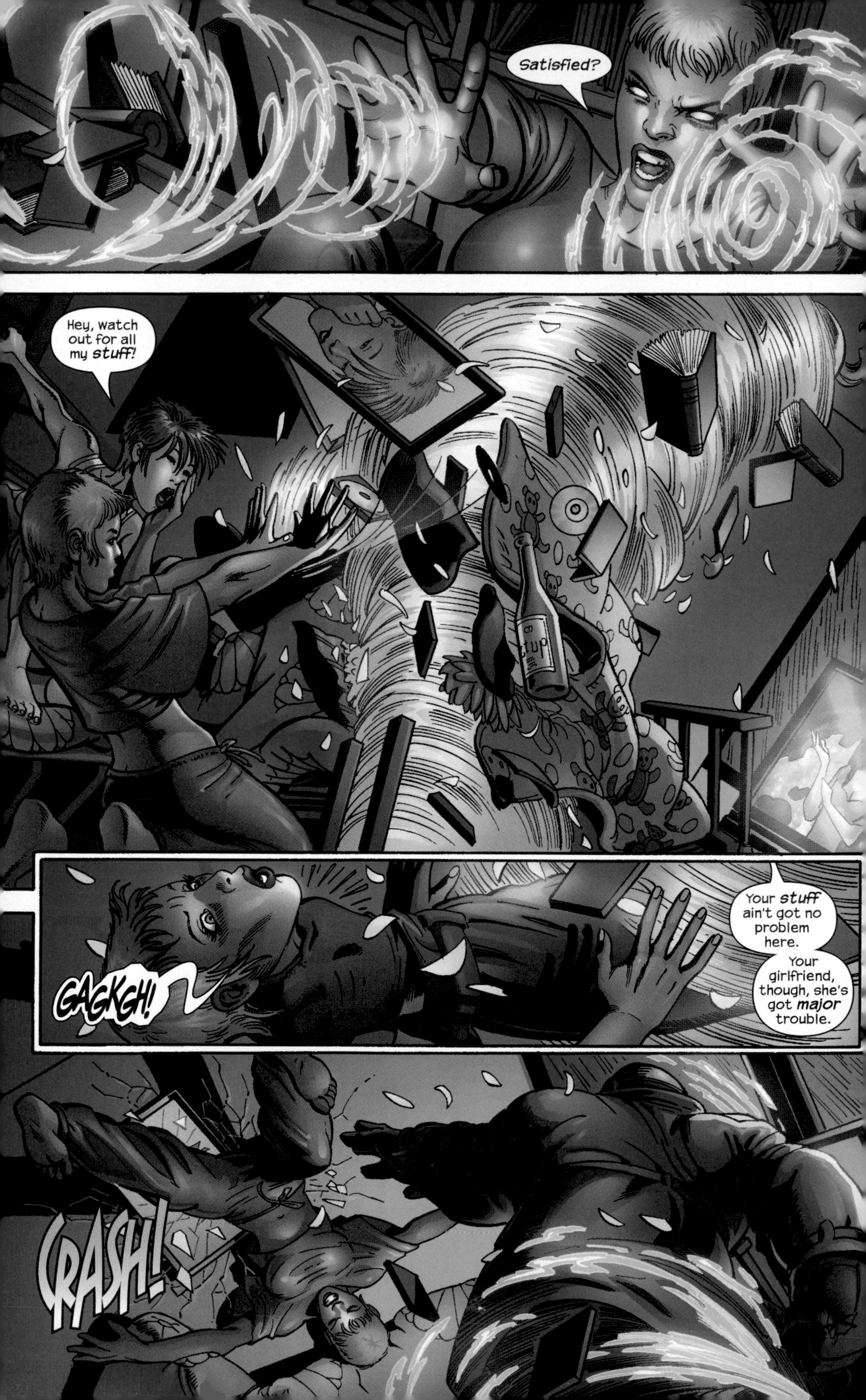
Satisfied?
Hey, watch out for all my stuff!
GAGKGH!
Your stuff ain't got no problem here.
Your girlfriend, though, she's got major trouble.
CRASH!

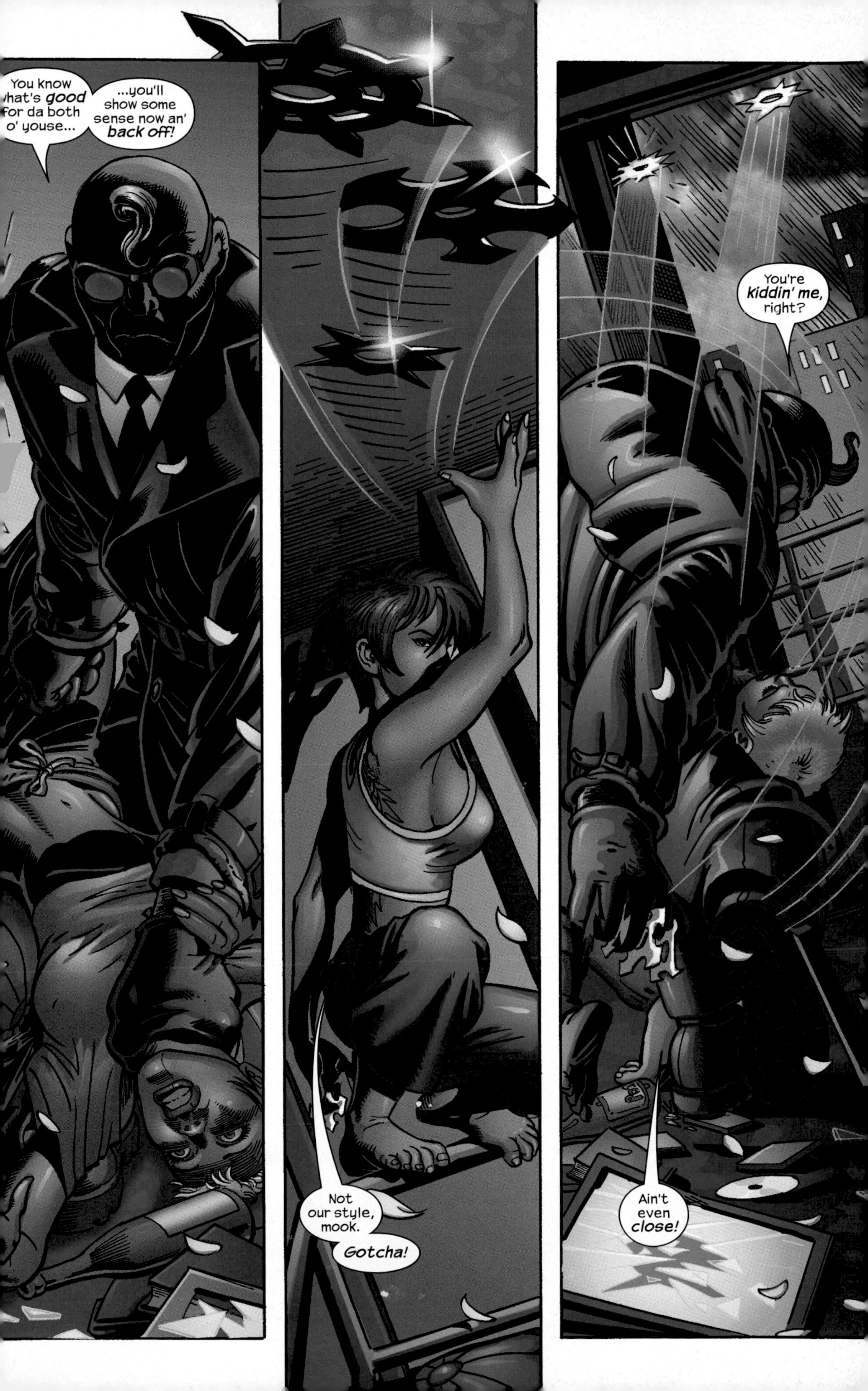
You know what's good for da both o' youse...
...you'll show some sense now an' back off!
Not our style, mook.
Gotcha!
You're kiddin' me, right?
Ain't even close!

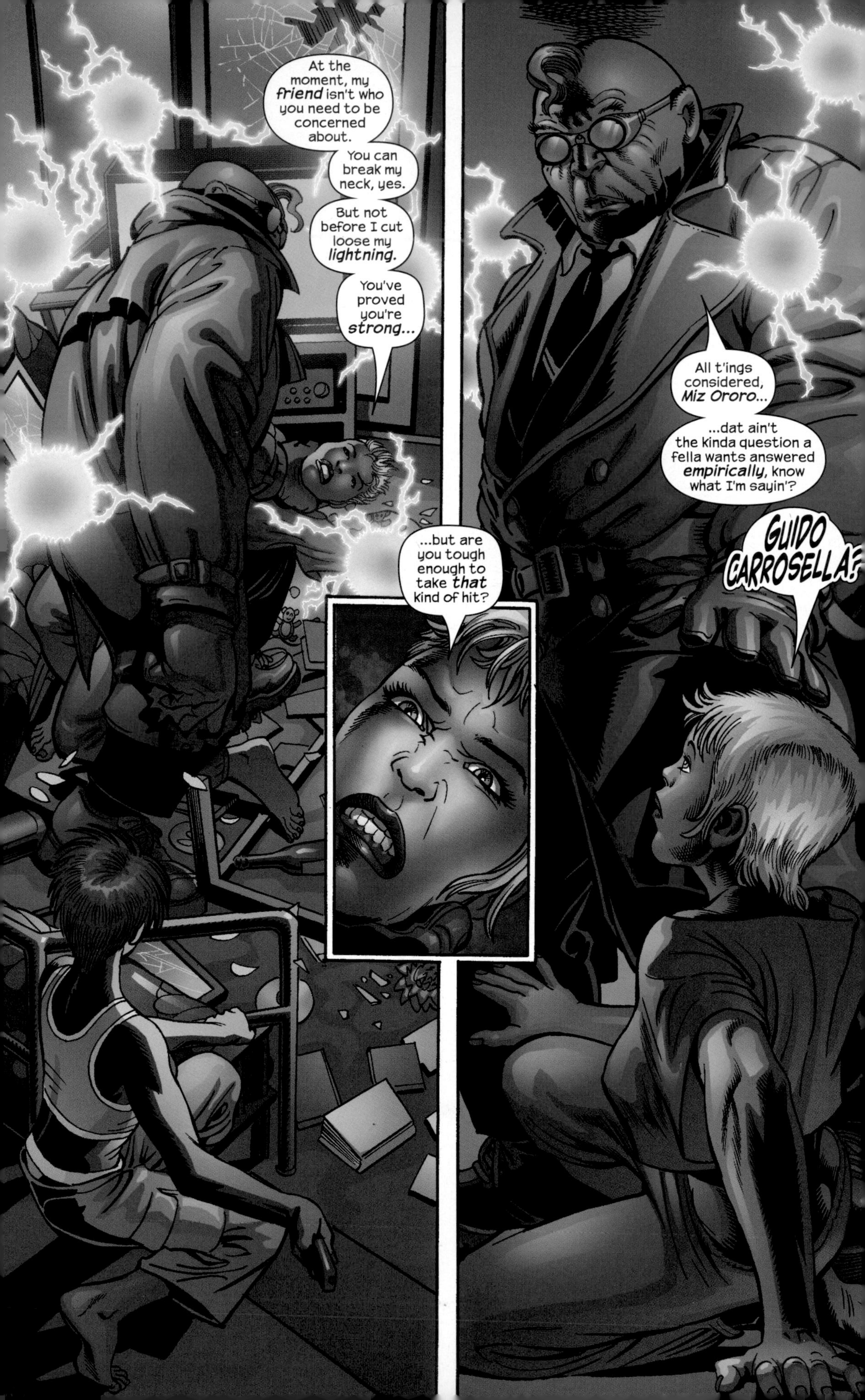
At the moment, my *friend* isn't who you need to be concerned about.
You can break my neck, yes.
But not before I cut loose my *lightning.*
You've proved you're *strong...*
...but are you tough enough to take *that* kind of hit?
All t'ings considered, *Miz Ororo...*
...dat ain't the kinda question a fella wants answered *empirically*, know what I'm sayin'?
GUIDO CARROSELLA!

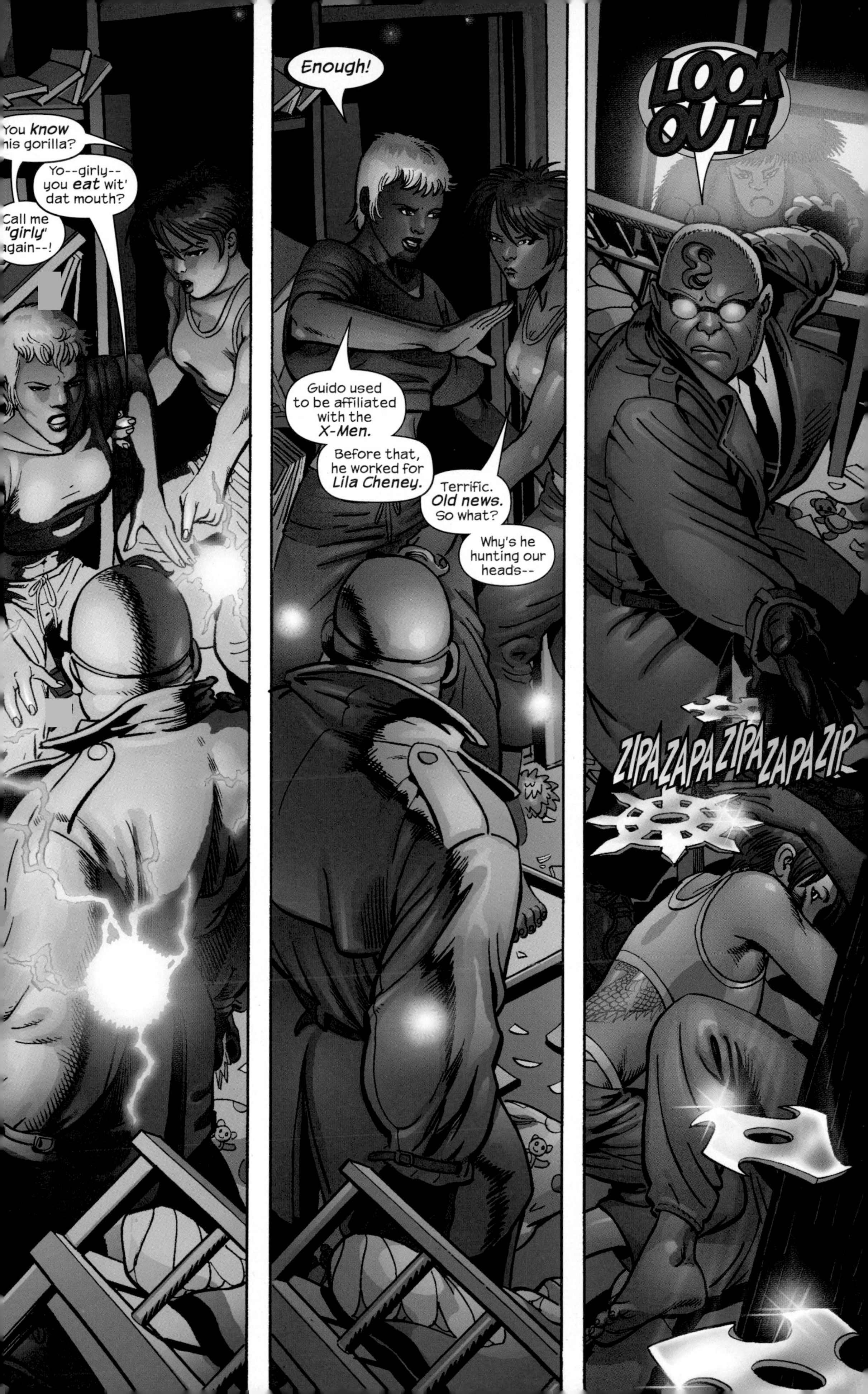
You know his gorilla?
Yo--girly--you eat wit' dat mouth?
Call me "girly" again--!
Enough!
Guido used to be affiliated with the X-Men.
Before that, he worked for Lila Cheney.
Terrific. Old news. So what?
Why's he hunting our heads--
LOOK OUT!
ZIPA ZAPA ZIPA ZAPA ZIP

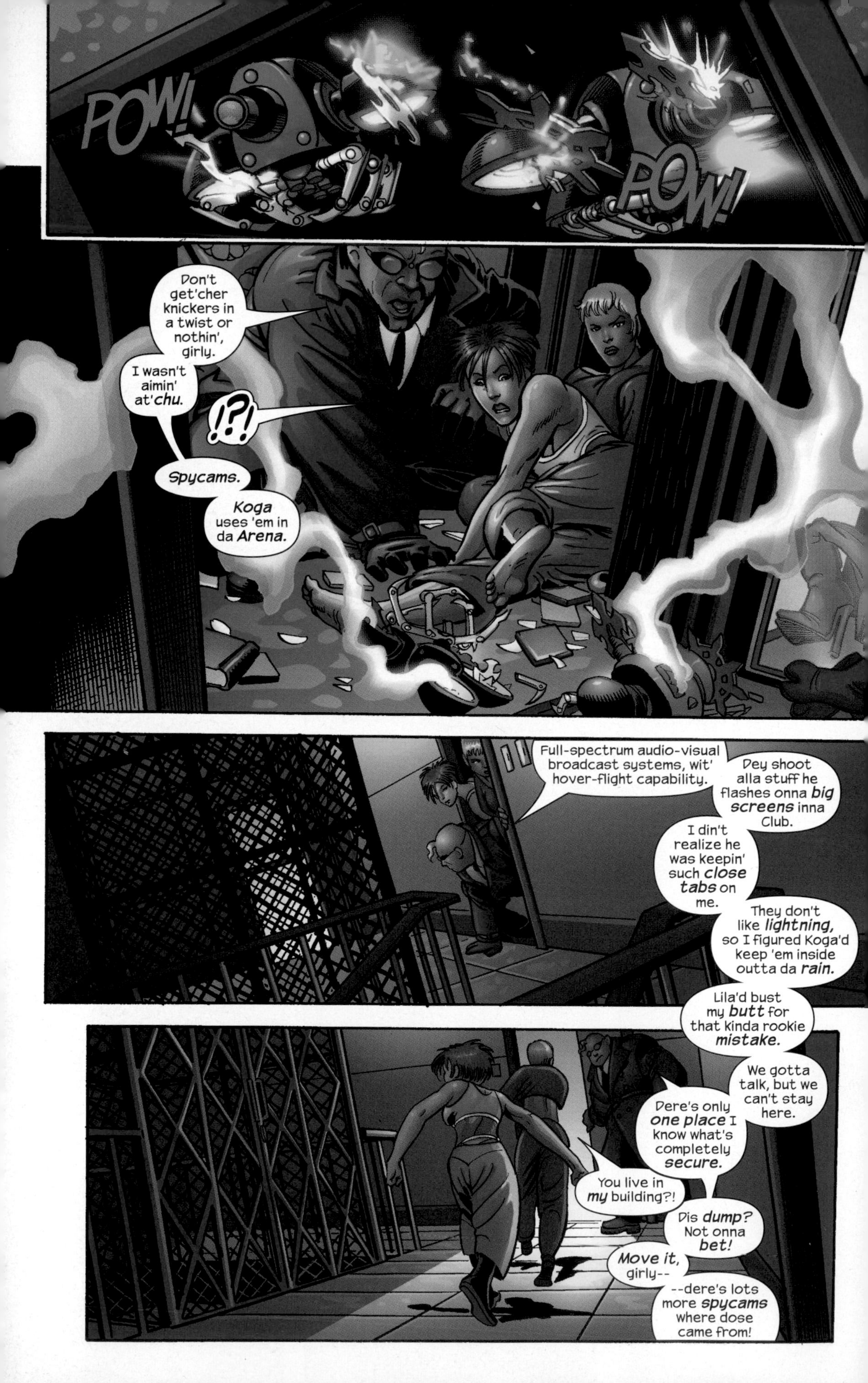
POW!
POW!
Don't get'cher knickers in a twist or nothin', girly.
I wasn't aimin' at'chu.
!?!
Spycams.
Koga uses 'em in da Arena.
Full-spectrum audio-visual broadcast systems, wit' hover-flight capability.
Dey shoot alla stuff he flashes onna big screens inna Club.
I din't realize he was keepin' such close tabs on me.
They don't like lightning, so I figured Koga'd keep 'em inside outta da rain.
Lila'd bust my butt for that kinda rookie mistake.
We gotta talk, but we can't stay here.
Dere's only one place I know what's completely secure.
You live in my building?!
Dis dump? Not onna bet!
Move it, girly--
--dere's lots more spycams where dose came from!

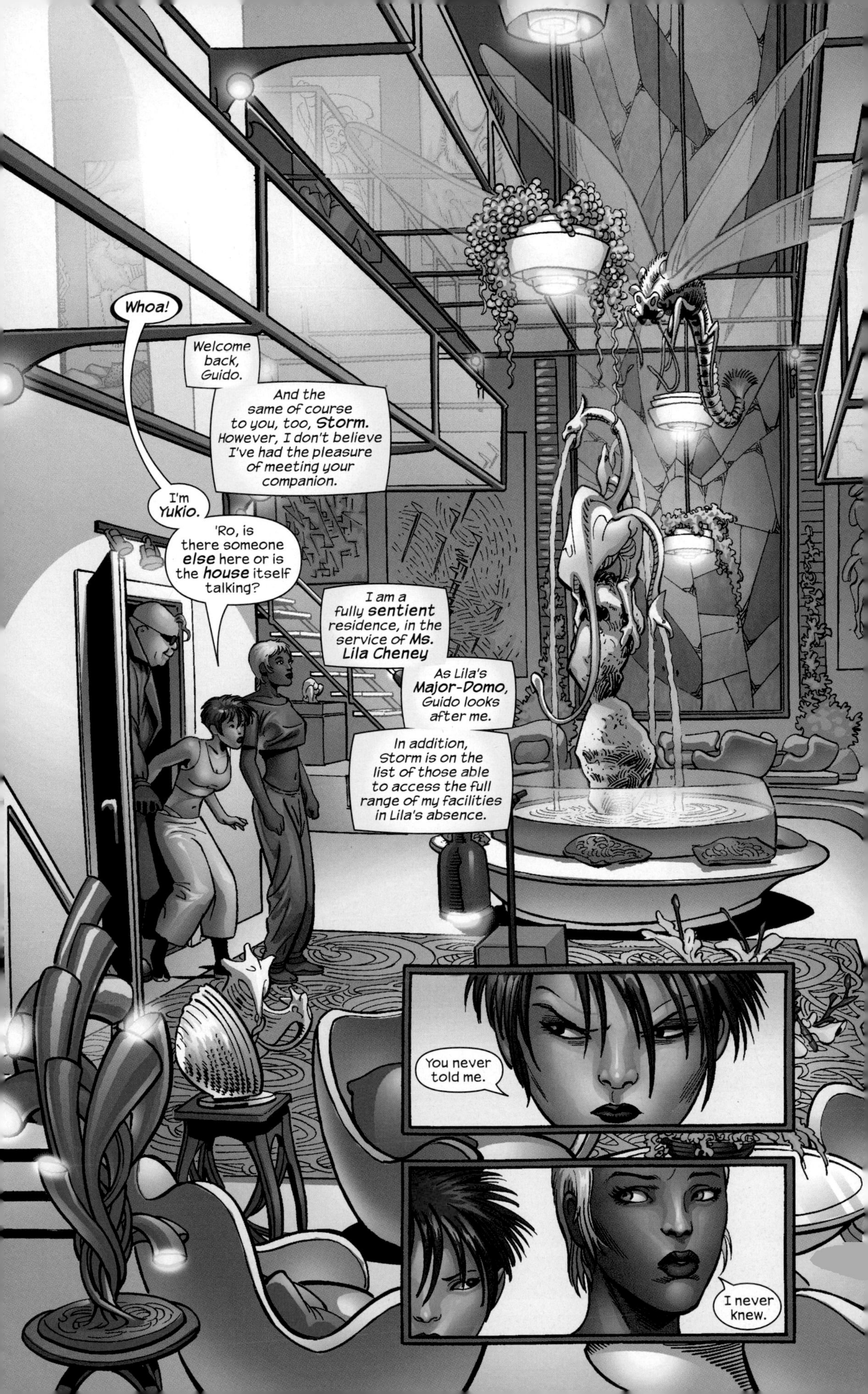
Whoa!
Welcome back, Guido.
And the same of course to you, too, **Storm.** However, I don't believe I've had the pleasure of meeting your companion.
I'm **Yukio.**
'Ro, is there someone **else** here or is the **house** itself talking?
I am a fully **sentient** residence, in the service of **Ms. Lila Cheney**
As Lila's **Major-Domo,** Guido looks after me.
In addition, Storm is on the list of those able to access the full range of my facilities in Lila's absence.
You never told me.
I never knew.

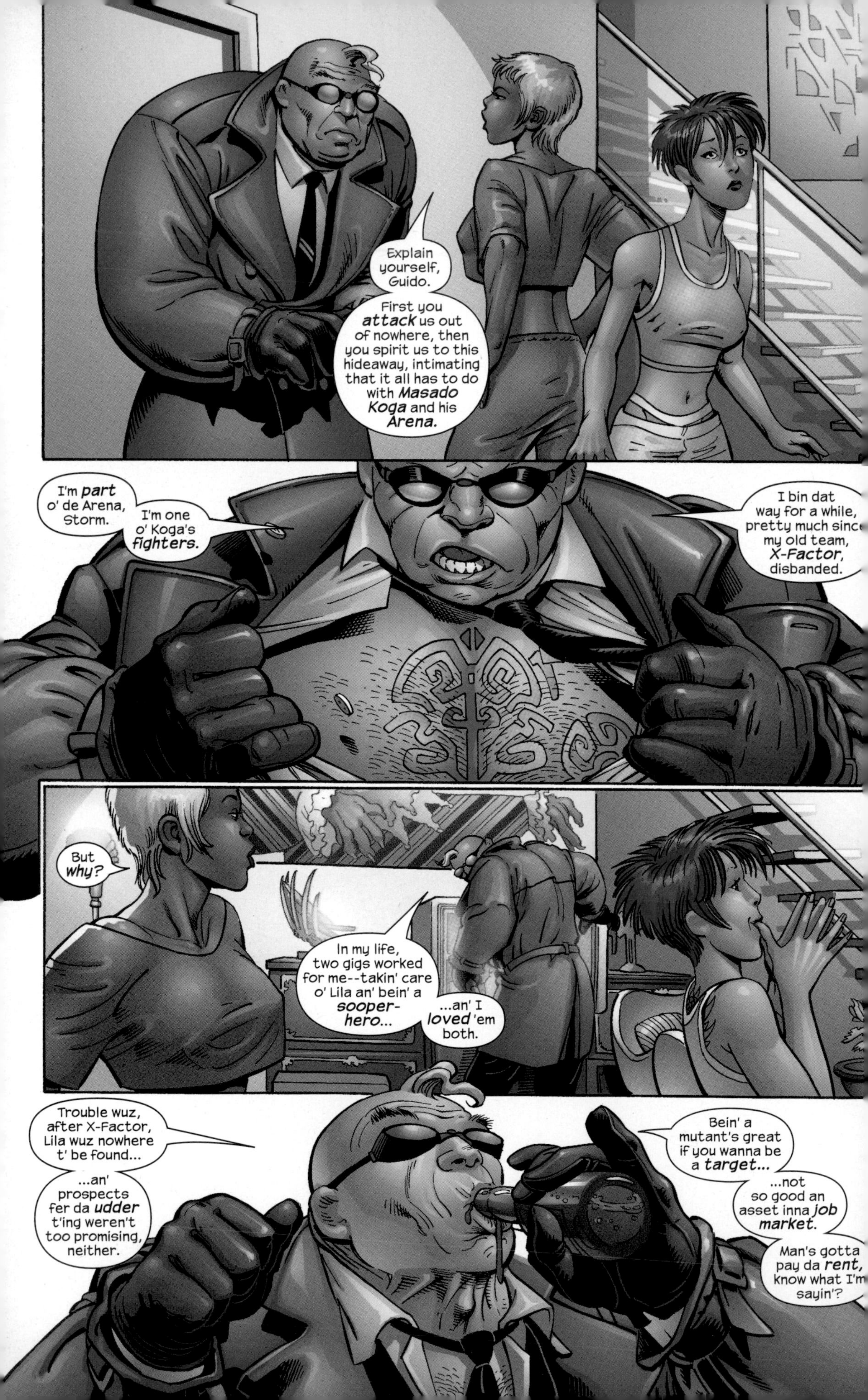
Explain yourself, Guido.
First you attack us out of nowhere, then you spirit us to this hideaway, intimating that it all has to do with Masado Koga and his Arena.
I'm part o' de Arena, Storm.
I'm one o' Koga's fighters.
I bin dat way for a while, pretty much since my old team, X-Factor, disbanded.
But why?
In my life, two gigs worked for me--takin' care o' Lila an' bein' a sooper-hero...
...an' I loved 'em both.
Trouble wuz, after X-Factor, Lila wuz nowhere t' be found...
...an' prospects fer da udder t'ing weren't too promising, neither.
Bein' a mutant's great if you wanna be a target...
...not so good an asset inna job market.
Man's gotta pay da rent, know what I'm sayin'?

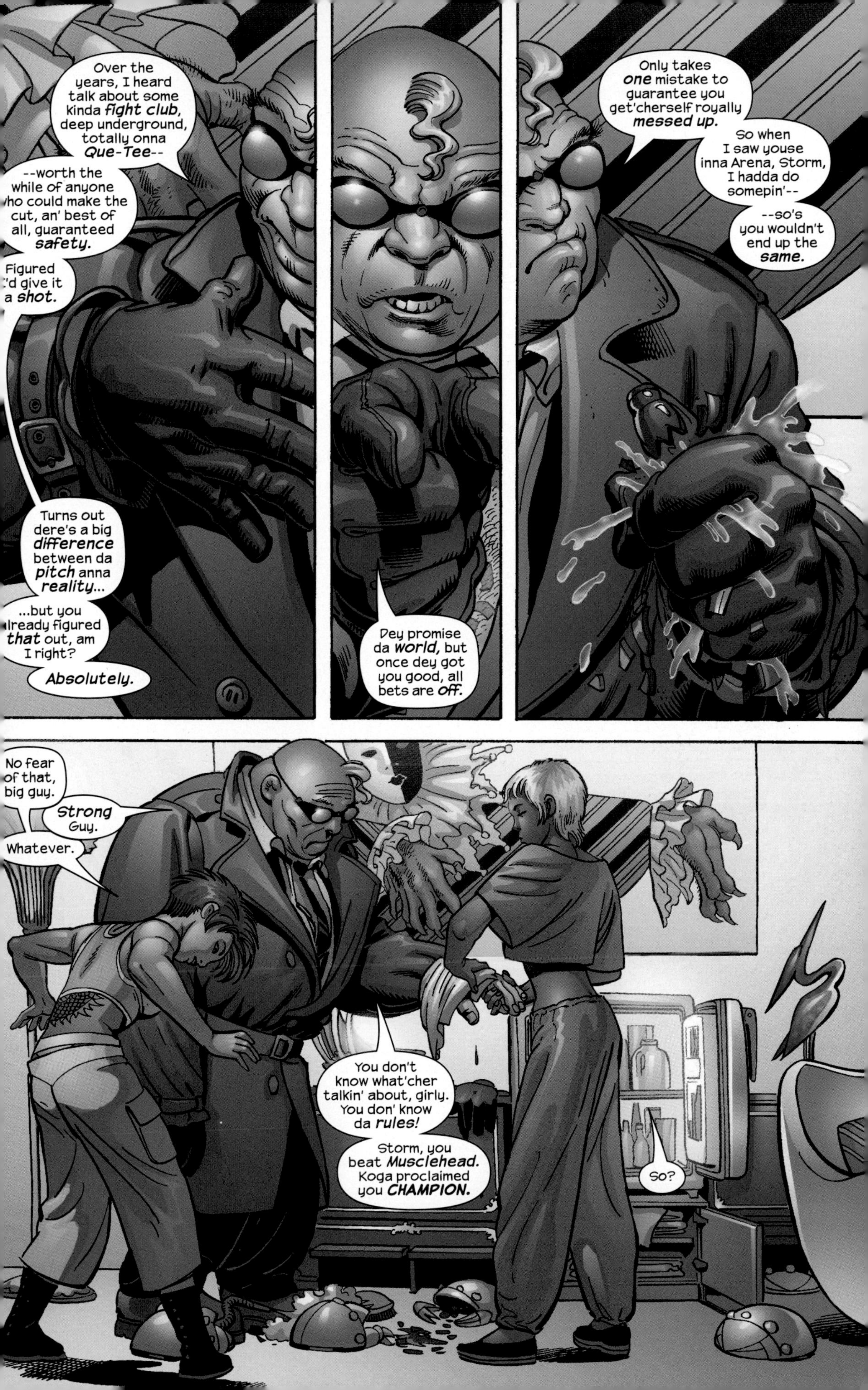
Over the years, I heard talk about some kinda fight club, deep underground, totally onna Que-Tee--
--worth the while of anyone who could make the cut, an' best of all, guaranteed safety.
Figured I'd give it a shot.
Turns out dere's a big difference between da pitch anna reality...
...but you already figured that out, am I right?
Absolutely.
Dey promise da world, but once dey got you good, all bets are off.
Only takes one mistake to guarantee you get'cherself royally messed up.
So when I saw youse inna Arena, Storm, I hadda do somepin'--
--so's you wouldn't end up the same.
No fear of that, big guy.
Strong Guy.
Whatever.
You don't know what'cher talkin' about, girly. You don' know da rules!
Storm, you beat Musclehead. Koga proclaimed you CHAMPION.
So?

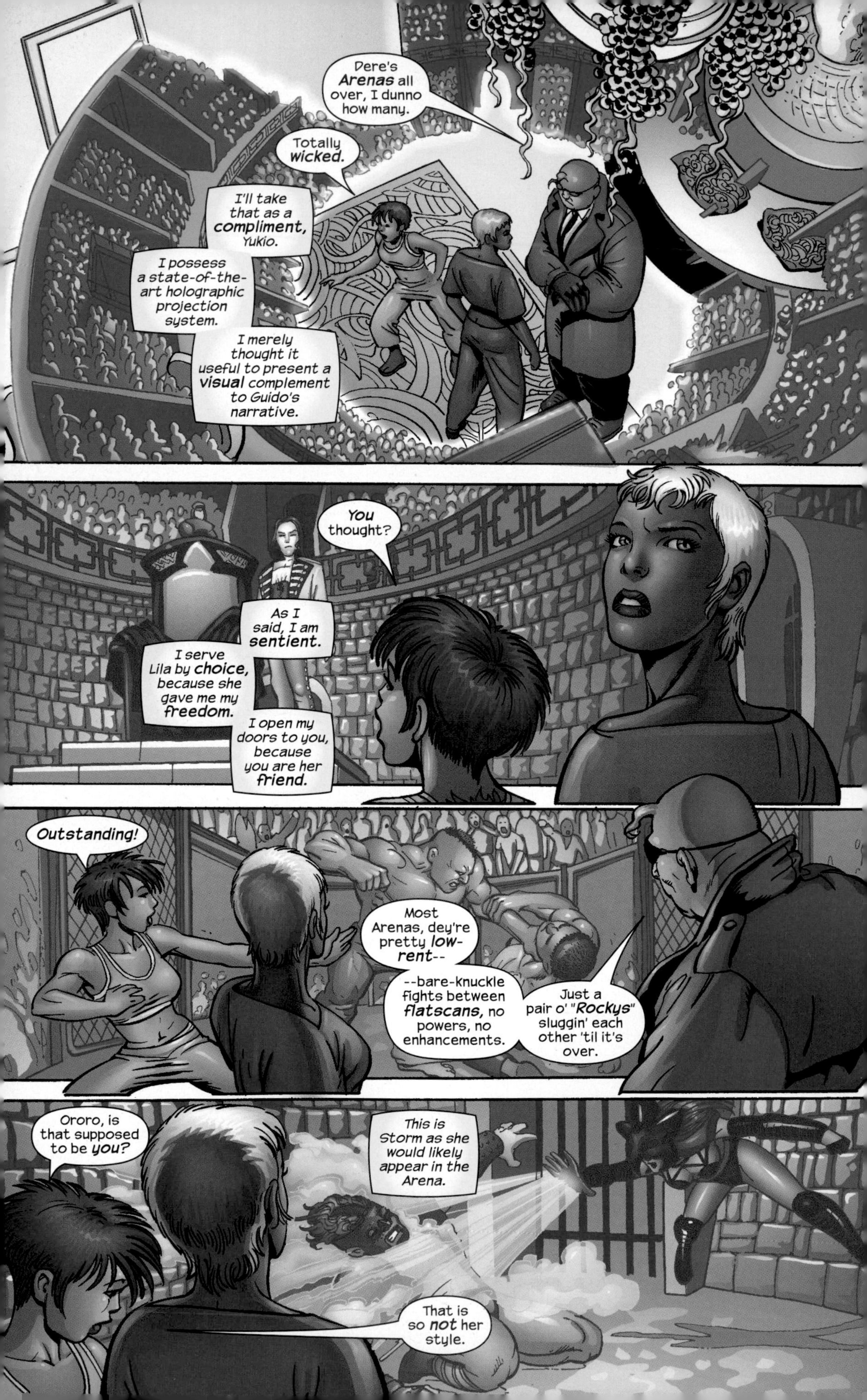
Dere's Arenas all over, I dunno how many.
Totally wicked.
I'll take that as a compliment, Yukio.
I possess a state-of-the-art holographic projection system.
I merely thought it useful to present a visual complement to Guido's narrative.
You thought?
As I said, I am sentient.
I serve Lila by choice, because she gave me my freedom.
I open my doors to you, because you are her friend.
Outstanding!
Most Arenas, dey're pretty low-rent--
--bare-knuckle fights between flatscans, no powers, no enhancements.
Just a pair o' "Rockys" sluggin' each other 'til it's over.
Ororo, is that supposed to be you?
This is Storm as she would likely appear in the Arena.
That is so not her style.

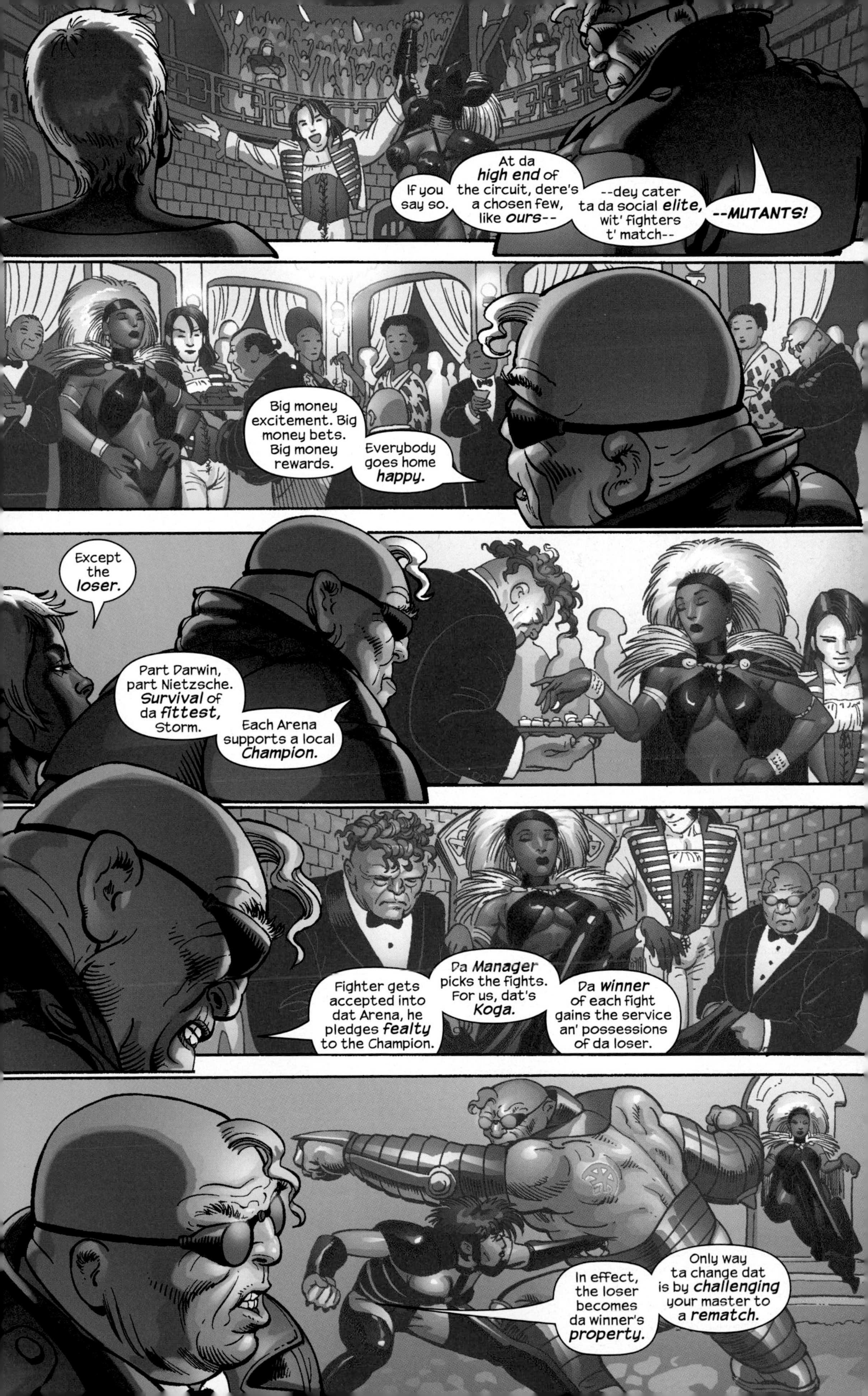

If you say so.
At da *high end* of the circuit, dere's a chosen few, like *ours*--
--dey cater ta da social *elite*, wit' fighters t' match--
--MUTANTS!
Big money excitement. Big money bets. Big money rewards.
Everybody goes home *happy*.
Except the *loser*.
Part Darwin, part Nietzsche. *Survival* of da *fittest*, Storm.
Each Arena supports a local *Champion*.
Fighter gets accepted into dat Arena, he pledges *fealty* to the Champion.
Da *Manager* picks the fights. For us, dat's *Koga*.
Da *winner* of each fight gains the service an' possessions of da loser.
In effect, the loser becomes da winner's *property*.
Only way ta change dat is by *challenging* your master to a *rematch*.

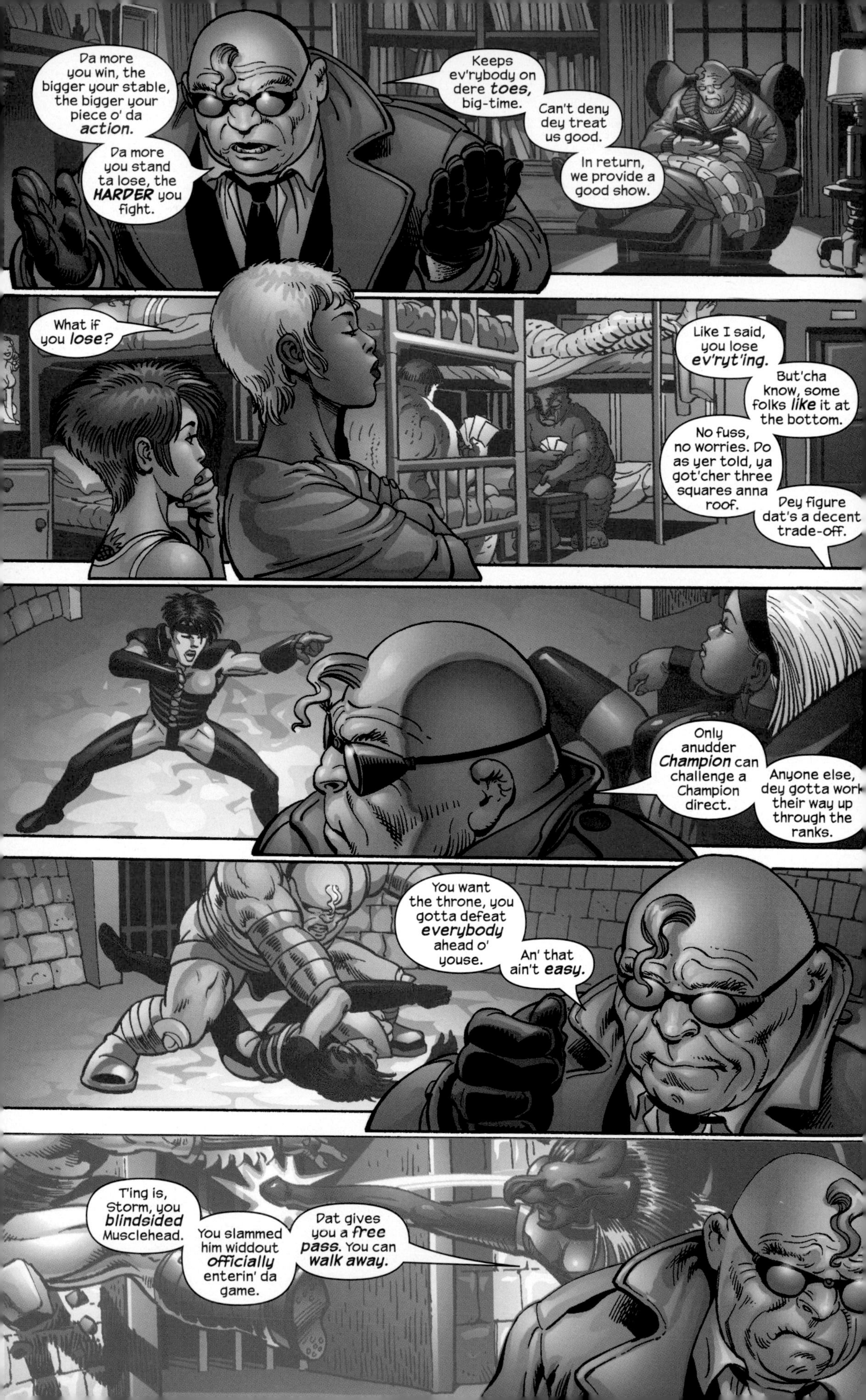

Da more you win, the bigger your stable, the bigger your piece o' da action.
Da more you stand ta lose, the HARDER you fight.
Keeps ev'rybody on dere toes, big-time.
Can't deny dey treat us good.
In return, we provide a good show.
What if you lose?
Like I said, you lose ev'ryt'ing.
But'cha know, some folks like it at the bottom.
No fuss, no worries. Do as yer told, ya got'cher three squares anna roof.
Dey figure dat's a decent trade-off.
Only anudder Champion can challenge a Champion direct.
Anyone else, dey gotta work their way up through the ranks.
You want the throne, you gotta defeat everybody ahead o' youse.
An' that ain't easy.
T'ing is, Storm, you blindsided Musclehead.
You slammed him widout officially enterin' da game.
Dat gives you a free pass. You can walk away.

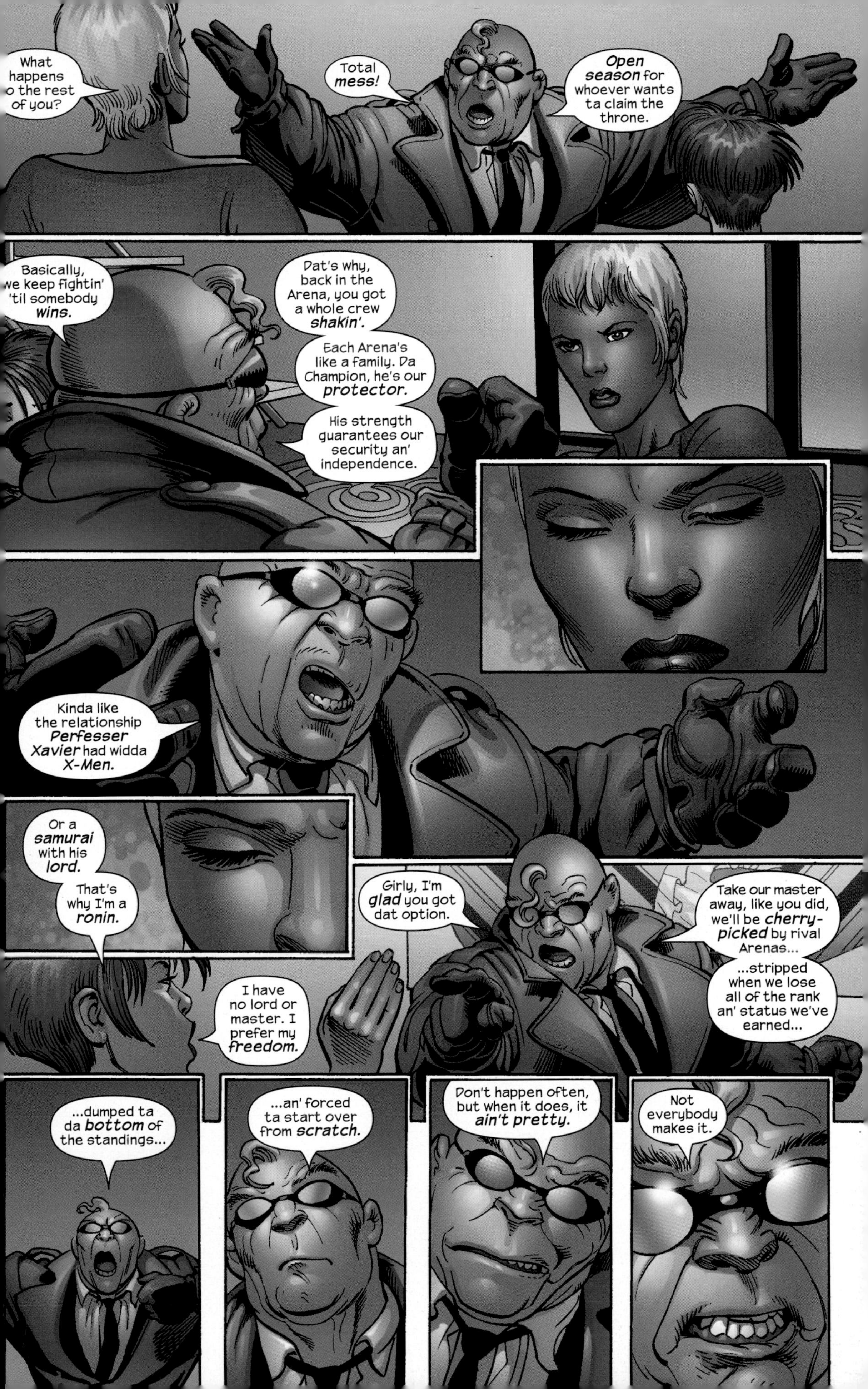

What happens to the rest of you?
Total mess!
Open season for whoever wants ta claim the throne.
Basically, we keep fightin' 'til somebody wins.
Dat's why, back in the Arena, you got a whole crew shakin'.
Each Arena's like a family. Da Champion, he's our protector.
His strength guarantees our security an' independence.
Kinda like the relationship Perfesser Xavier had widda X-Men.
Or a samurai with his lord.
That's why I'm a ronin.
Girly, I'm glad you got dat option.
Take our master away, like you did, we'll be cherry-picked by rival Arenas...
...stripped when we lose all of the rank an' status we've earned...
I have no lord or master. I prefer my freedom.
...dumped ta da bottom of the standings...
...an' forced ta start over from scratch.
Don't happen often, but when it does, it ain't pretty.
Not everybody makes it.

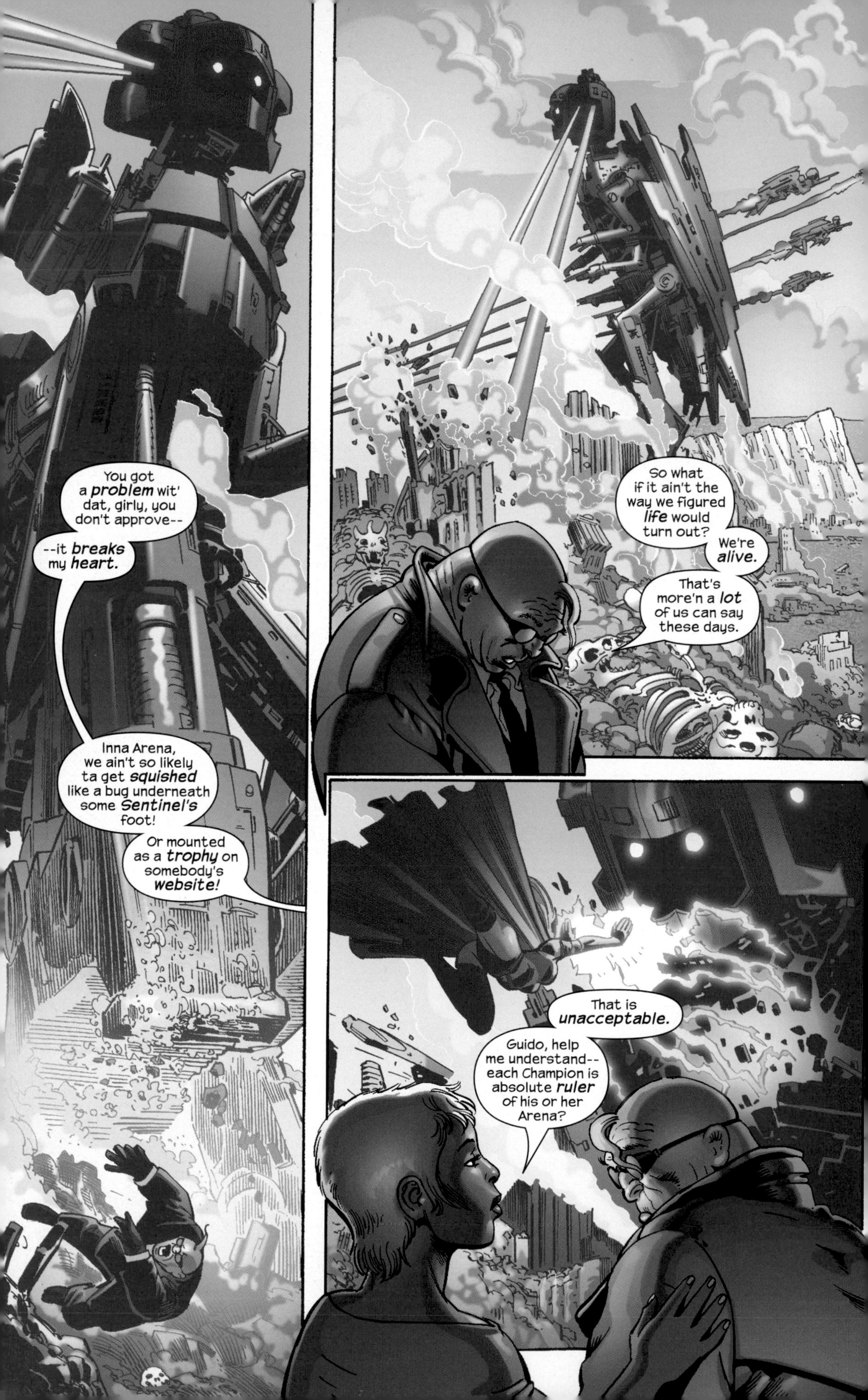

You got a problem wit' dat, girly, you don't approve--
--it breaks my heart.
Inna Arena, we ain't so likely ta get squished like a bug underneath some Sentinel's foot!
Or mounted as a trophy on somebody's website!
So what if it ain't the way we figured life would turn out?
We're alive.
That's more'n a lot of us can say these days.
That is unacceptable.
Guido, help me understand-- each Champion is absolute ruler of his or her Arena?

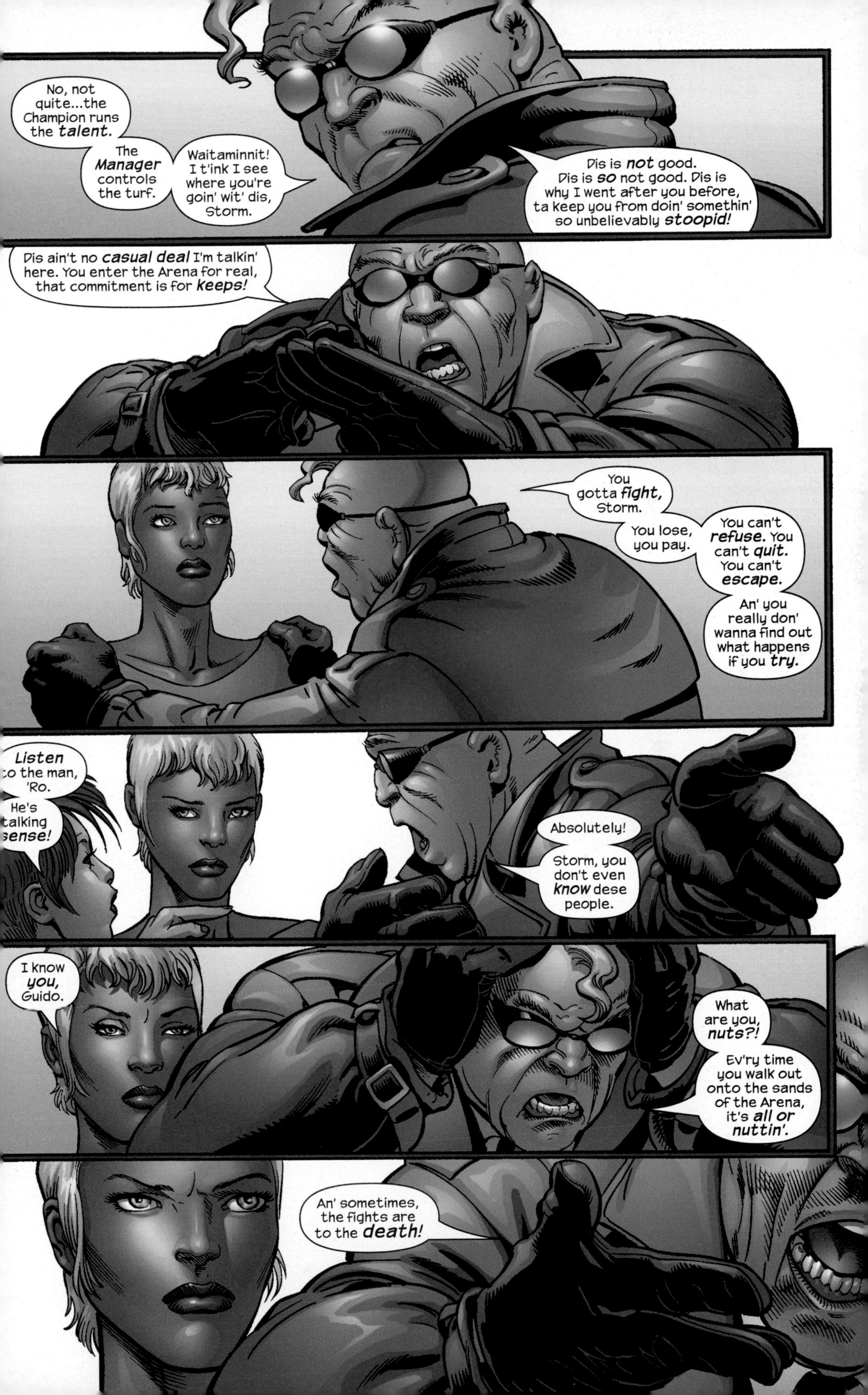
No, not quite...the Champion runs the *talent*.
The *Manager* controls the turf.
Waitaminnit! I t'ink I see where you're goin' wit' dis, Storm.
Dis is *not* good. Dis is *so* not good. Dis is why I went after you before, ta keep you from doin' somethin' so unbelievably *stoopid!*
Dis ain't no *casual deal* I'm talkin' here. You enter the Arena for real, that commitment is for *keeps!*
You gotta *fight,* Storm.
You lose, you pay.
You can't *refuse.* You can't *quit.* You can't *escape.*
An' you really don' wanna find out what happens if you *try.*
Listen to the man, 'Ro.
He's talking *sense!*
Absolutely!
Storm, you don't even *know* dese people.
I know *you,* Guido.
What are you, *nuts?!*
Ev'ry time you walk out onto the sands of the Arena, it's *all or nuttin'.*
An' sometimes, the fights are to the *death!*

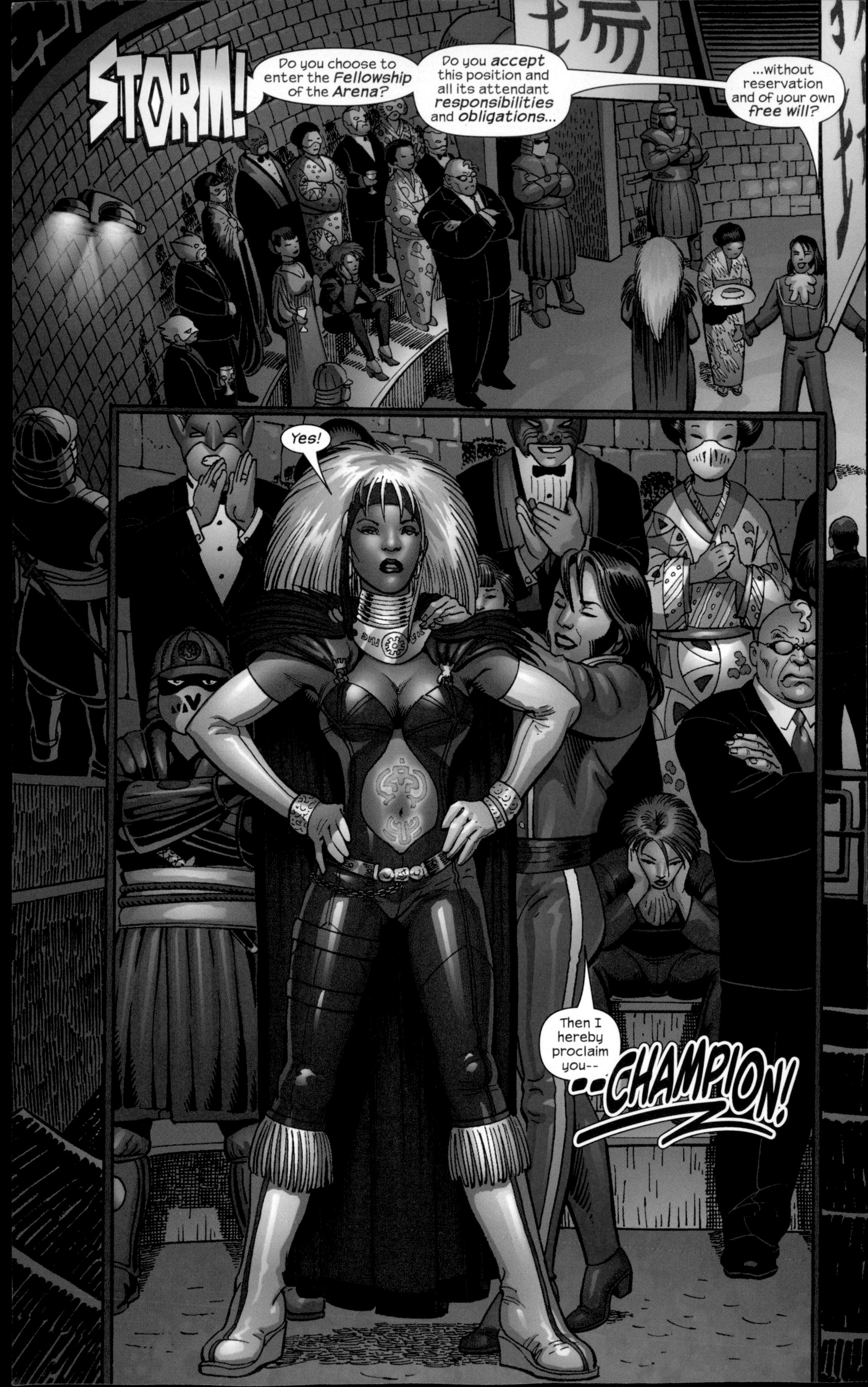
STORM!
Do you choose to enter the *Fellowship* of the *Arena?*
Do you *accept* this position and all its attendant *responsibilities* and *obligations...*
...without reservation and of your own *free will?*
Yes!
Then I hereby proclaim you--
--CHAMPION!

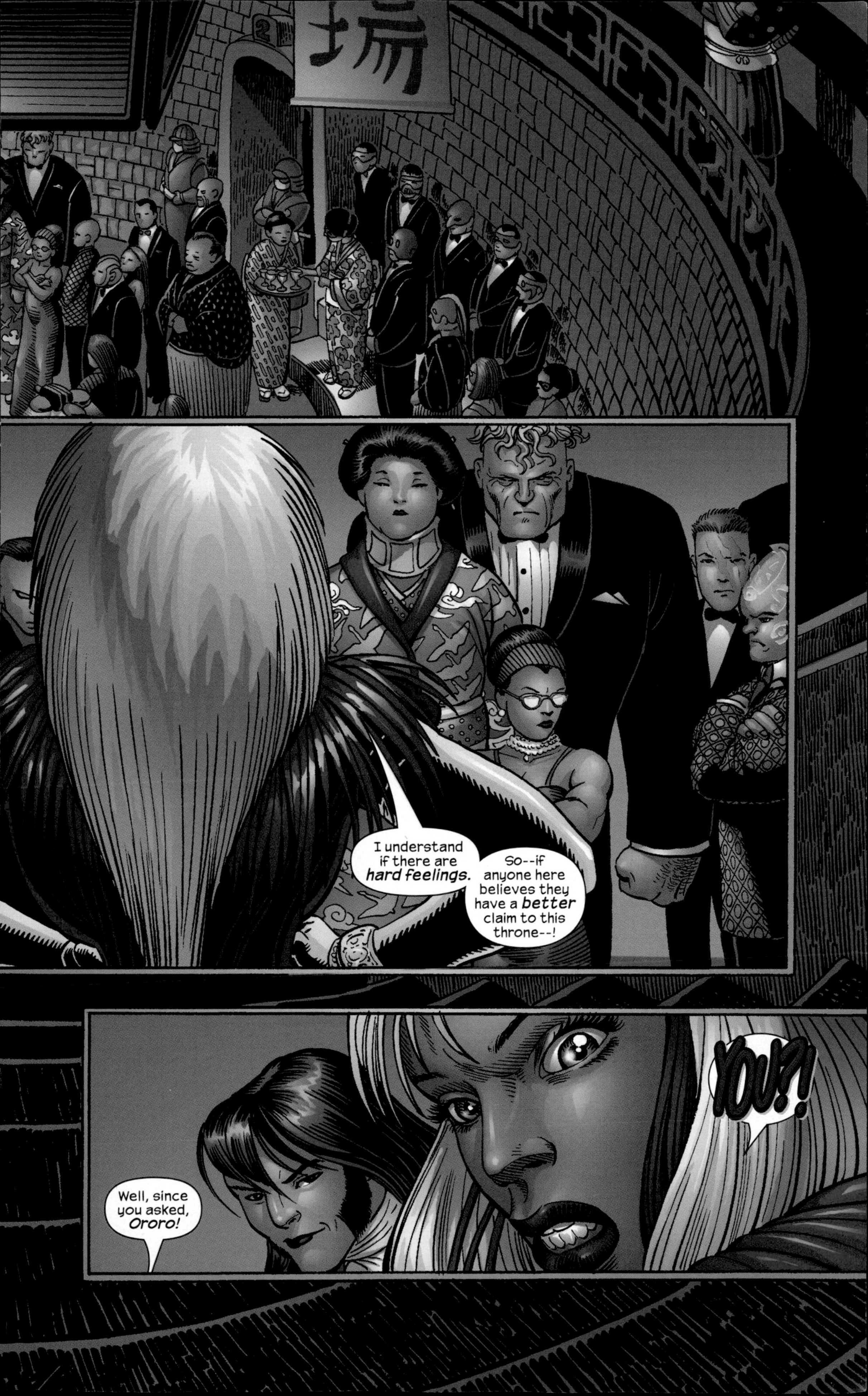
I understand if there are **hard feelings.**
So--if anyone here believes they have a **better** claim to this throne--!
Well, since you asked, *Ororo!*
YOU?!

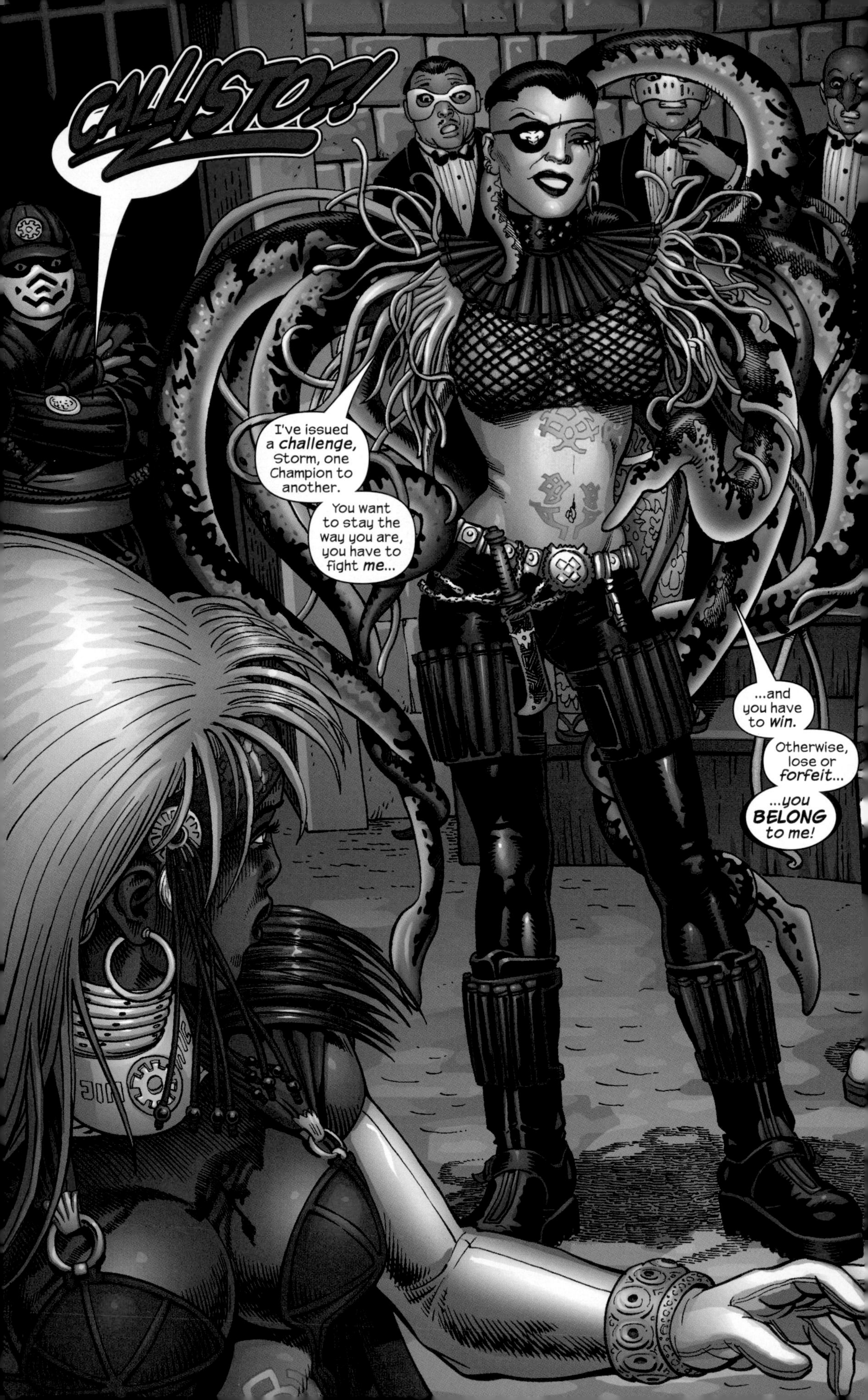
CALLISTO?!
I've issued a challenge, Storm, one Champion to another.
You want to stay the way you are, you have to fight me...
...and you have to win.
Otherwise, lose or forfeit...
...you BELONG to me!

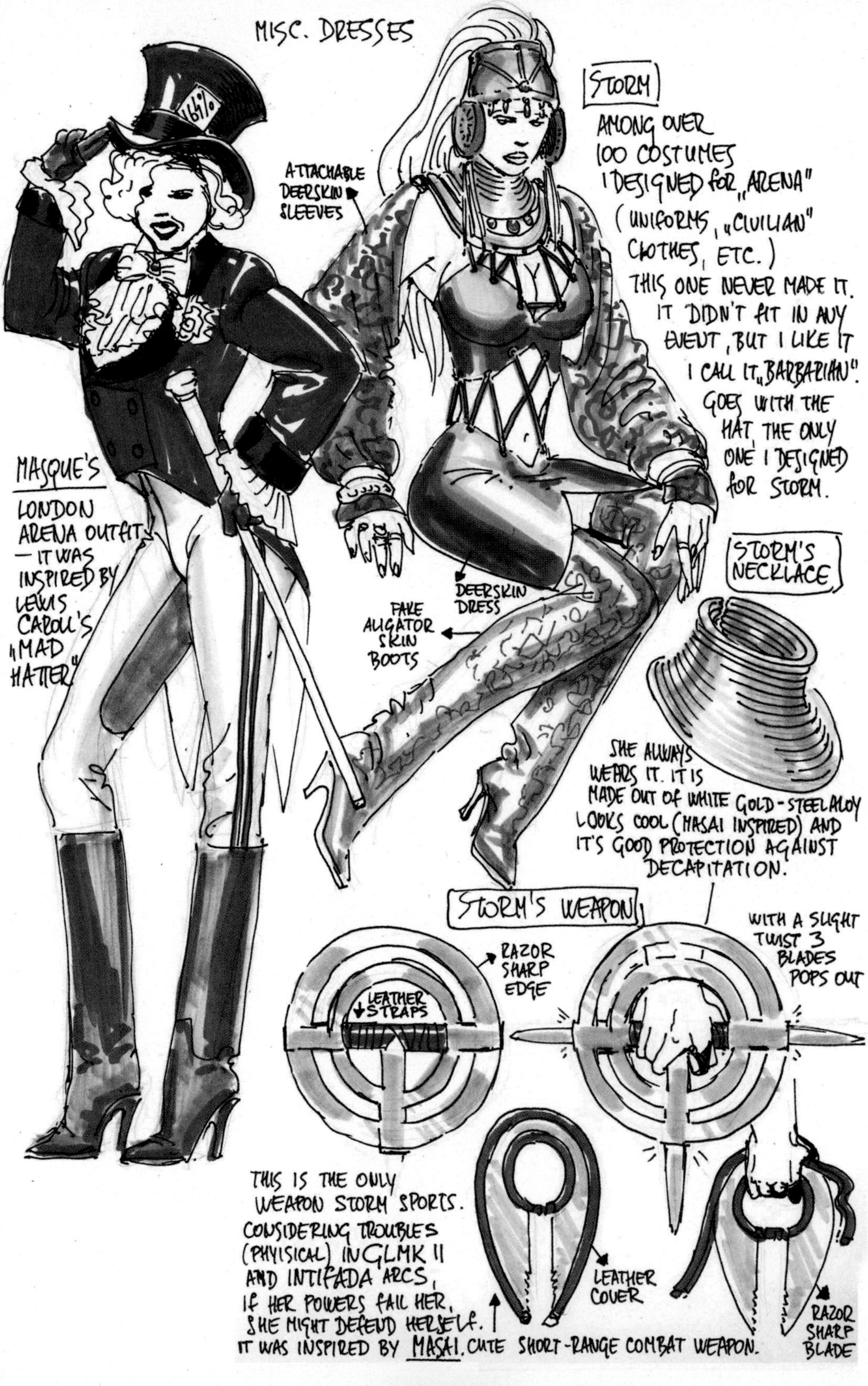
MISC. DRESSES
STORM
AMONG OVER 100 COSTUMES I DESIGNED FOR „ARENA" (UNIFORMS, „CIVILIAN" CLOTHES, ETC.) THIS ONE NEVER MADE IT. IT DIDN'T FIT IN ANY EVENT, BUT I LIKE IT I CALL IT „BARBARIAN". GOES WITH THE HAT, THE ONLY ONE I DESIGNED FOR STORM.
ATTACHABLE DEERSKIN SLEEVES
MASQUE'S
LONDON ARENA OUTFIT — IT WAS INSPIRED BY LEWIS CAROLL'S „MAD HATTER"
DEERSKIN DRESS
FAKE ALLIGATOR SKIN BOOTS
STORM'S NECKLACE
SHE ALWAYS WEARS IT. IT IS MADE OUT OF WHITE GOLD-STEEL ALLOY LOOKS COOL (MASAI INSPIRED) AND IT'S GOOD PROTECTION AGAINST DECAPITATION.
STORM'S WEAPON
RAZOR SHARP EDGE
LEATHER STRAPS
WITH A SLIGHT TWIST 3 BLADES POPS OUT
LEATHER COVER
RAZOR SHARP BLADE
THIS IS THE ONLY WEAPON STORM SPORTS. CONSIDERING TROUBLES (PHYISICAL) IN GLMK II AND INTIFADA ARCS, IF HER POWERS FAIL HER, SHE MIGHT DEFEND HERSELF. IT WAS INSPIRED BY MASAI. CUTE SHORT-RANGE COMBAT WEAPON.

Sketches by Igor Kordey

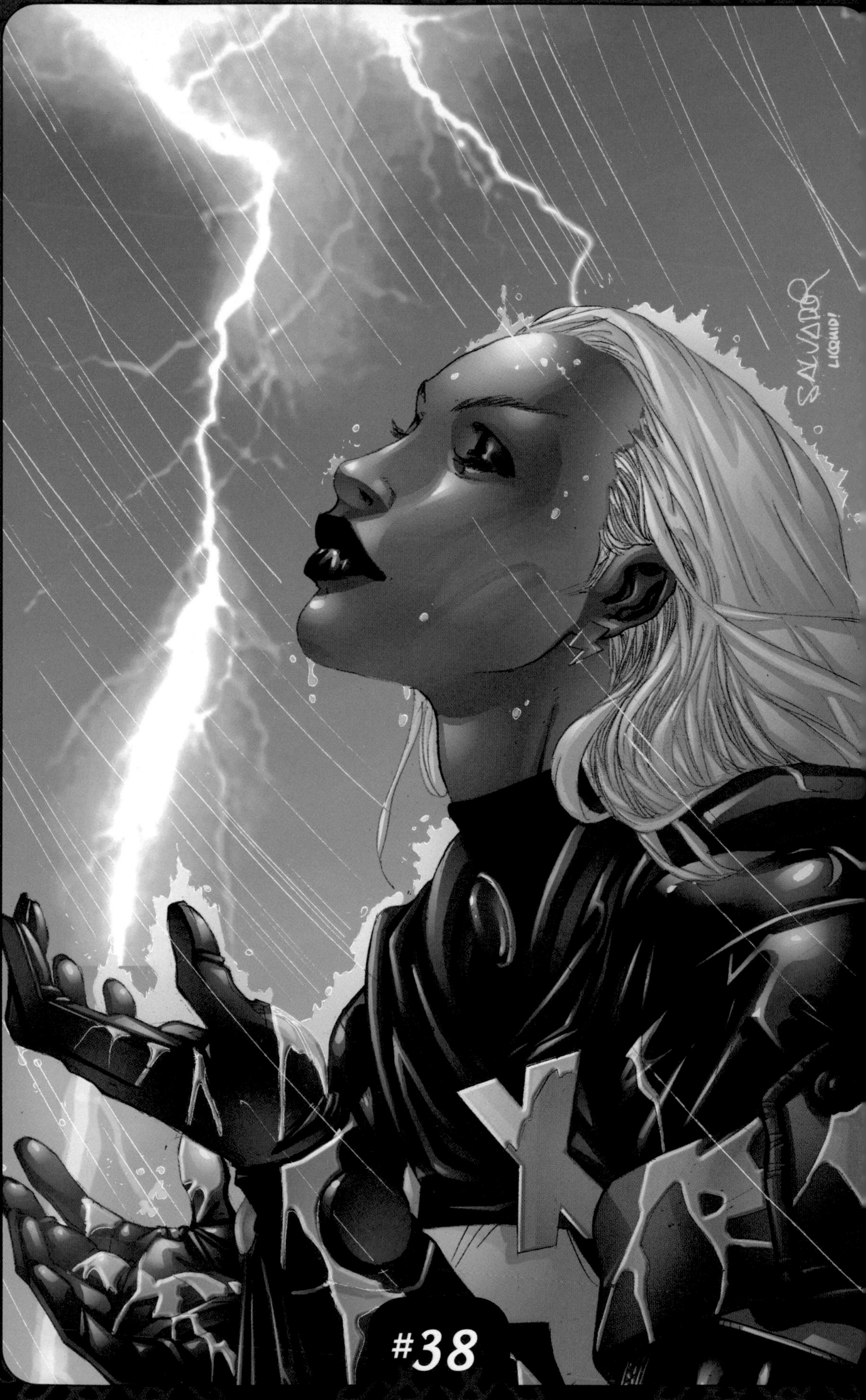
SALVADOR
LIQUID!

#38

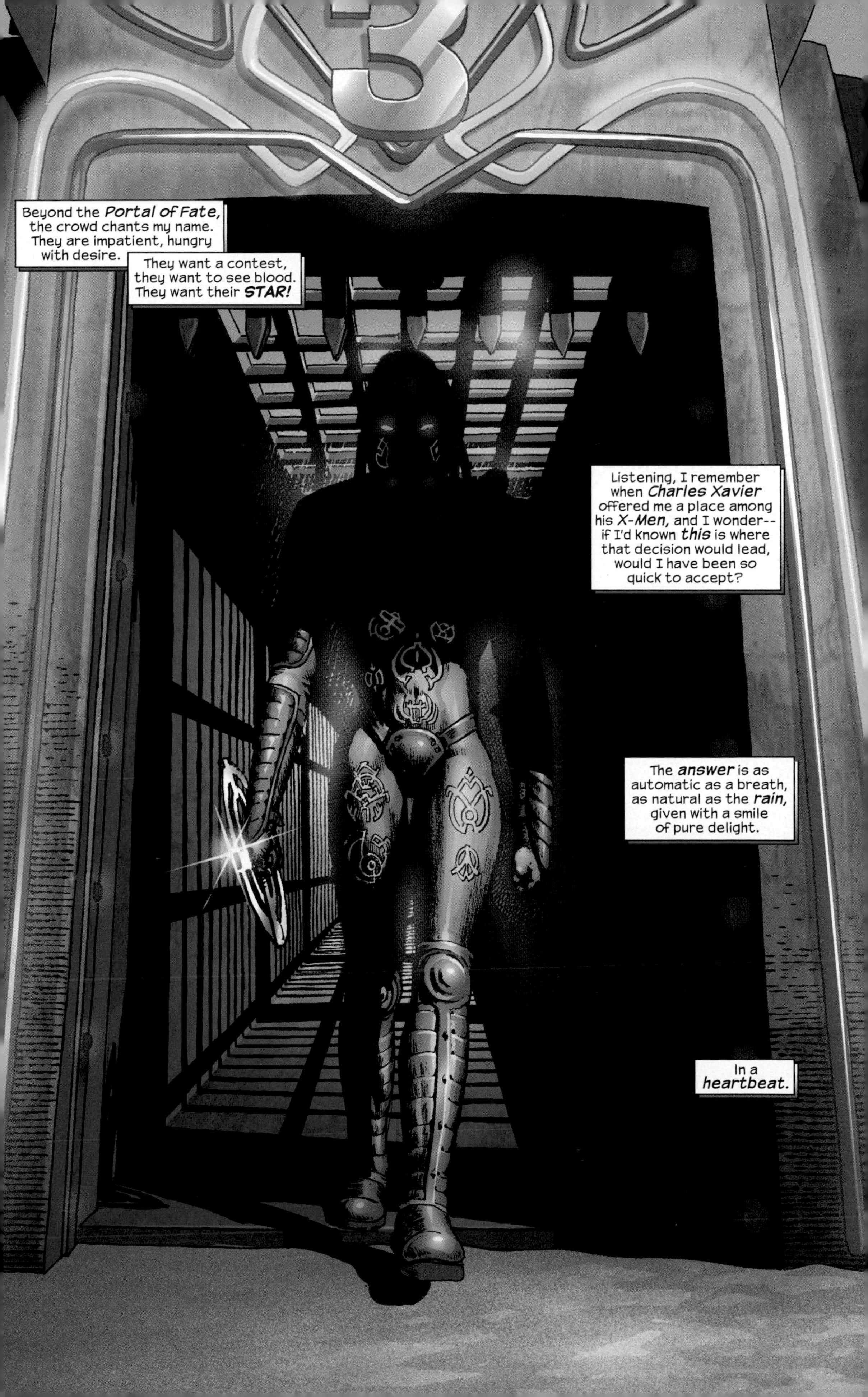
Beyond the Portal of Fate, the crowd chants my name. They are impatient, hungry with desire.
They want a contest, they want to see blood. They want their STAR!
Listening, I remember when Charles Xavier offered me a place among his X-Men, and I wonder-- if I'd known this is where that decision would lead, would I have been so quick to accept?
The answer is as automatic as a breath, as natural as the rain, given with a smile of pure delight.
In a heartbeat.

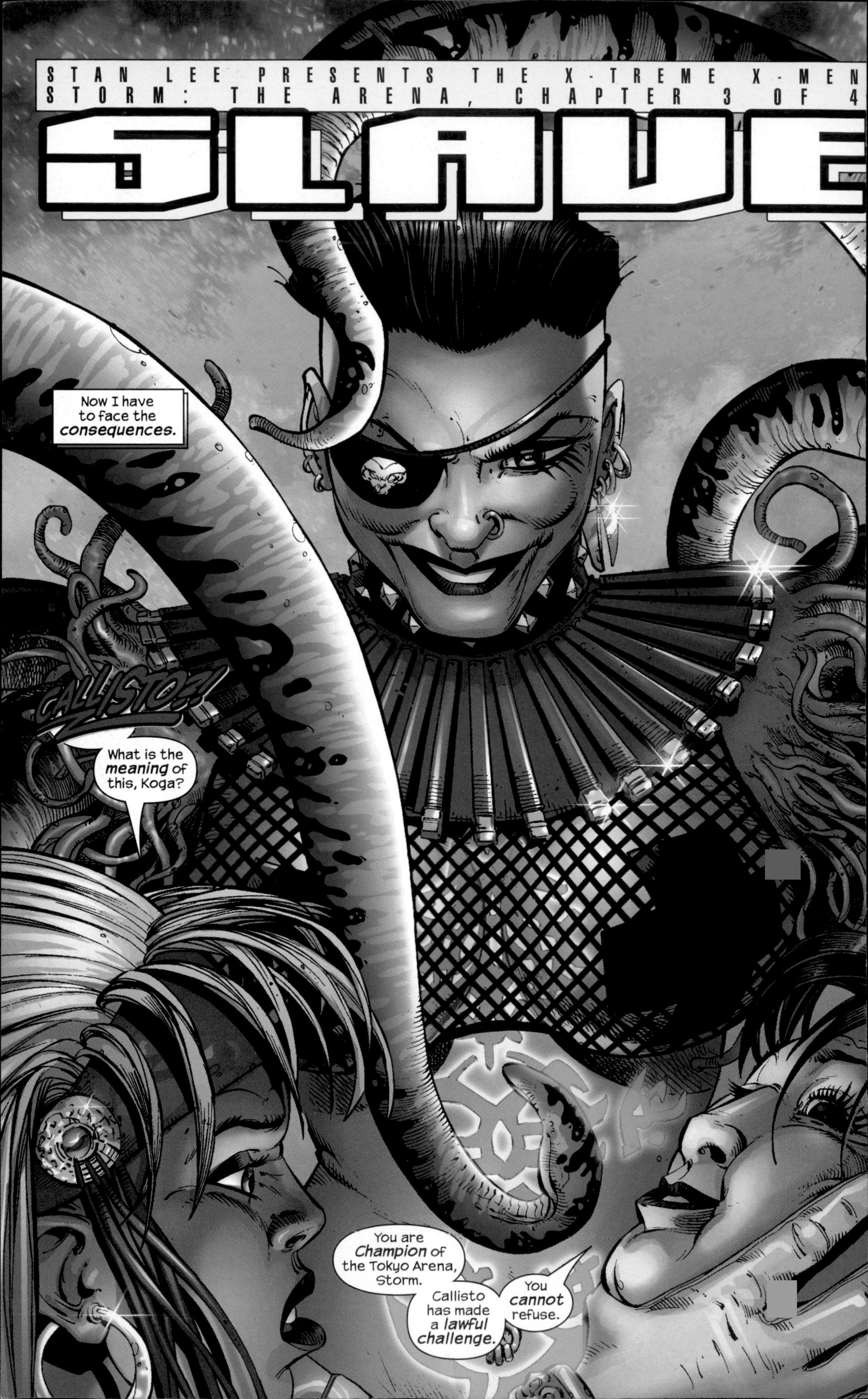
STAN LEE PRESENTS THE X-TREME X-MEN
STORM: THE ARENA, CHAPTER 3 OF 4
SLAVE
Now I have to face the *consequences*.
CALLISTO?!
What is the *meaning* of this, Koga?
You are *Champion* of the Tokyo Arena, Storm.
Callisto has made a *lawful challenge*.
You *cannot* refuse.

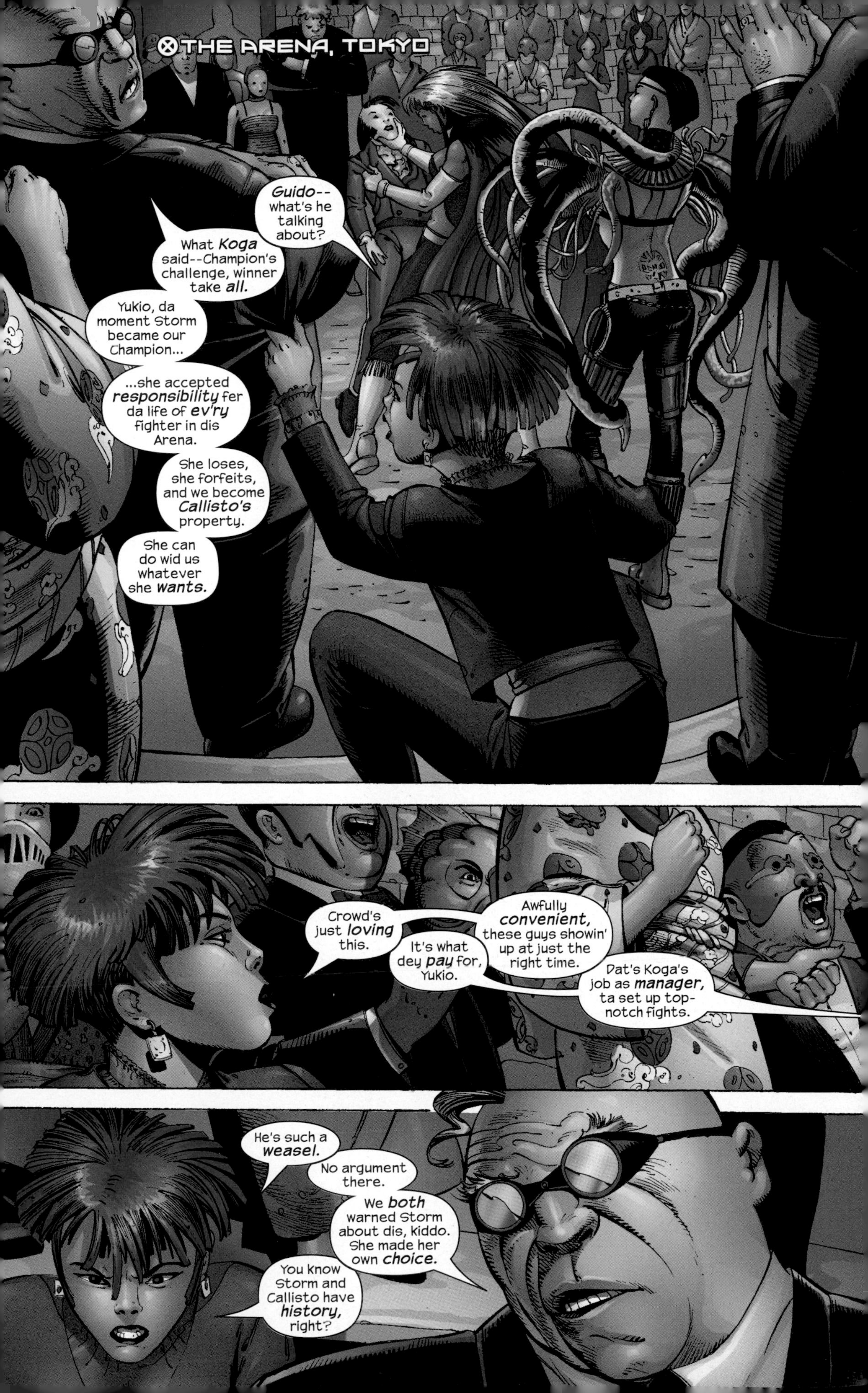
THE ARENA, TOKYO
Guido--what's he talking about?
What Koga said--Champion's challenge, winner take all.
Yukio, da moment Storm became our Champion...
...she accepted responsibility fer da life of ev'ry fighter in dis Arena.
She loses, she forfeits, and we become Callisto's property.
She can do wid us whatever she wants.
Crowd's just loving this.
It's what dey pay for, Yukio.
Awfully convenient, these guys showin' up at just the right time.
Dat's Koga's job as manager, ta set up top-notch fights.
He's such a weasel.
No argument there.
We both warned Storm about dis, kiddo. She made her own choice.
You know Storm and Callisto have history, right?

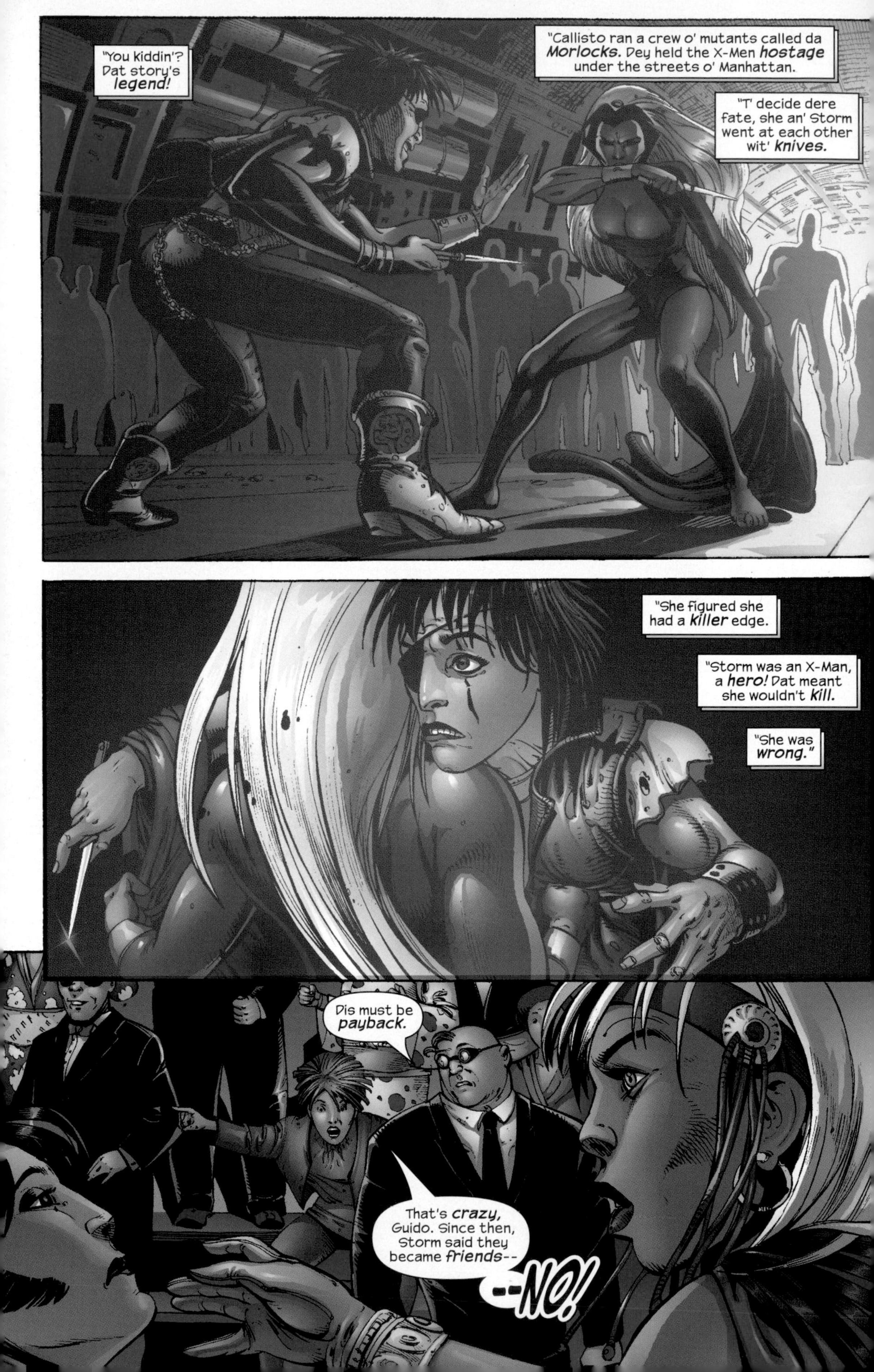
"You kiddin'? Dat story's legend!
"Callisto ran a crew o' mutants called da Morlocks. Dey held the X-Men hostage under the streets o' Manhattan.
"T' decide dere fate, she an' Storm went at each other wit' knives.
"She figured she had a killer edge.
"Storm was an X-Man, a hero! Dat meant she wouldn't kill.
"She was wrong."
Dis must be payback.
That's crazy, Guido. Since then, Storm said they became friends--
--NO!

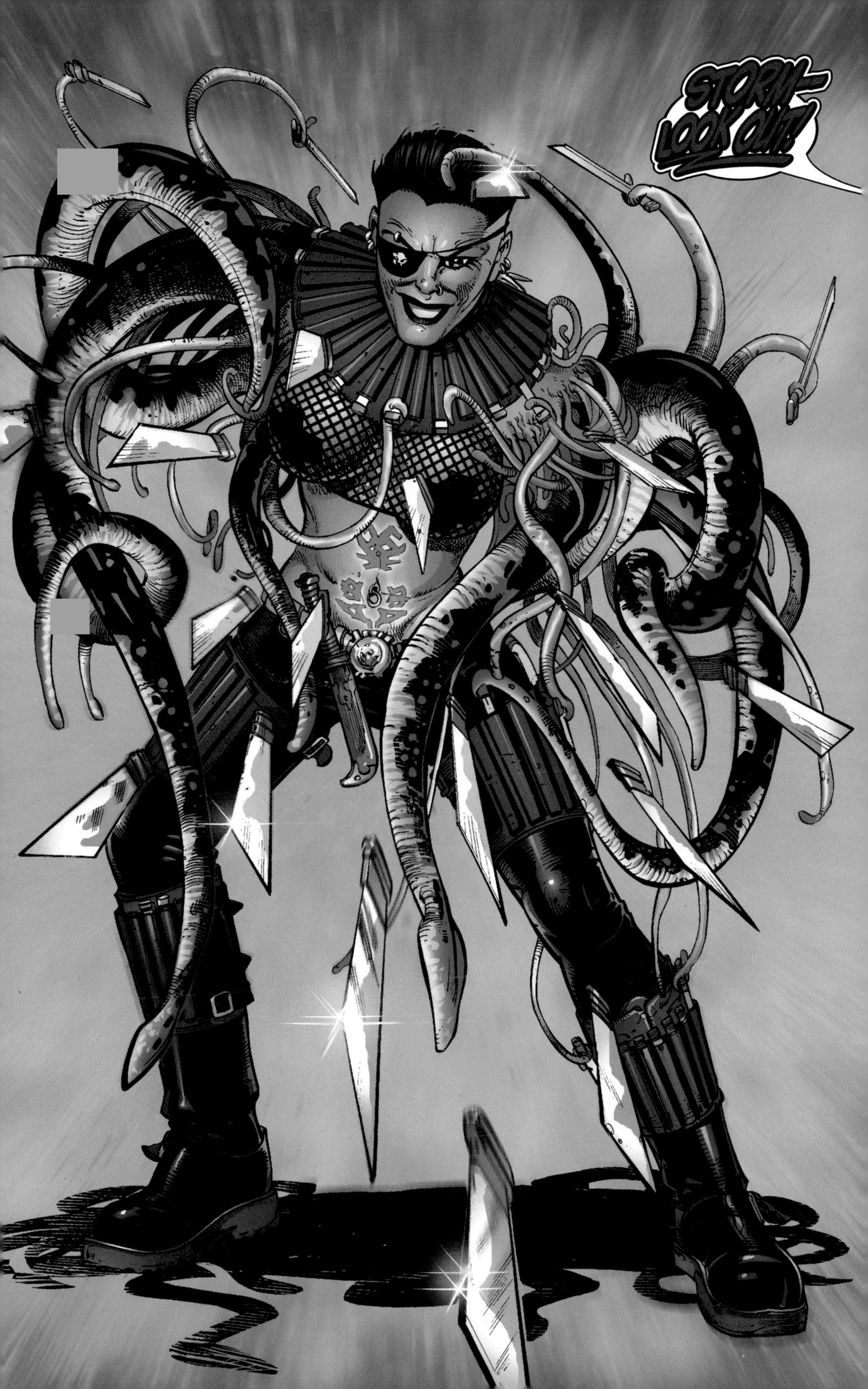
STORM--
LOOK OUT!

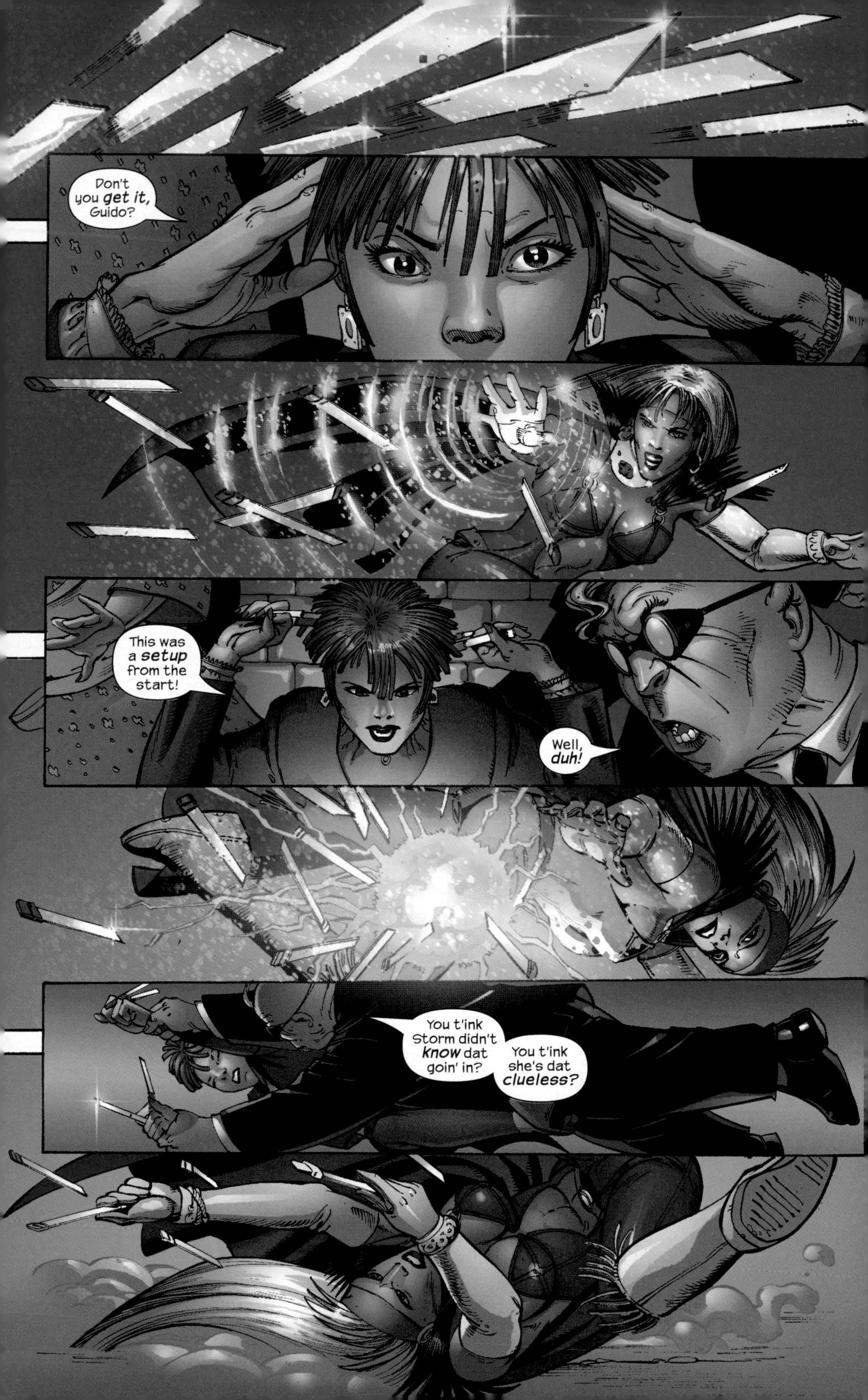
Don't you get it, Guido?
This was a setup from the start!
Well, duh!
You t'ink Storm didn't know dat goin' in?
You t'ink she's dat clueless?

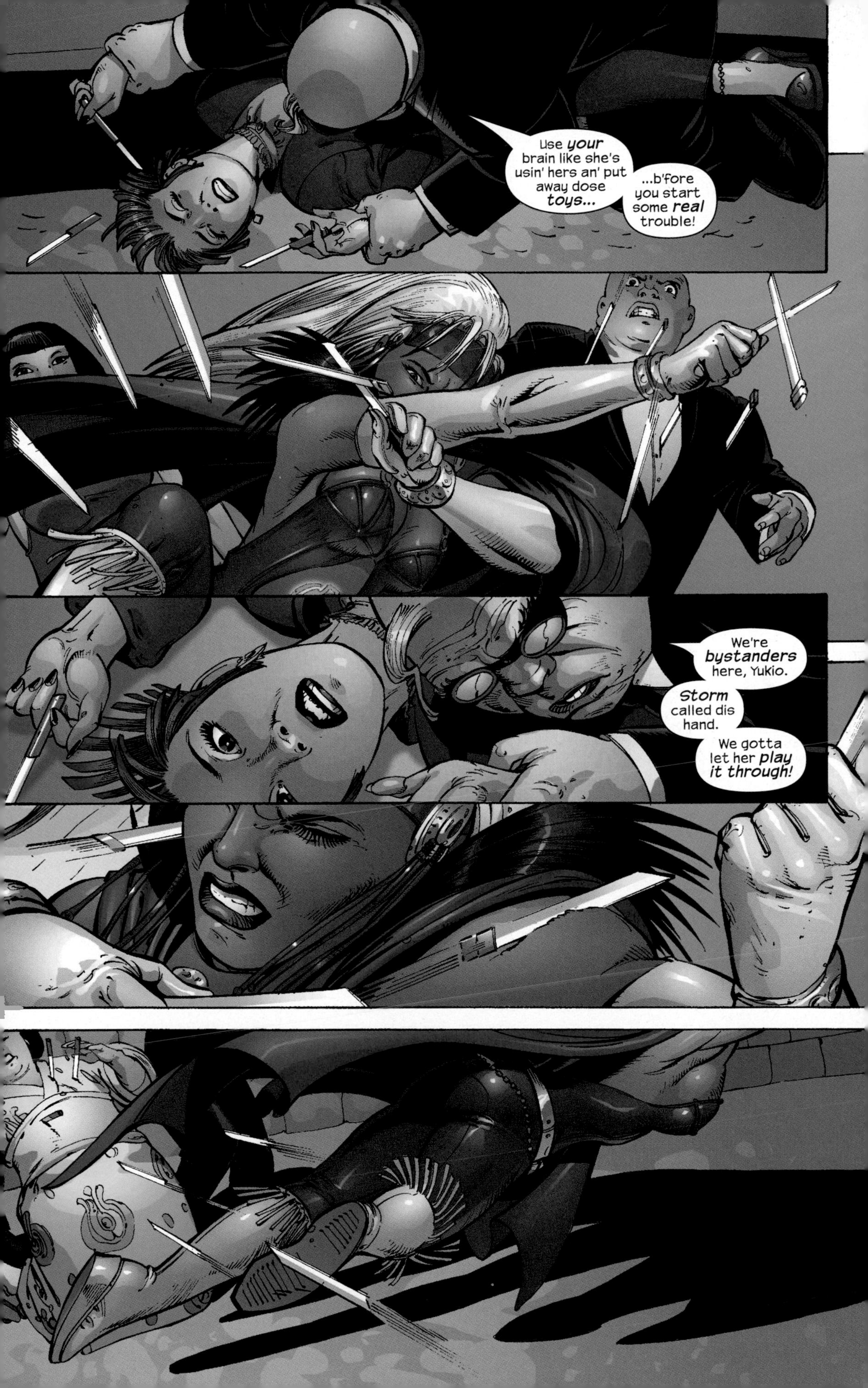
Use your brain like she's usin' hers an' put away dose toys...
...b'fore you start some real trouble!
We're bystanders here, Yukio.
Storm called dis hand.
We gotta let her play it through!

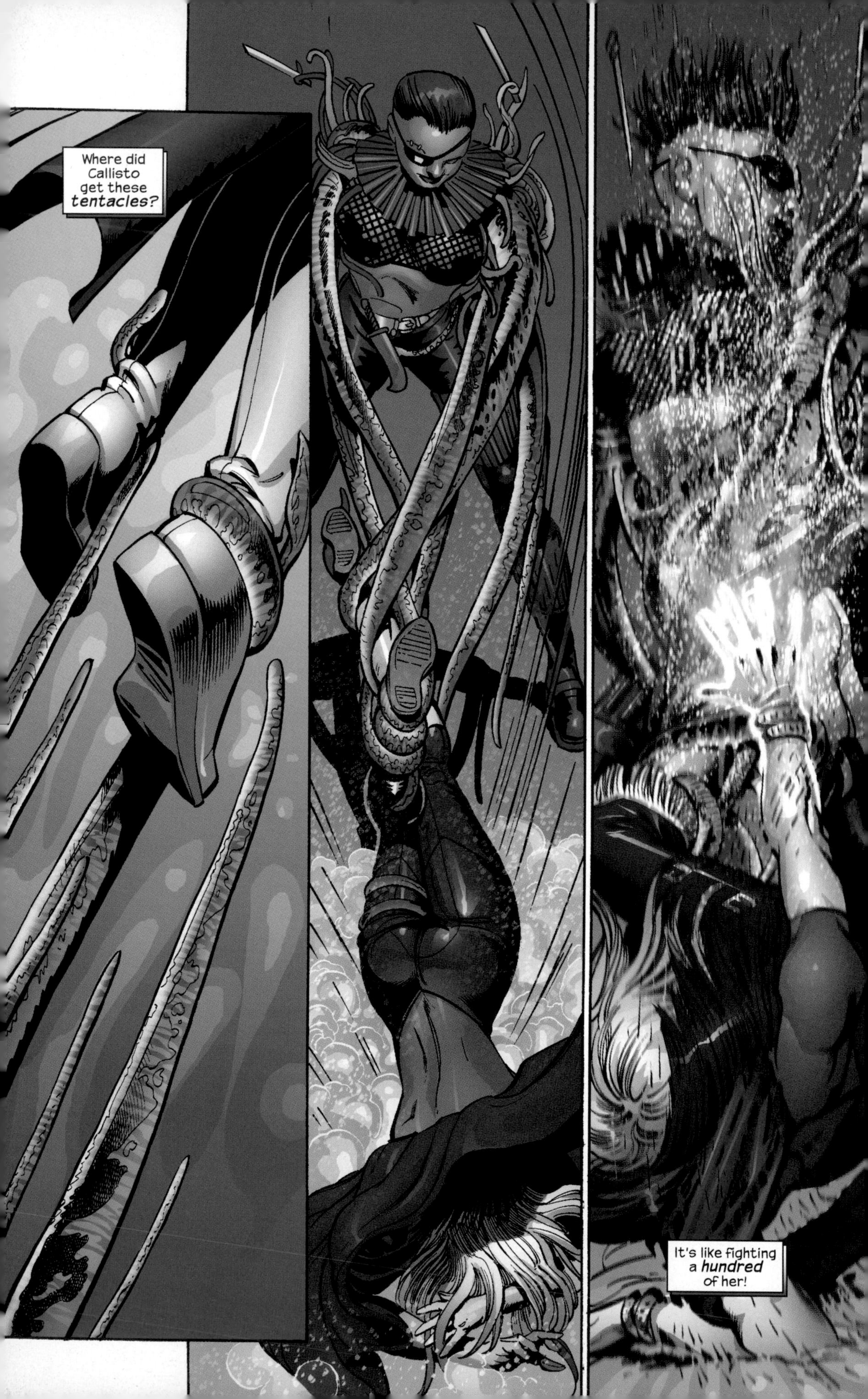
Where did Callisto get these tentacles?
It's like fighting a hundred of her!

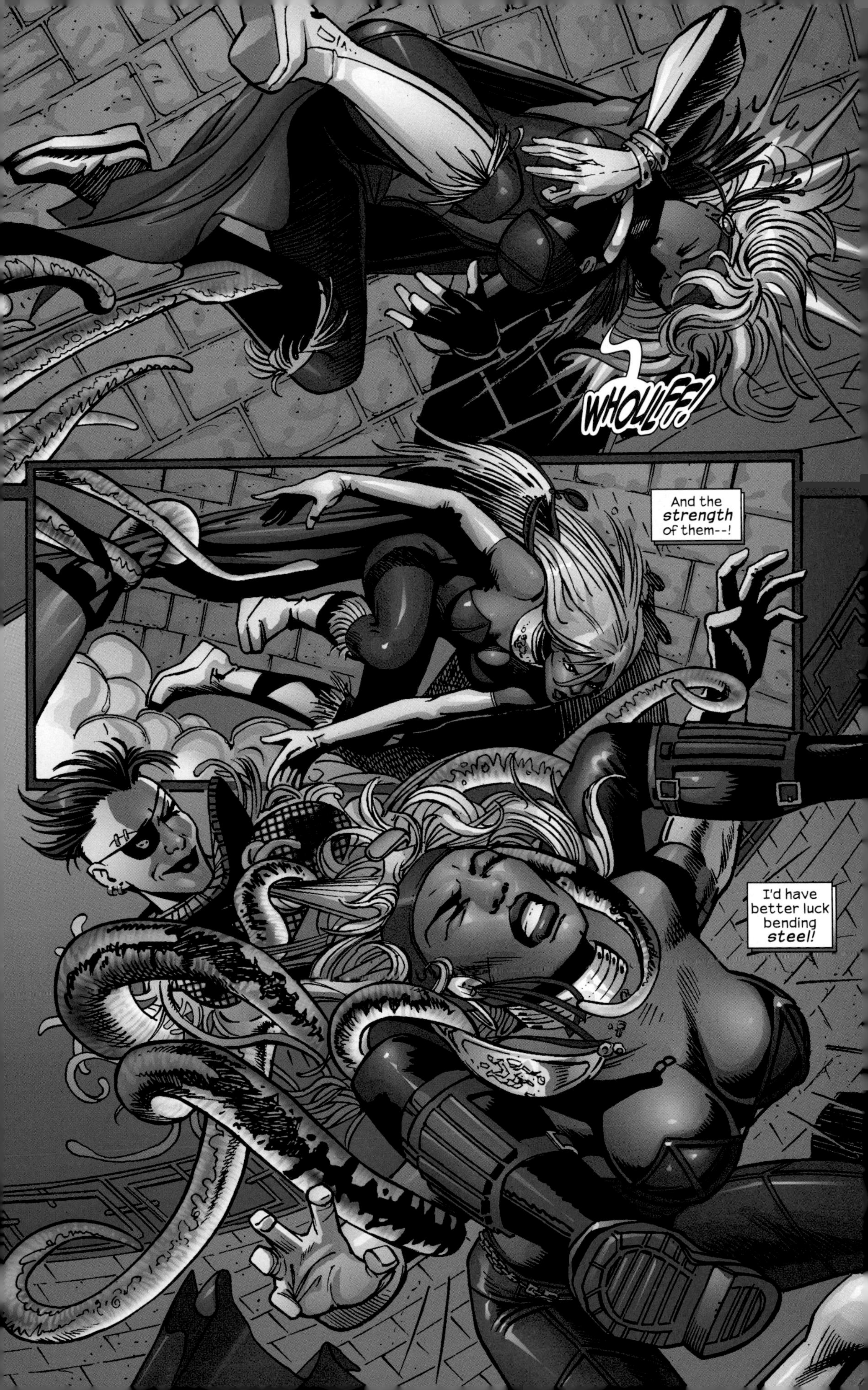
WHOULFF!
And the *strength* of them--!
I'd have better luck bending *steel!*

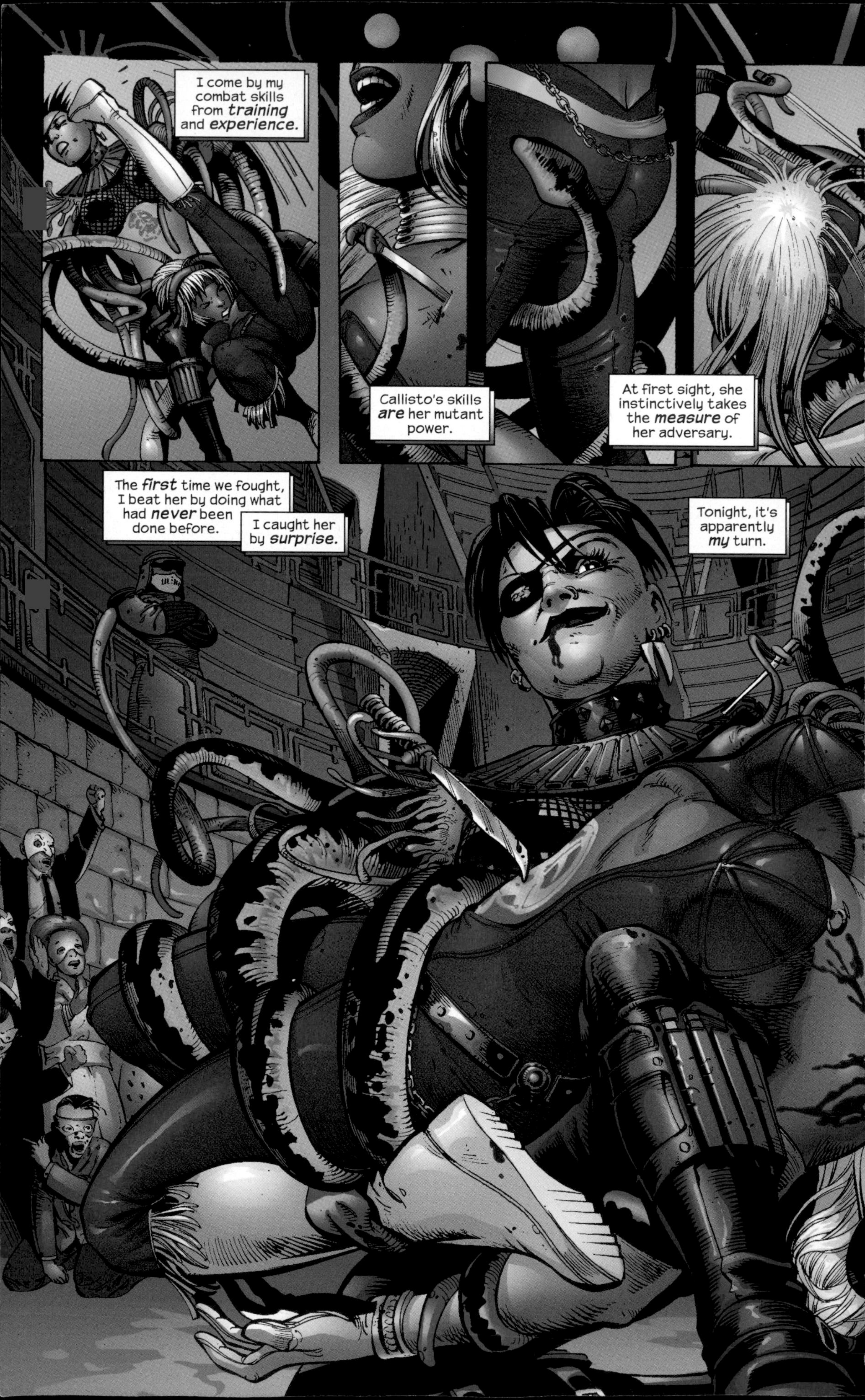

I come by my combat skills from *training* and *experience.*
Callisto's skills *are* her mutant power.
At first sight, she instinctively takes the *measure* of her adversary.
The *first* time we fought, I beat her by doing what had *never* been done before.
I caught her by *surprise.*
Tonight, it's apparently *my* turn.

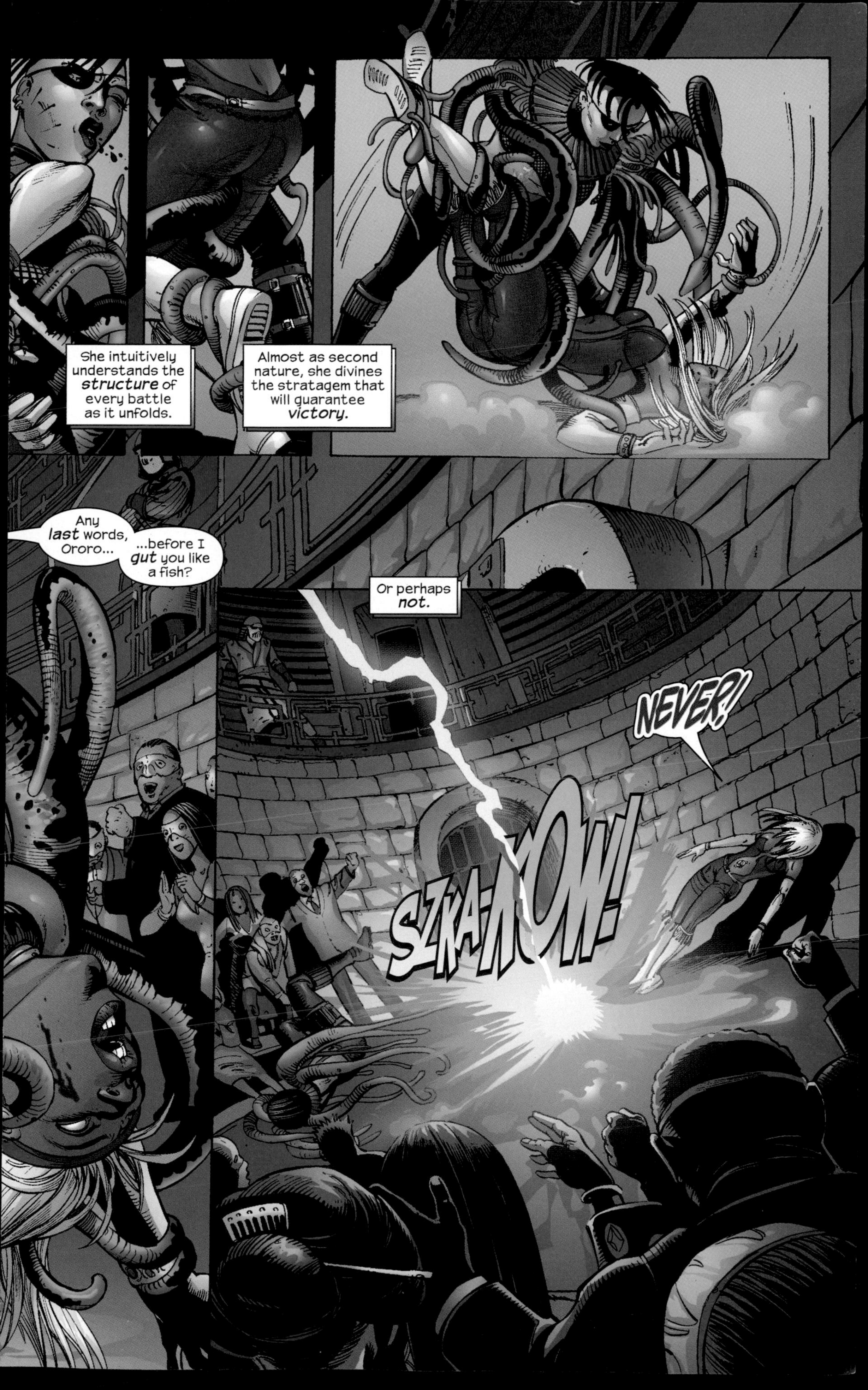
She intuitively understands the structure of every battle as it unfolds.
Almost as second nature, she divines the stratagem that will guarantee victory.
Any last words, Ororo...
...before I gut you like a fish?
Or perhaps not.
NEVER!
SZKA-KOOM!

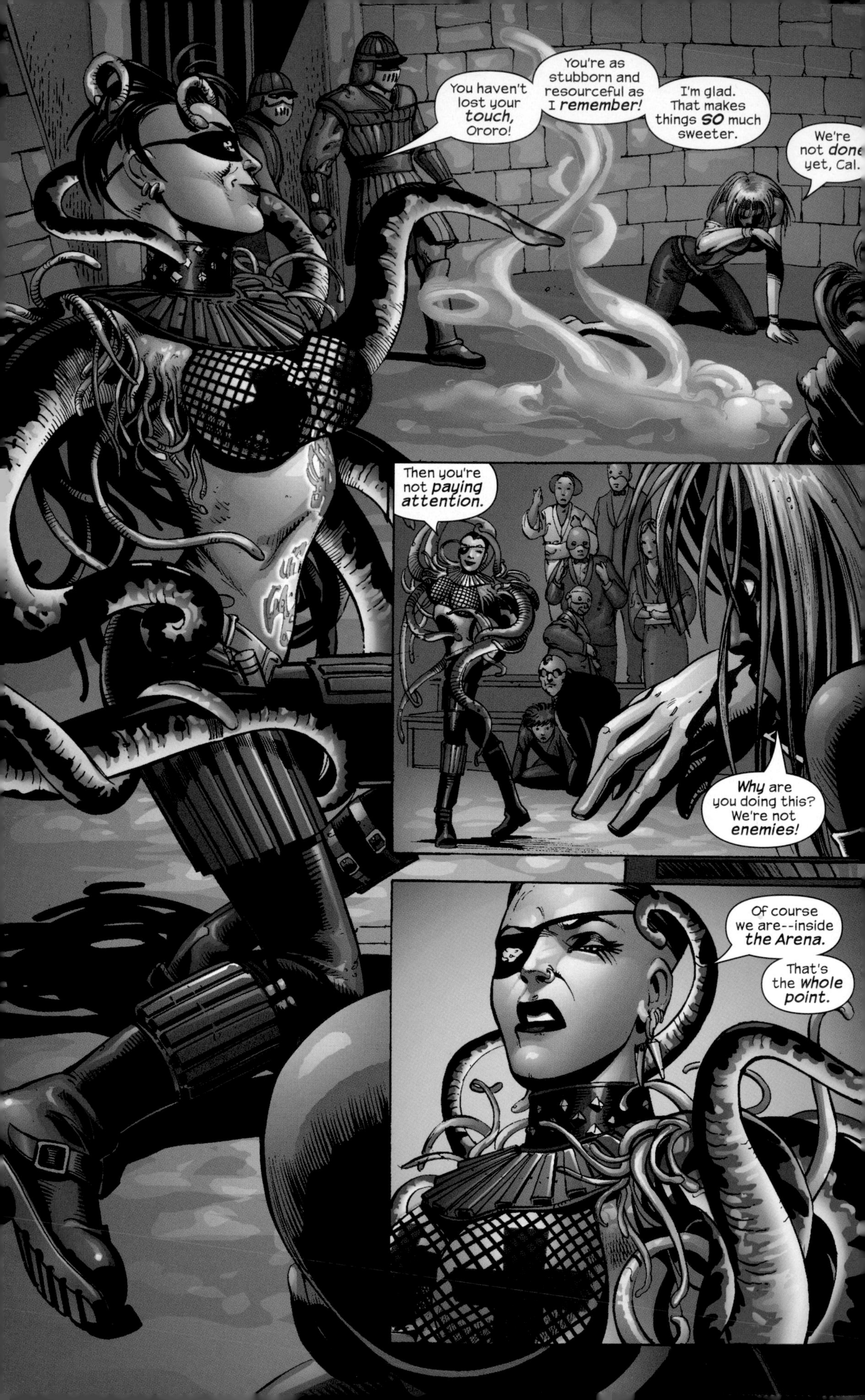
You haven't lost your touch, Ororo!
You're as stubborn and resourceful as I remember!
I'm glad. That makes things SO much sweeter.
We're not done yet, Cal.
Then you're not paying attention.
Why are you doing this? We're not enemies!
Of course we are--inside the Arena.
That's the whole point.

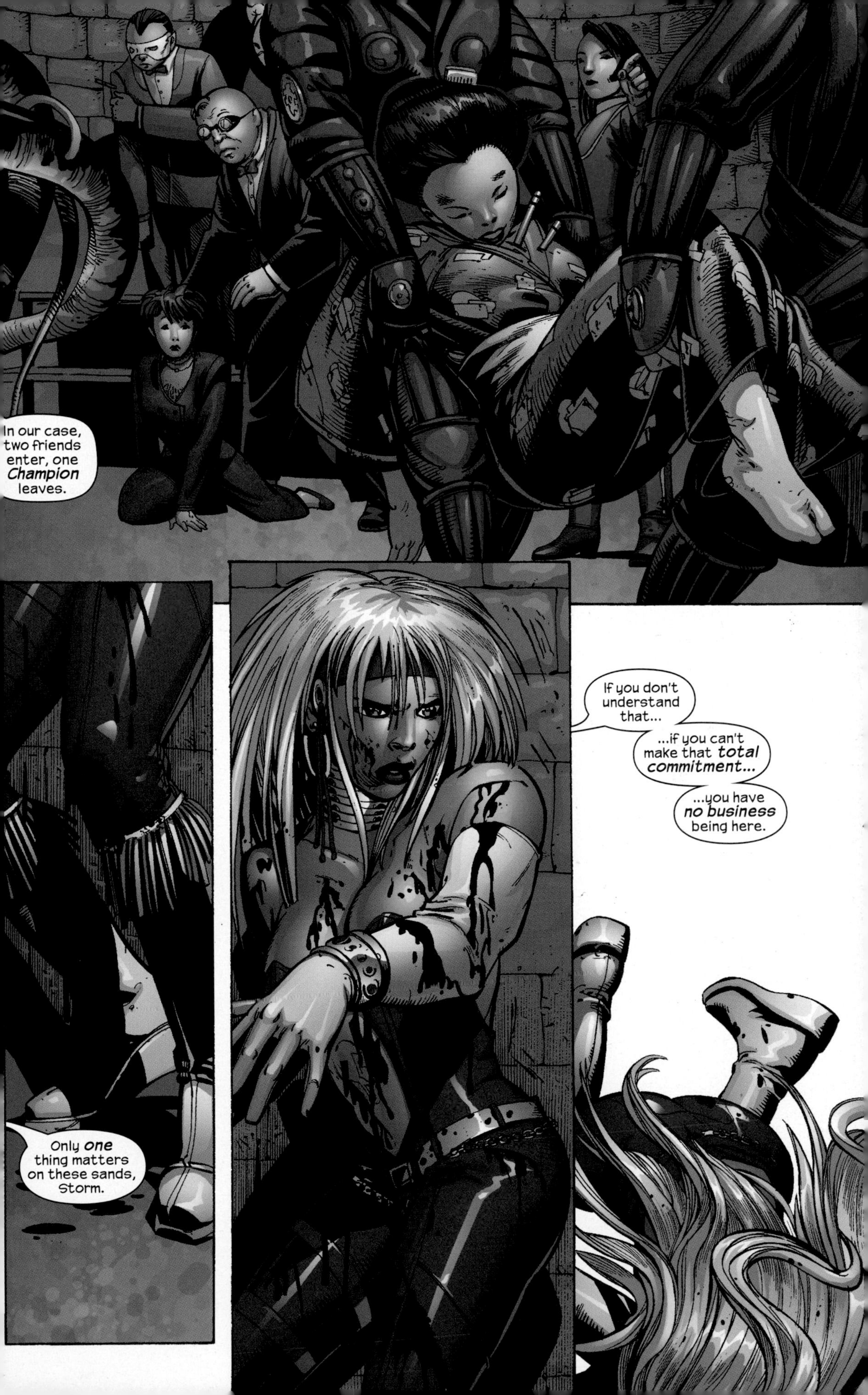
In our case, two friends enter, one *Champion* leaves.
Only *one* thing matters on these sands, Storm.
If you don't understand that...
...if you can't make that *total commitment...*
...you have *no business* being here.

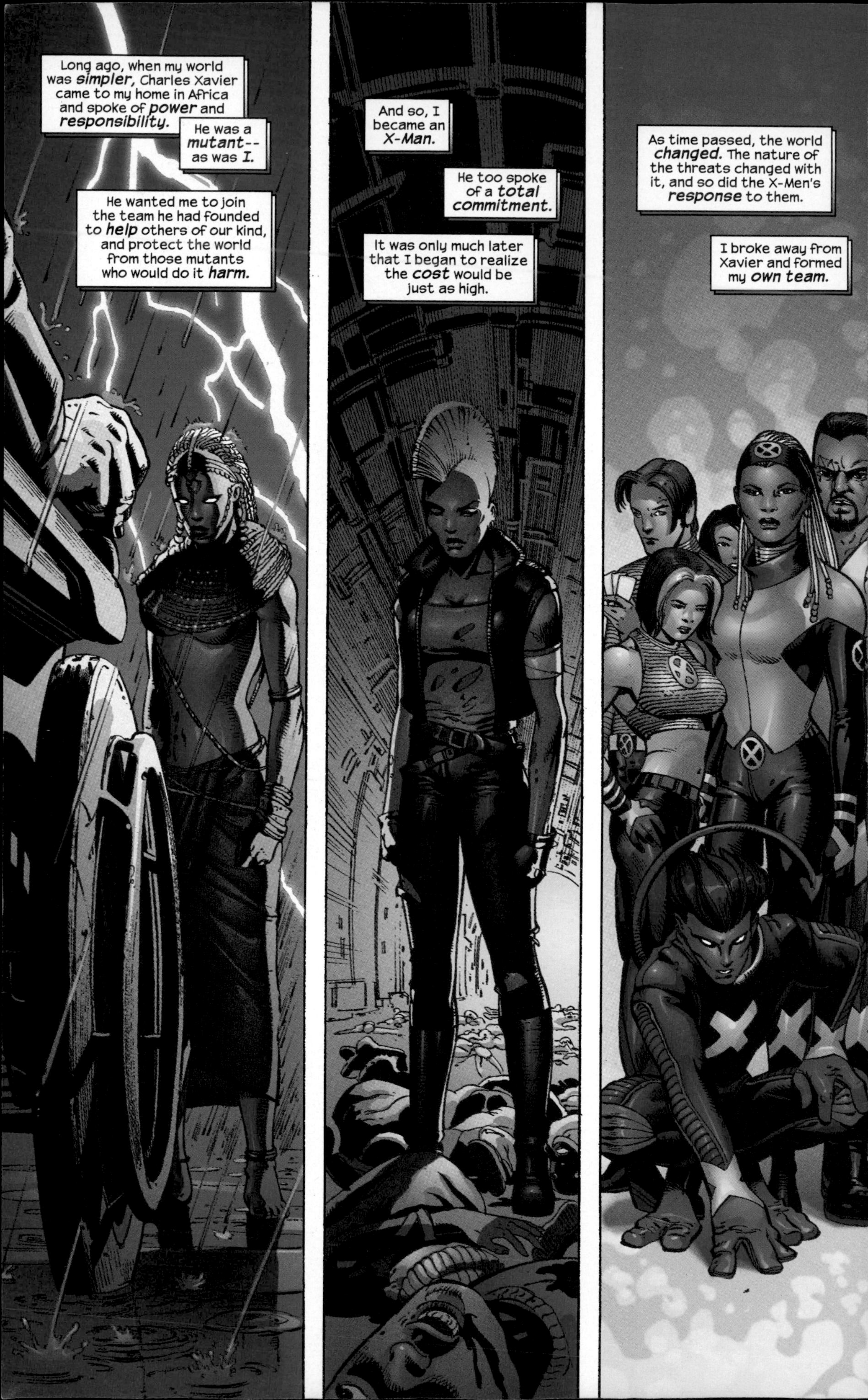

Long ago, when my world was simpler, Charles Xavier came to my home in Africa and spoke of power and responsibility.
He was a mutant-- as was I.
He wanted me to join the team he had founded to help others of our kind, and protect the world from those mutants who would do it harm.
And so, I became an X-Man.
He too spoke of a total commitment.
It was only much later that I began to realize the cost would be just as high.
As time passed, the world changed. The nature of the threats changed with it, and so did the X-Men's response to them.
I broke away from Xavier and formed my own team.

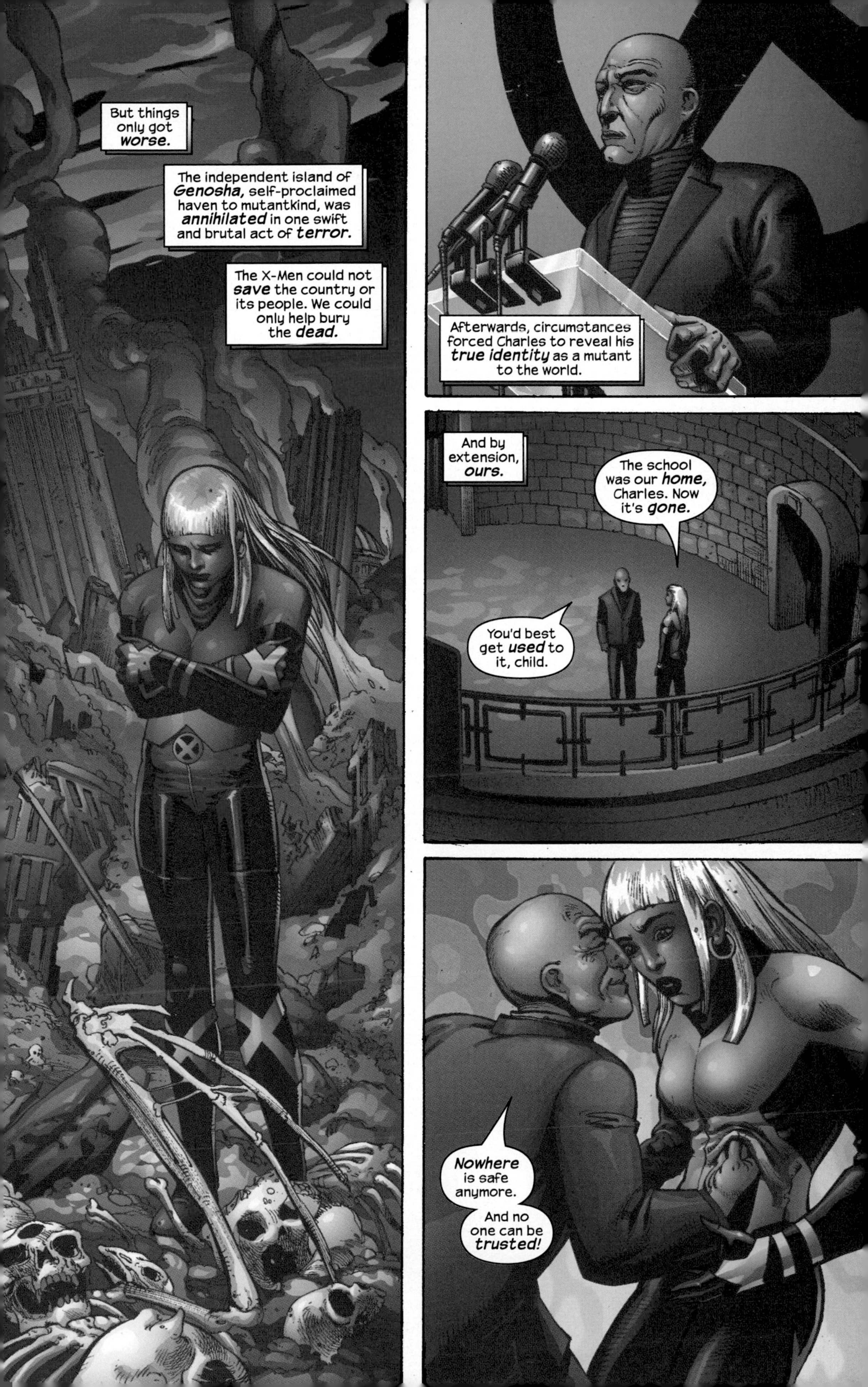
But things only got *worse.*
The independent island of *Genosha,* self-proclaimed haven to mutantkind, was *annihilated* in one swift and brutal act of *terror.*
The X-Men could not *save* the country or its people. We could only help bury the *dead.*
Afterwards, circumstances forced Charles to reveal his *true identity* as a mutant to the world.
And by extension, *ours.*
The school was our *home,* Charles. Now it's *gone.*
You'd best get *used* to it, child.
Nowhere is safe anymore.
And no one can be *trusted!*

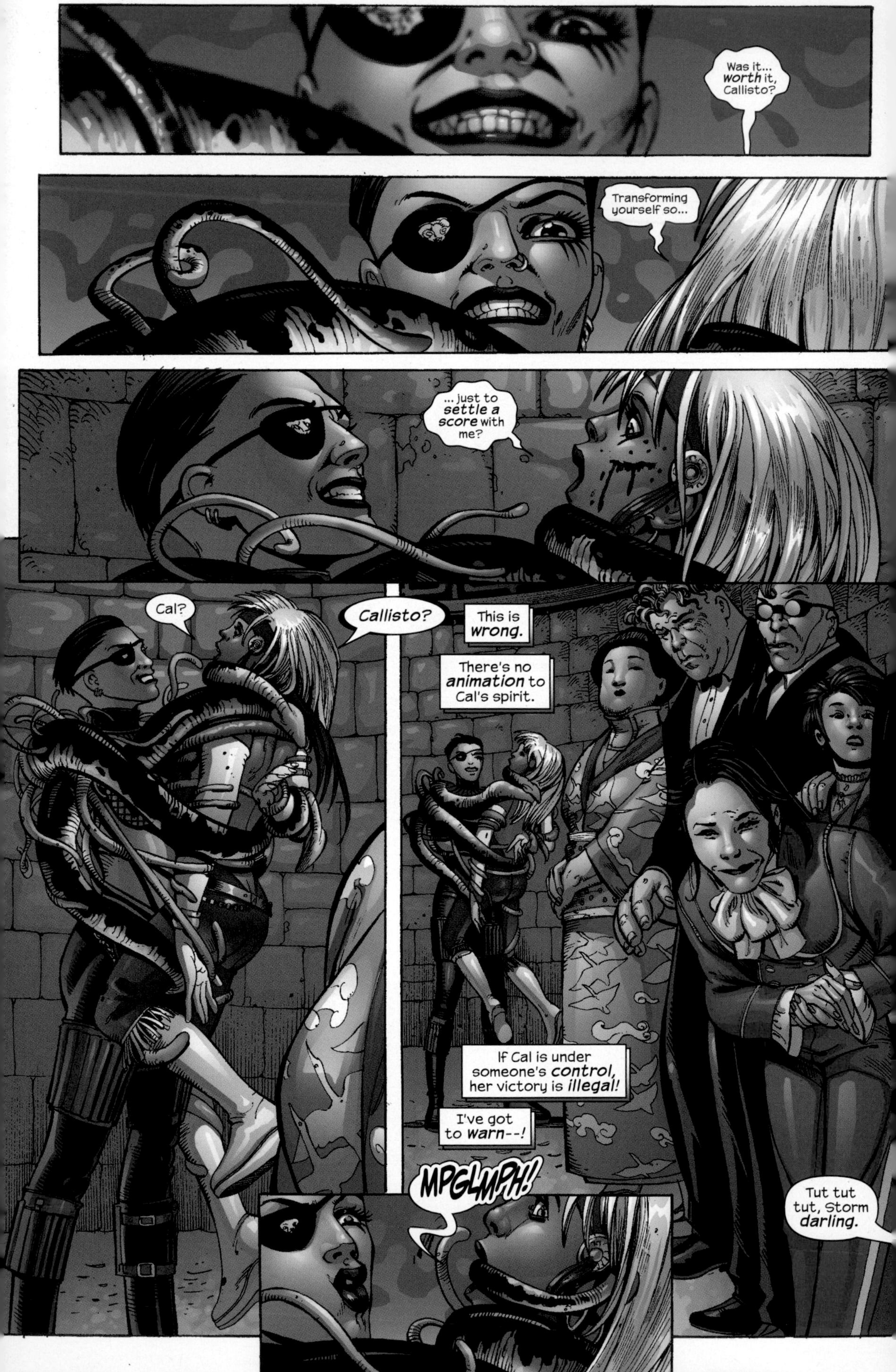

Was it... worth it, Callisto?
Transforming yourself so...
...just to settle a score with me?
Cal?
Callisto?
This is wrong.
There's no animation to Cal's spirit.
If Cal is under someone's control, her victory is illegal!
I've got to warn--!
MPGLMPH!
Tut tut tut, Storm darling.

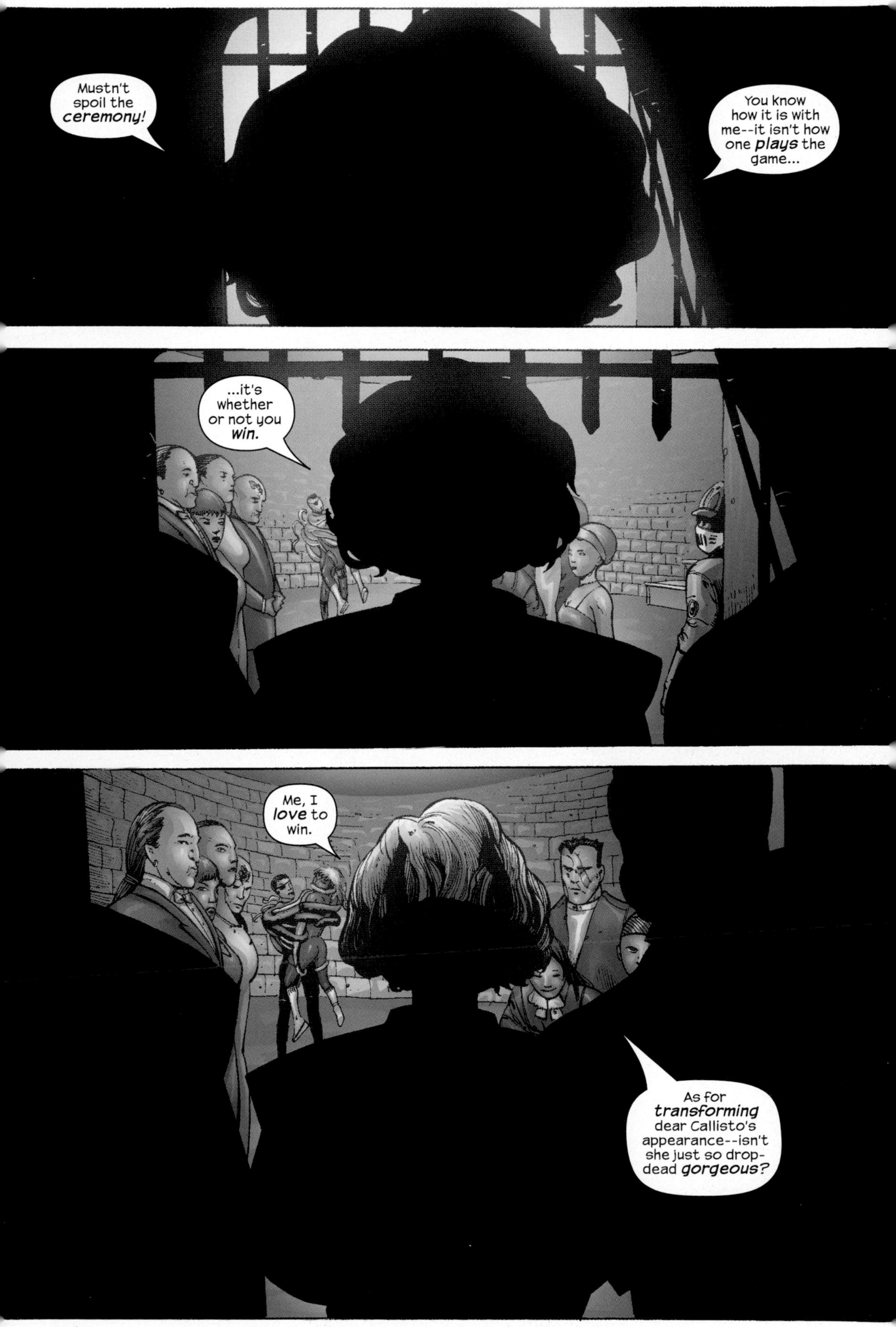
Mustn't spoil the ceremony!
You know how it is with me--it isn't how one plays the game...
...it's whether or not you win.
Me, I love to win.
As for transforming dear Callisto's appearance--isn't she just so drop-dead gorgeous?

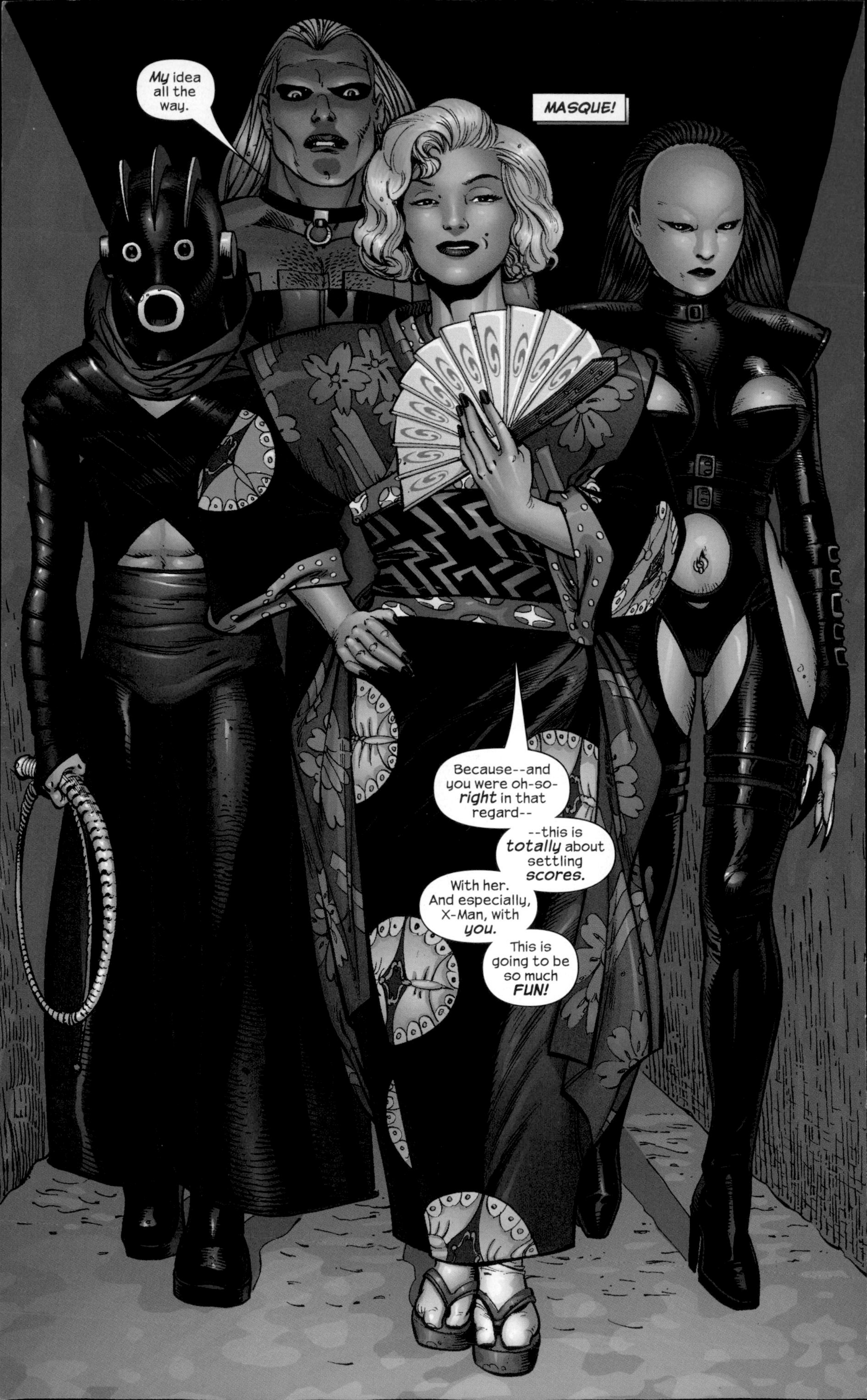
My idea all the way.
MASQUE!
Because--and you were oh-so-right in that regard--
--this is totally about settling scores.
With her. And especially, X-Man, with you.
This is going to be so much FUN!

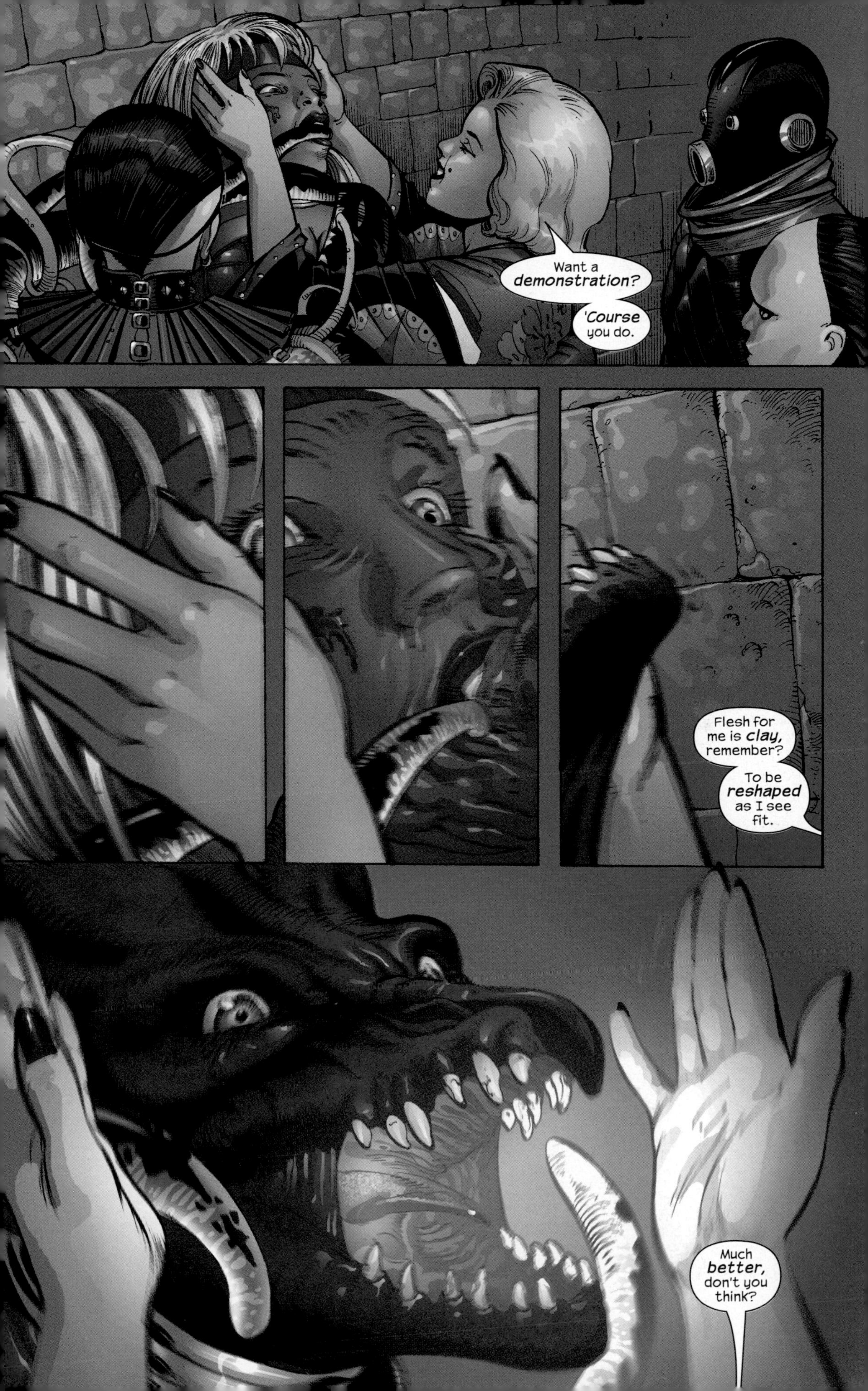
Want a *demonstration?*
'*Course* you do.
Flesh for me is *clay,* remember?
To be *reshaped* as I see fit.
Much *better,* don't you think?

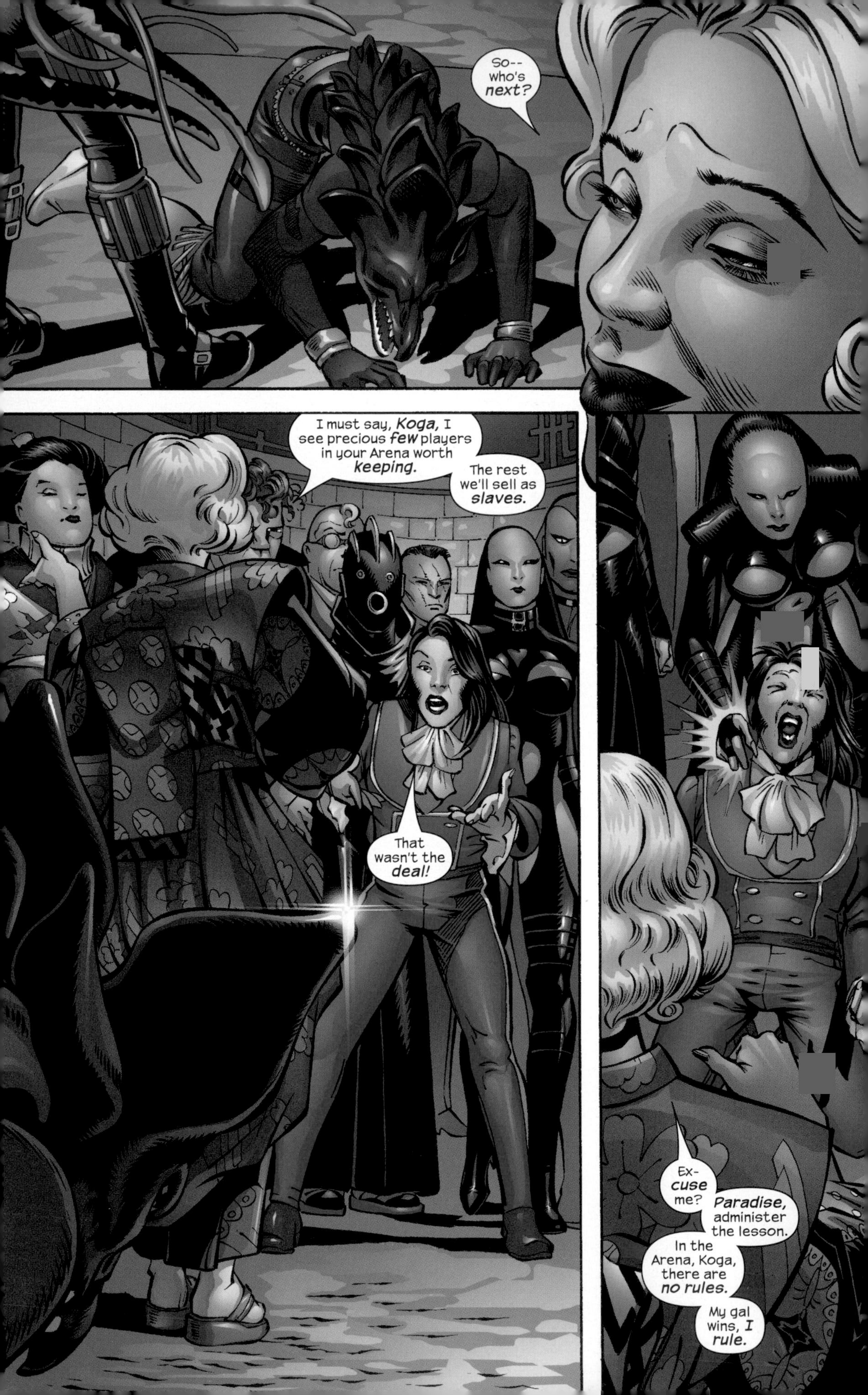
So--
who's
next?
I must say, Koga, I see precious few players in your Arena worth keeping.
The rest we'll sell as slaves.
That wasn't the deal!
Ex-cuse me?
Paradise, administer the lesson.
In the Arena, Koga, there are no rules.
My gal wins, I rule.

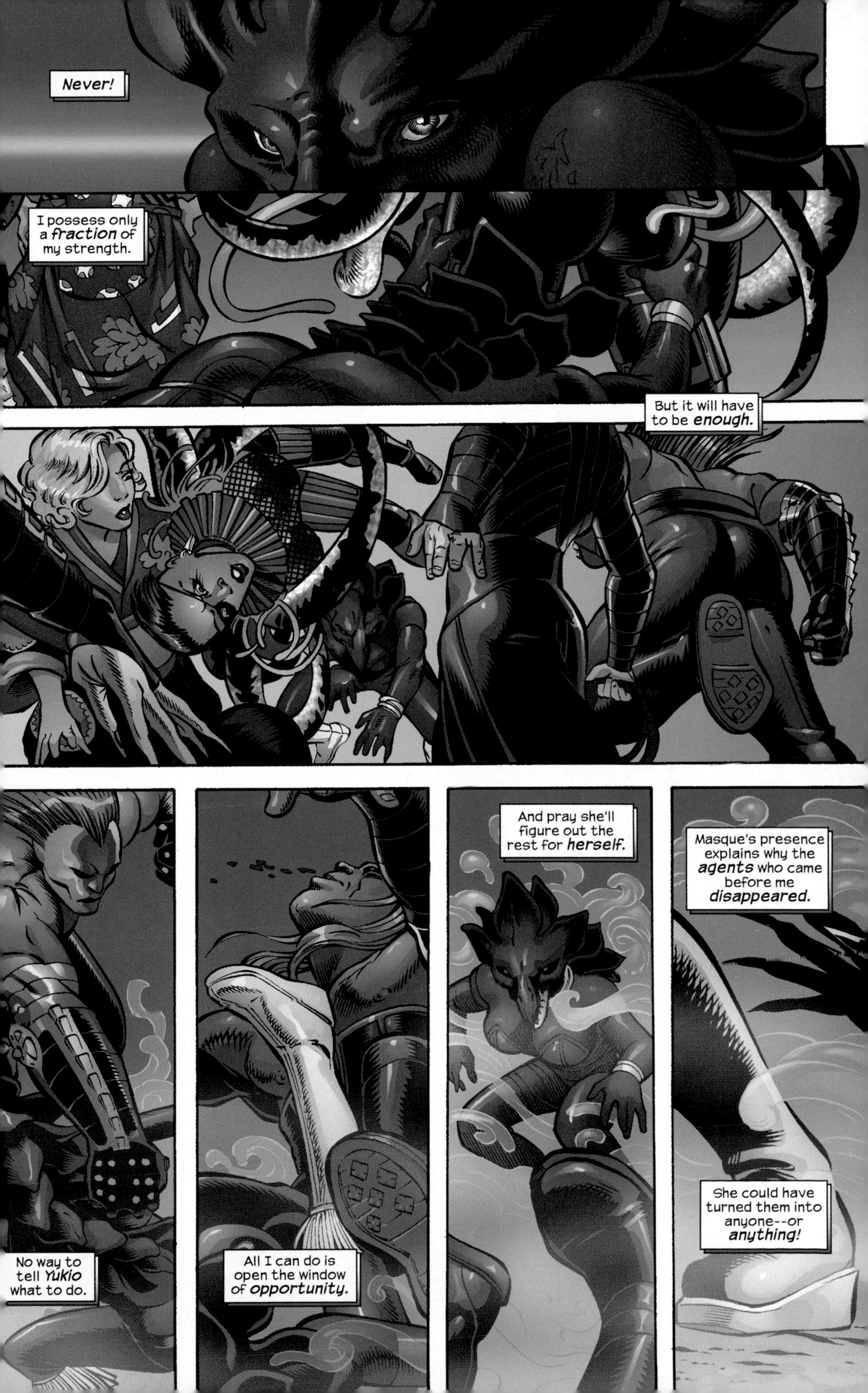
Never!
I possess only a fraction of my strength.
But it will have to be enough.
No way to tell Yukio what to do.
All I can do is open the window of opportunity.
And pray she'll figure out the rest for herself.
Masque's presence explains why the agents who came before me disappeared.
She could have turned them into anyone--or anything!

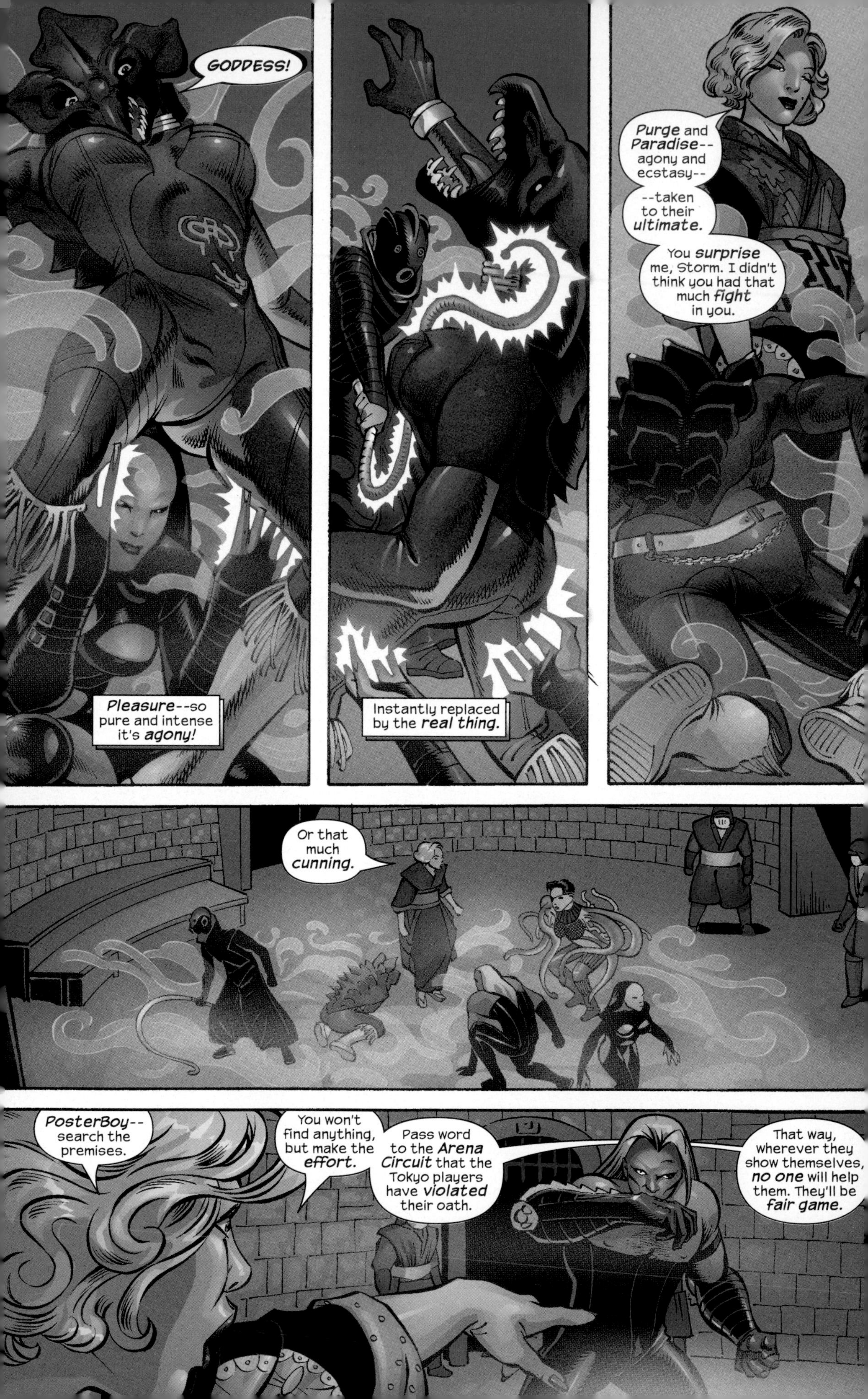
GODDESS!
Pleasure--so pure and intense it's agony!
Instantly replaced by the real thing.
Purge and Paradise--agony and ecstasy--
--taken to their ultimate.
You surprise me, Storm. I didn't think you had that much fight in you.
Or that much cunning.
PosterBoy--search the premises.
You won't find anything, but make the effort.
Pass word to the Arena Circuit that the Tokyo players have violated their oath.
That way, wherever they show themselves, no one will help them. They'll be fair game.

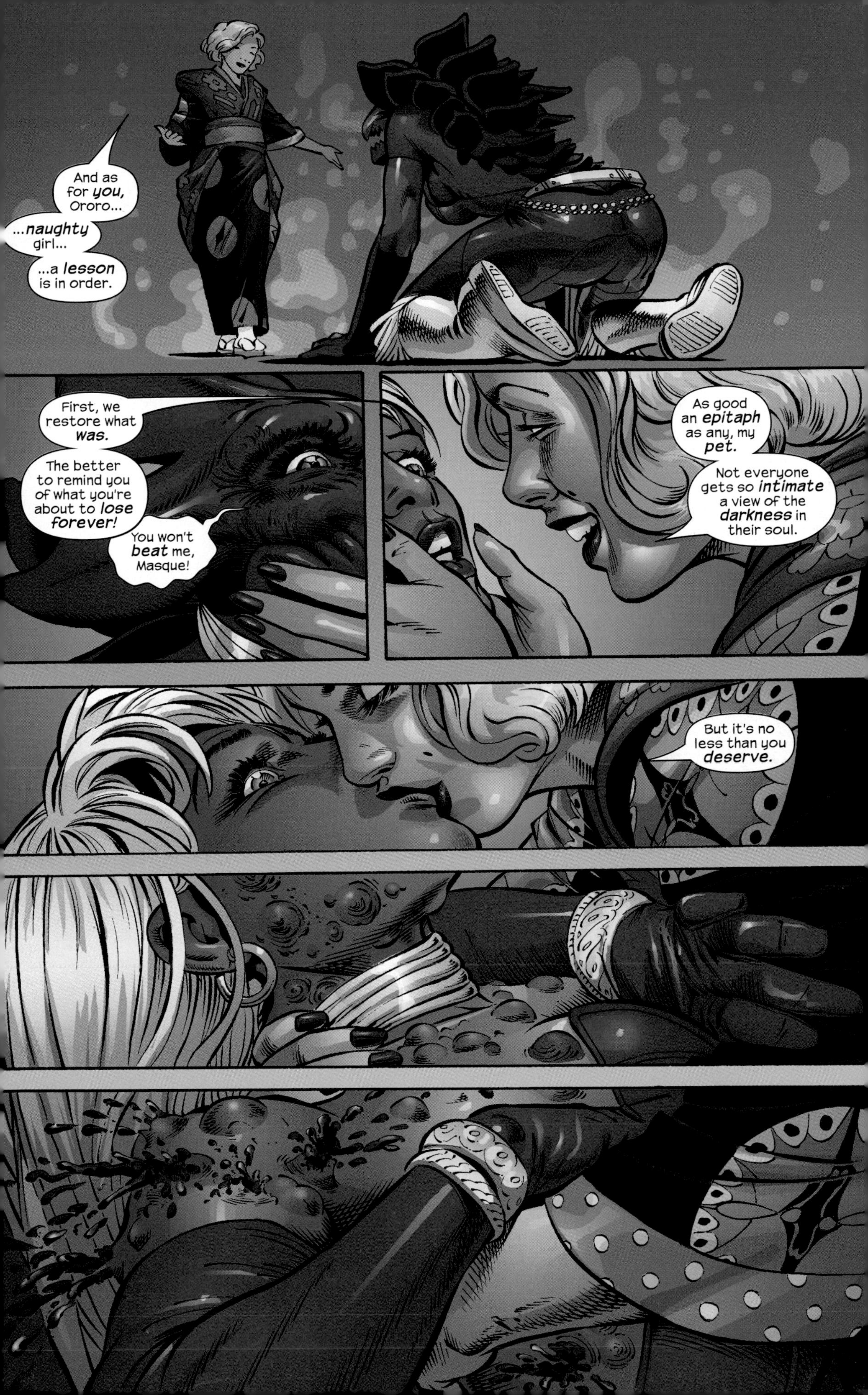
And as for you, Ororo...
...naughty girl...
...a lesson is in order.
First, we restore what was.
The better to remind you of what you're about to lose forever!
You won't beat me, Masque!
As good an epitaph as any, my pet.
Not everyone gets so intimate a view of the darkness in their soul.
But it's no less than you deserve.

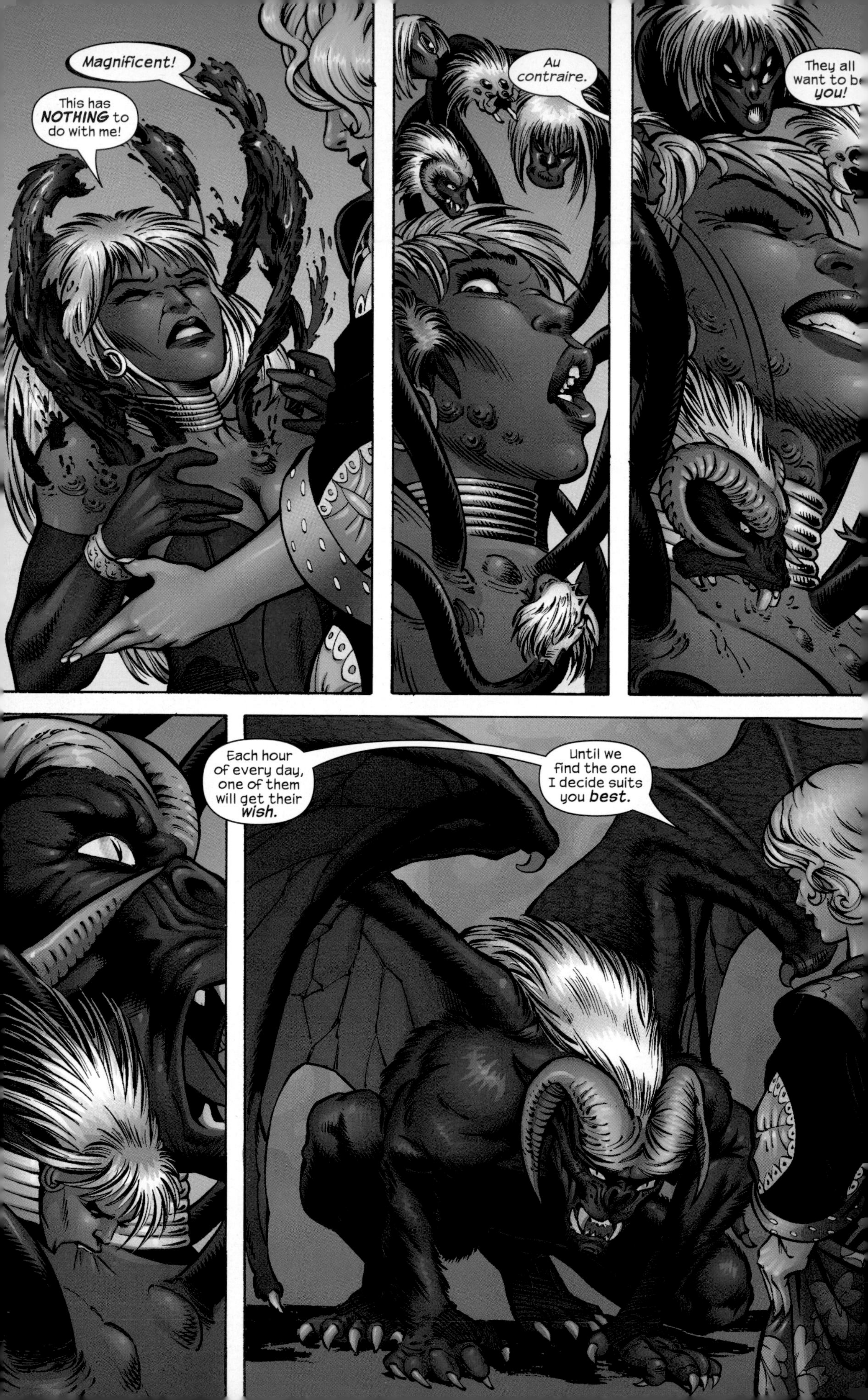
Magnificent!
This has NOTHING to do with me!
Au contraire.
They all want to be you!
Each hour of every day, one of them will get their wish.
Until we find the one I decide suits you best.

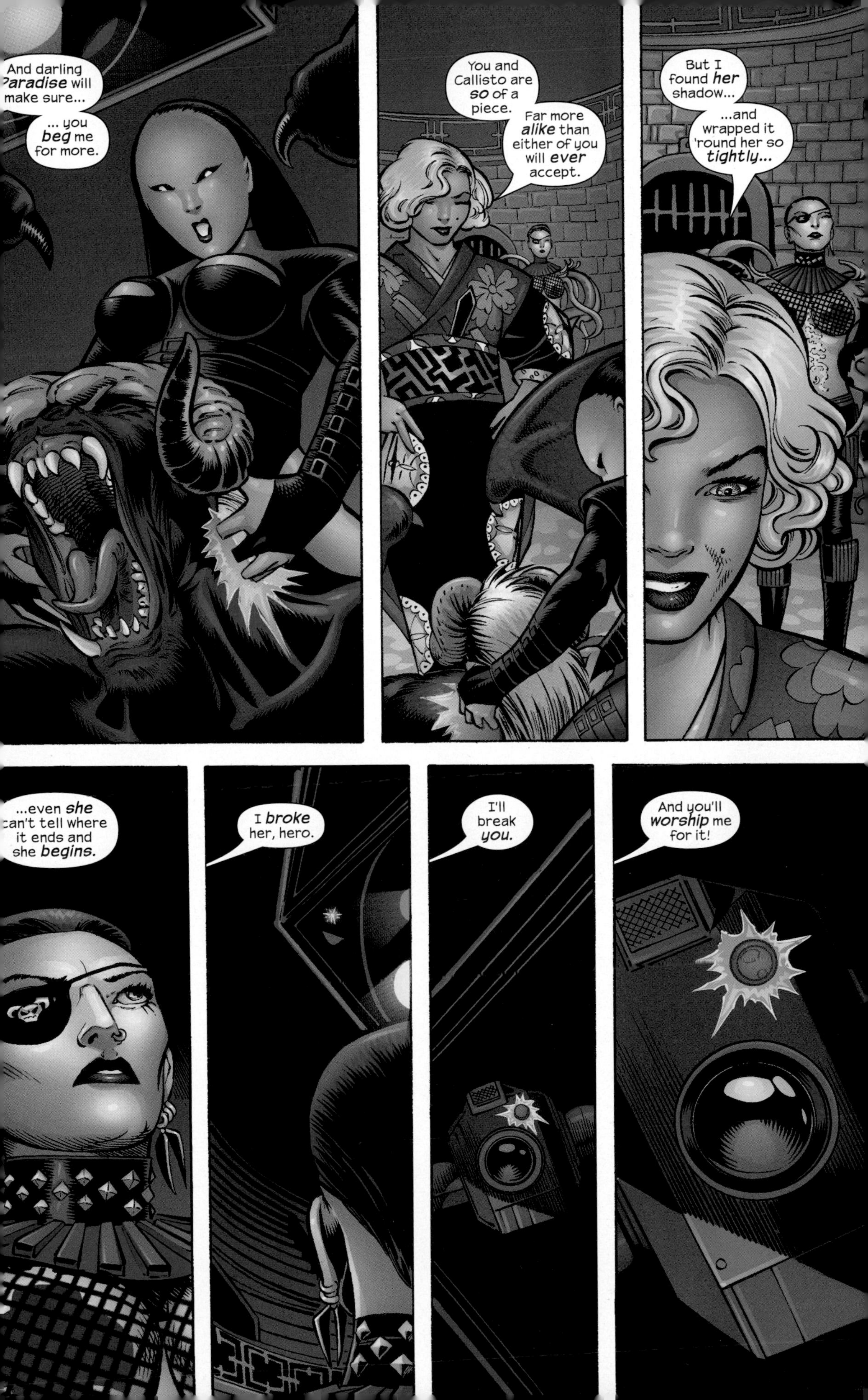
And darling Paradise will make sure...
... you beg me for more.
You and Callisto are so of a piece.
Far more alike than either of you will ever accept.
But I found her shadow...
...and wrapped it 'round her so tightly...
...even she can't tell where it ends and she begins.
I broke her, hero.
I'll break you.
And you'll worship me for it!

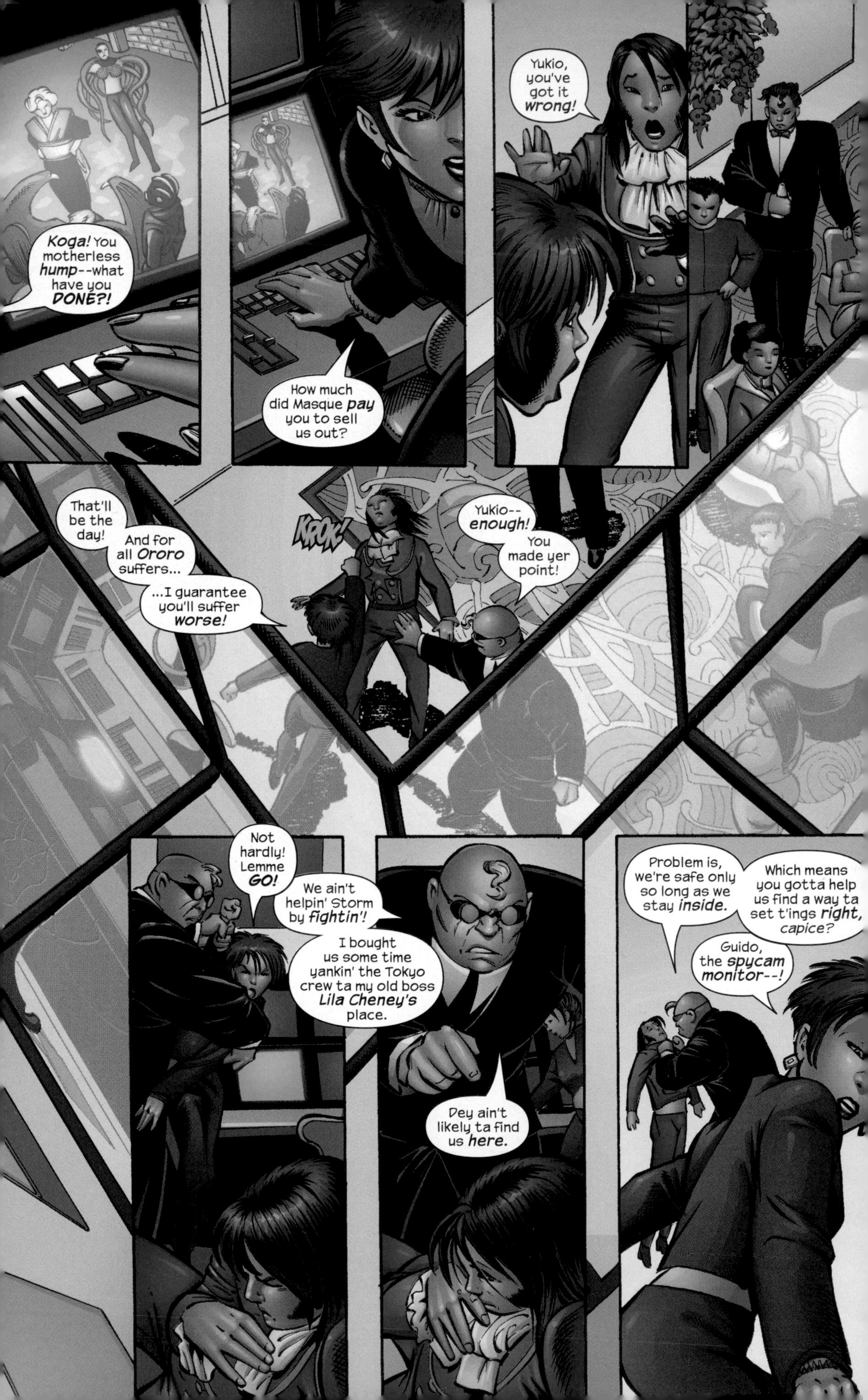

Koga! You motherless hump--what have you DONE?!
How much did Masque pay you to sell us out?
Yukio, you've got it wrong!
That'll be the day!
And for all Ororo suffers...
...I guarantee you'll suffer worse!
KROK!
Yukio--enough!
You made yer point!
Not hardly! Lemme GO!
We ain't helpin' Storm by fightin'!
I bought us some time yankin' the Tokyo crew ta my old boss Lila Cheney's place.
Dey ain't likely ta find us here.
Problem is, we're safe only so long as we stay inside.
Which means you gotta help us find a way ta set t'ings right, capice?
Guido, the spycam monitor--!

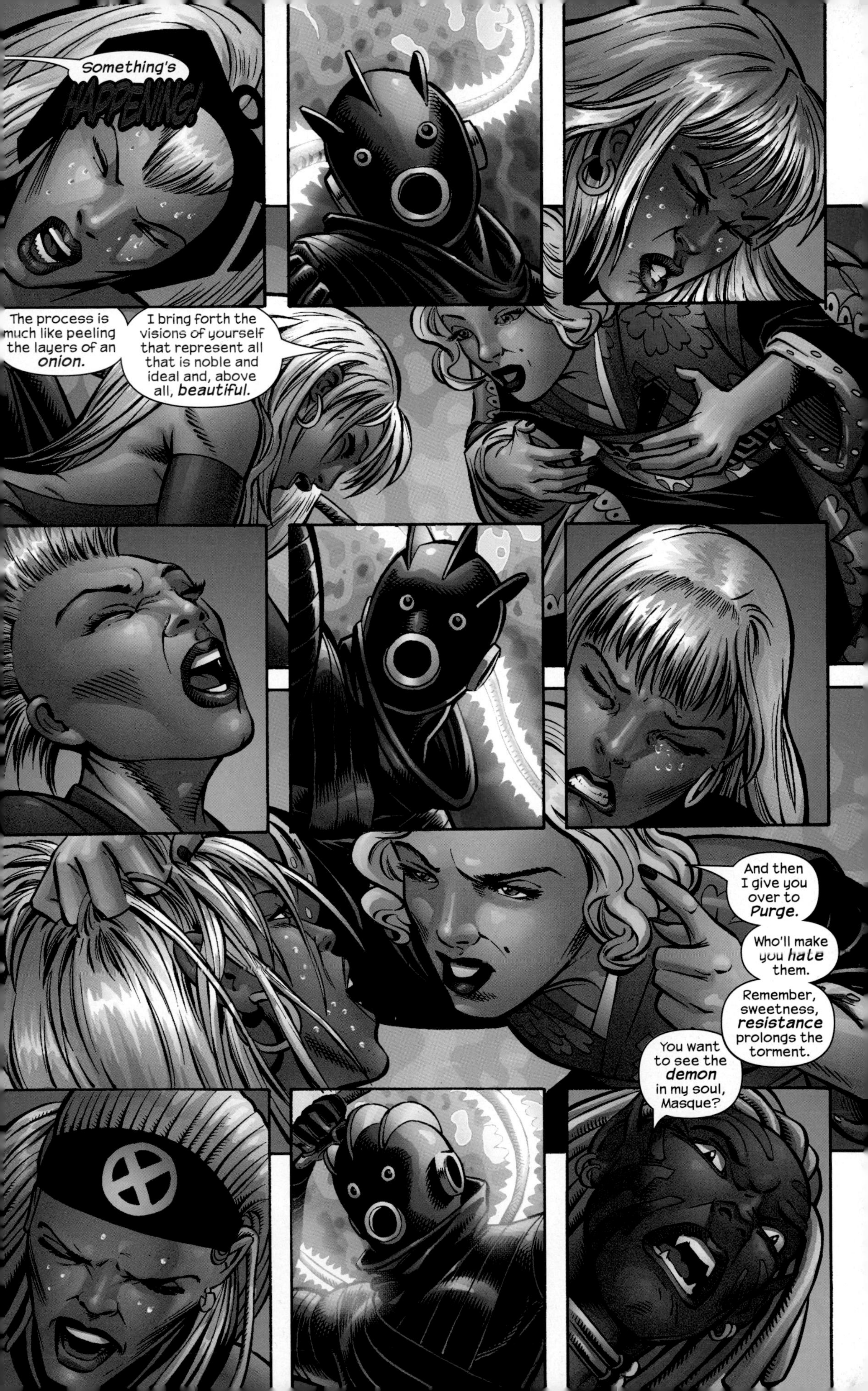
Something's HAPPENING!
The process is much like peeling the layers of an onion.
I bring forth the visions of yourself that represent all that is noble and ideal and, above all, beautiful.
And then I give you over to Purge.
Who'll make you hate them.
Remember, sweetness, resistance prolongs the torment.
You want to see the demon in my soul, Masque?

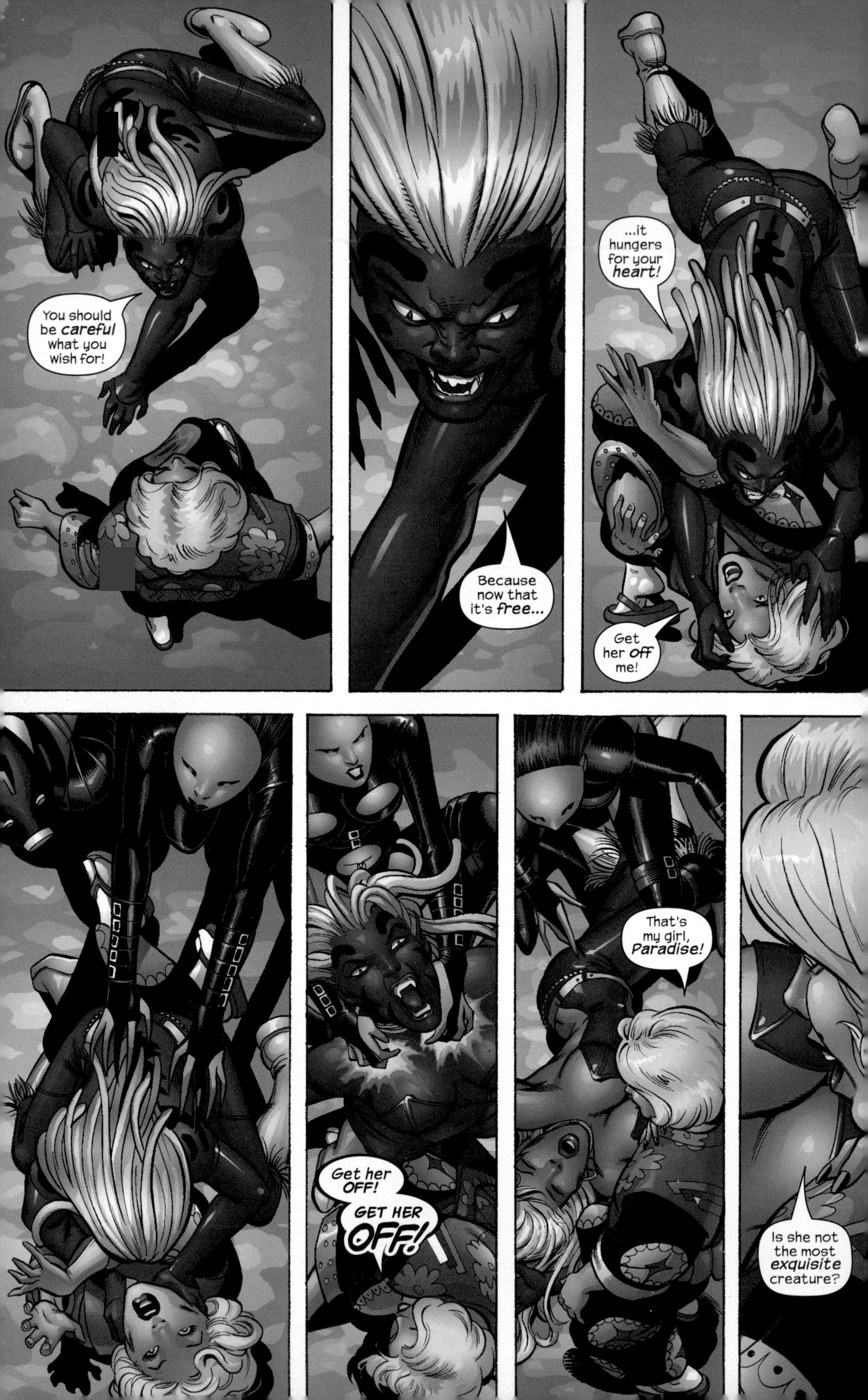
You should be *careful* what you wish for!
Because now that it's *free...*
...it hungers for your *heart!*
Get her *off* me!
Get her OFF!
GET HER OFF!
That's my girl, *Paradise!*
Is she not the most *exquisite* creature?

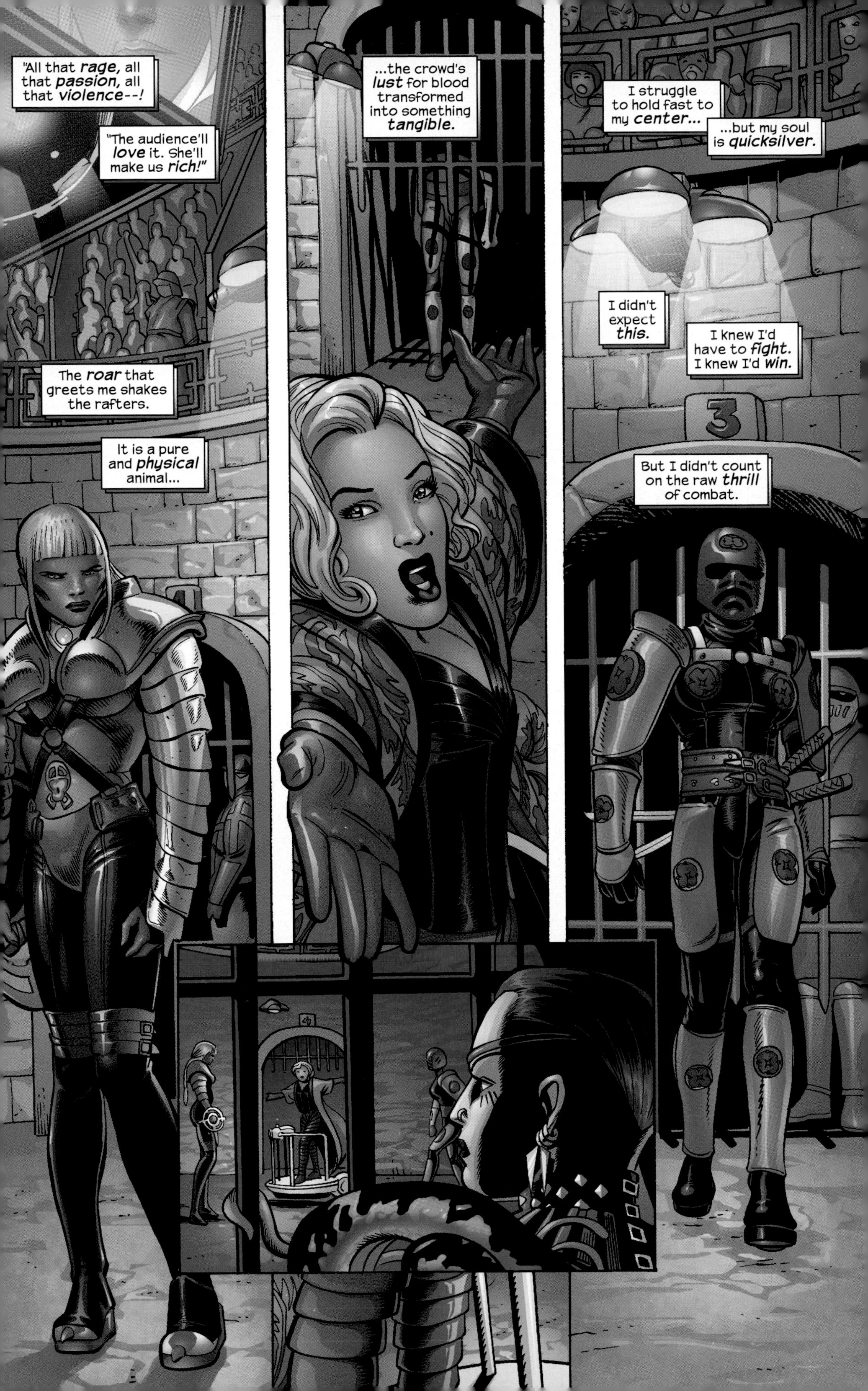
"All that rage, all that passion, all that violence--!
"The audience'll love it. She'll make us rich!"
The roar that greets me shakes the rafters.
It is a pure and physical animal...
...the crowd's lust for blood transformed into something tangible.
I struggle to hold fast to my center...
...but my soul is quicksilver.
I didn't expect this.
I knew I'd have to fight. I knew I'd win.
3
But I didn't count on the raw thrill of combat.

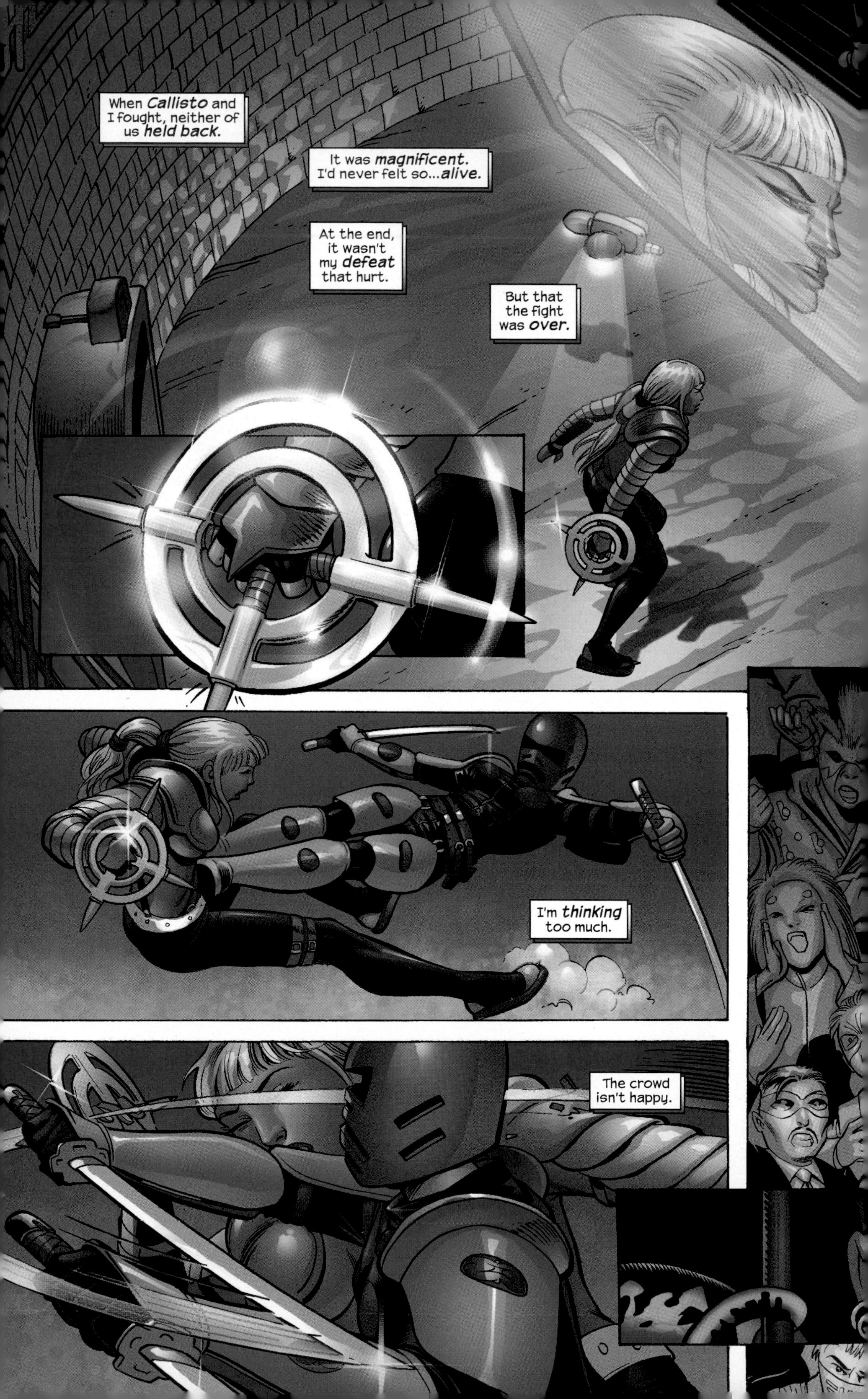
When Callisto and I fought, neither of us held back.
It was magnificent. I'd never felt so...alive.
At the end, it wasn't my defeat that hurt.
But that the fight was over.
I'm thinking too much.
The crowd isn't happy.

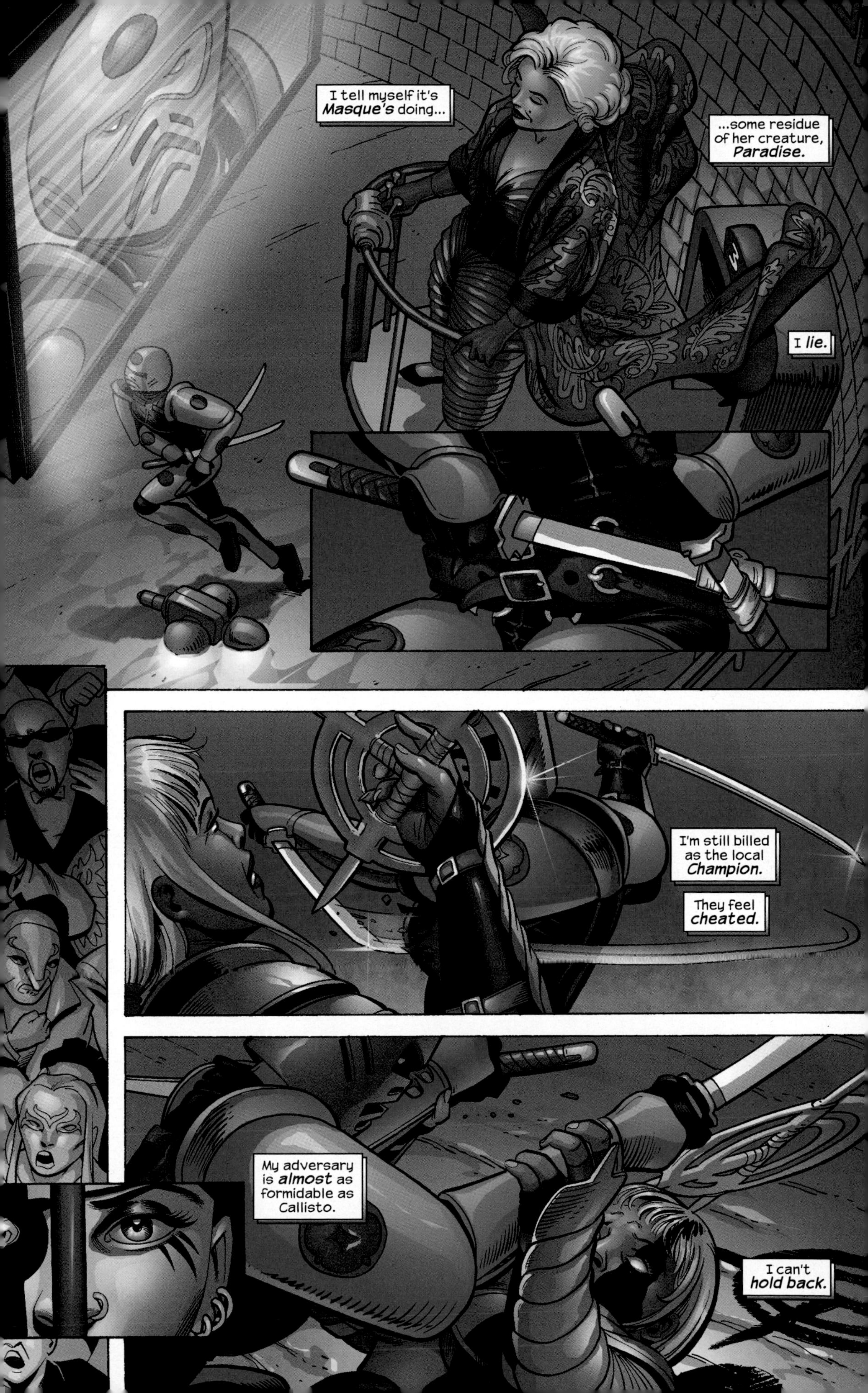
I tell myself it's *Masque's* doing...
...some residue of her creature, *Paradise.*
I *lie.*
I'm still billed as the local *Champion.*
They feel *cheated.*
My adversary is *almost* as formidable as Callisto.
I can't *hold back.*

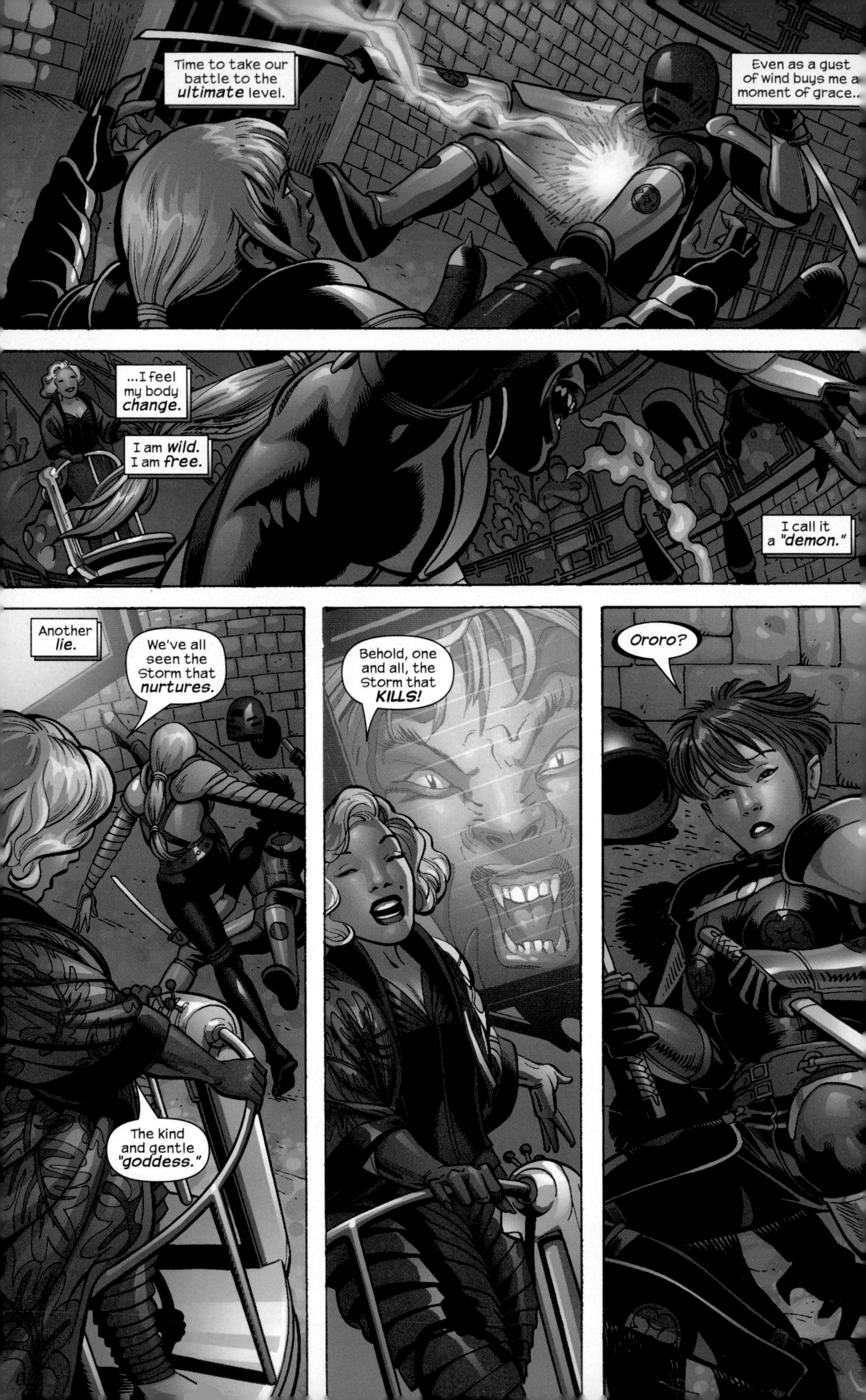
Time to take our battle to the ultimate level.
Even as a gust of wind buys me a moment of grace...
...I feel my body change.
I am wild. I am free.
I call it a "demon."
Another lie.
We've all seen the Storm that nurtures.
The kind and gentle "goddess."
Behold, one and all, the Storm that KILLS!
Ororo?

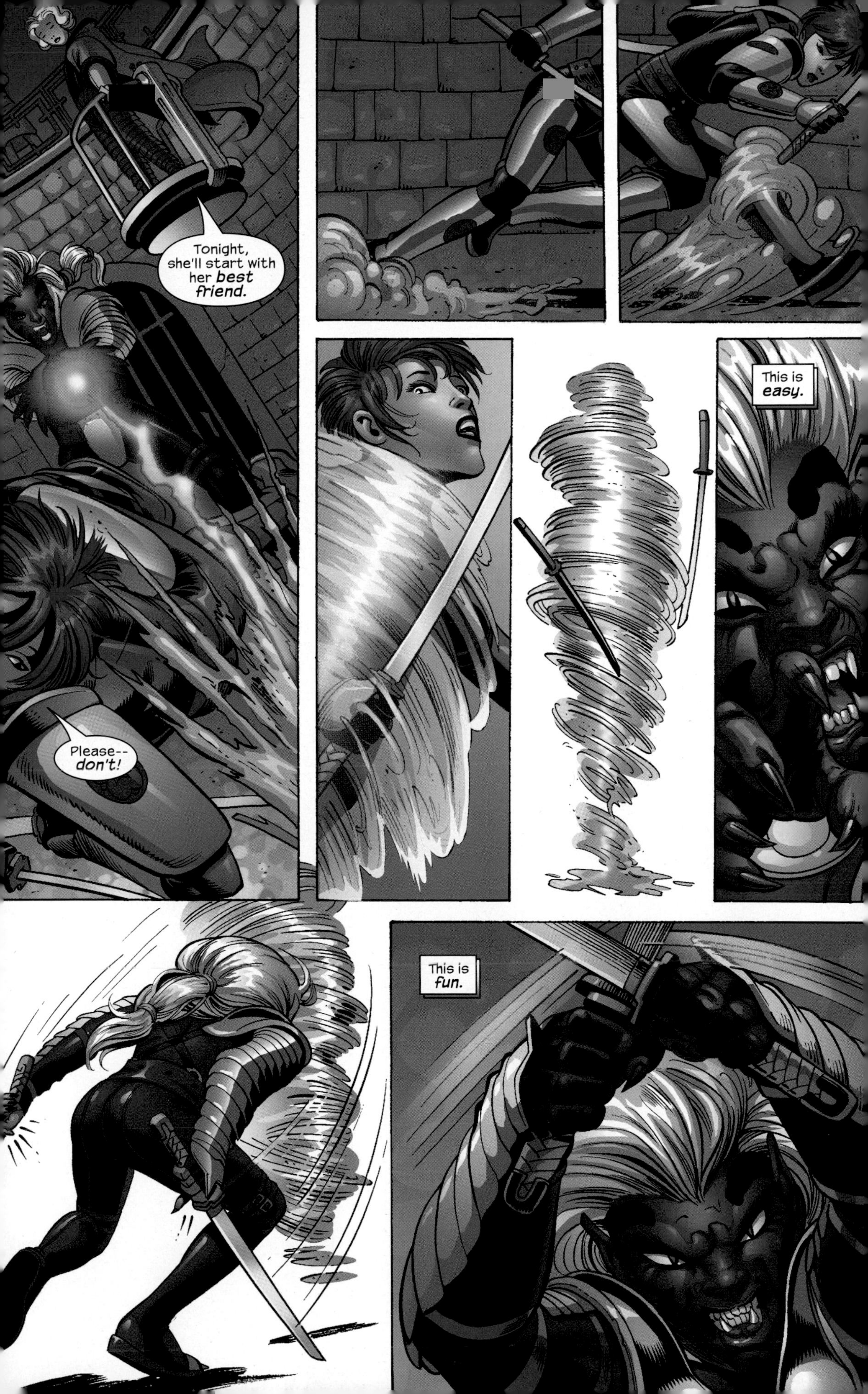
Tonight, she'll start with her best friend.
Please-- don't!
This is easy.
This is fun.

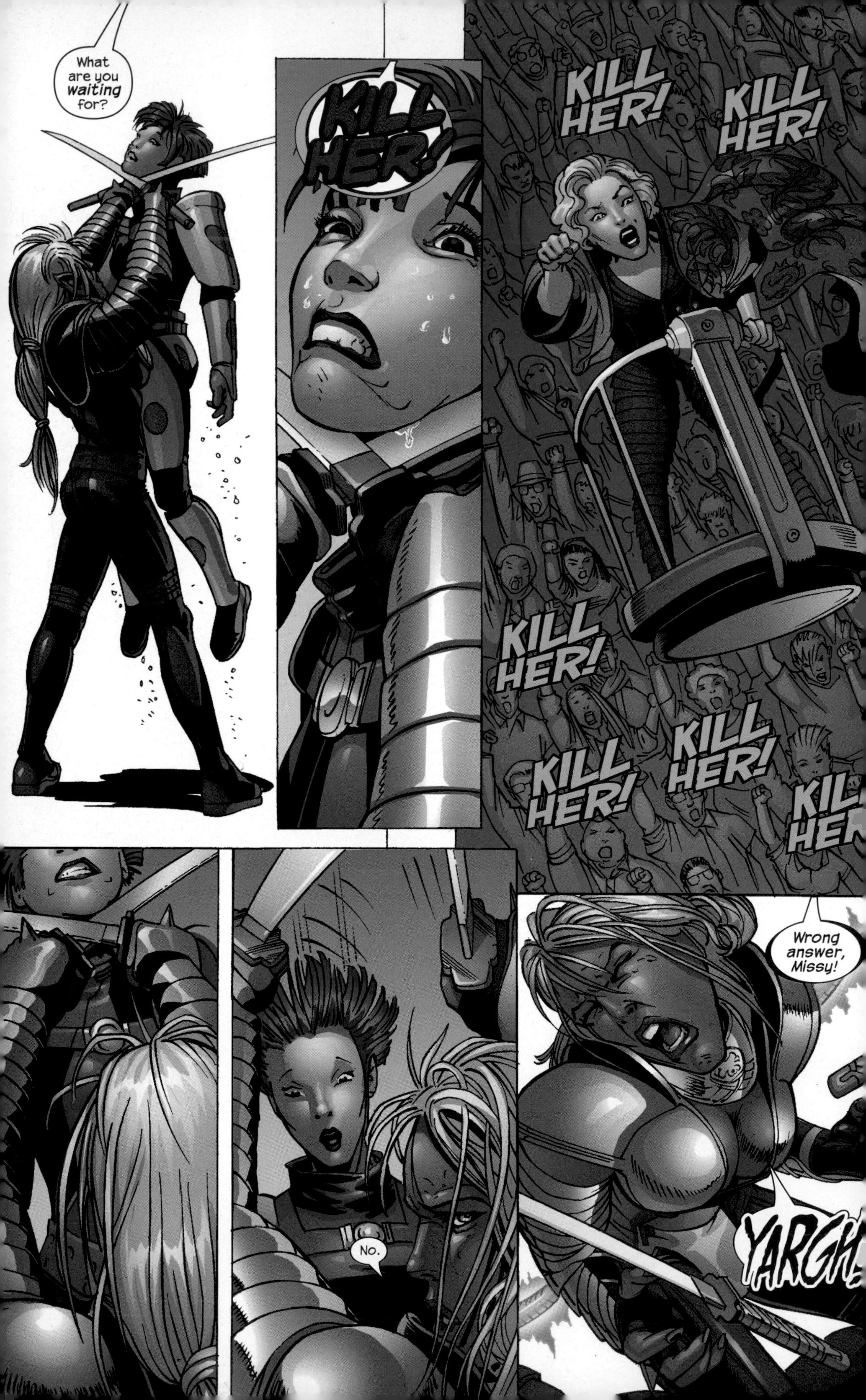
What are you waiting for?
KILL HER!
KILL HER! KILL HER!
KILL HER!
KILL HER! KILL HER!
No.
Wrong answer, Missy!
YARGH!

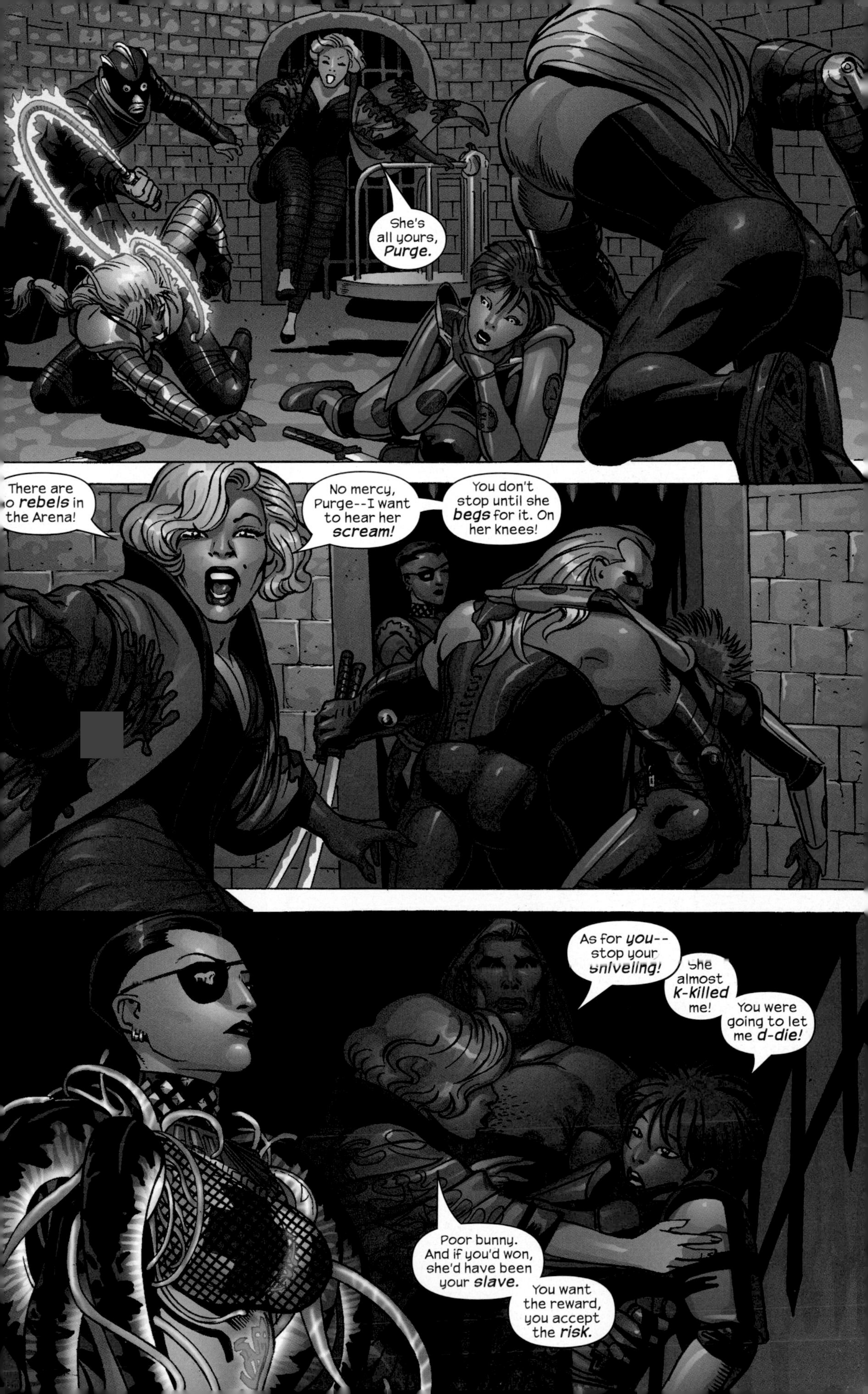
She's all yours, *Purge.*
There are o *rebels* in the Arena!
No mercy, Purge--I want to hear her *scream!*
You don't stop until she *begs* for it. On her knees!
As for *you*-- stop your *sniveling!*
She almost *k-killed* me!
You were going to let me *d-die!*
Poor bunny. And if you'd won, she'd have been your *slave.*
You want the reward, you accept the *risk.*

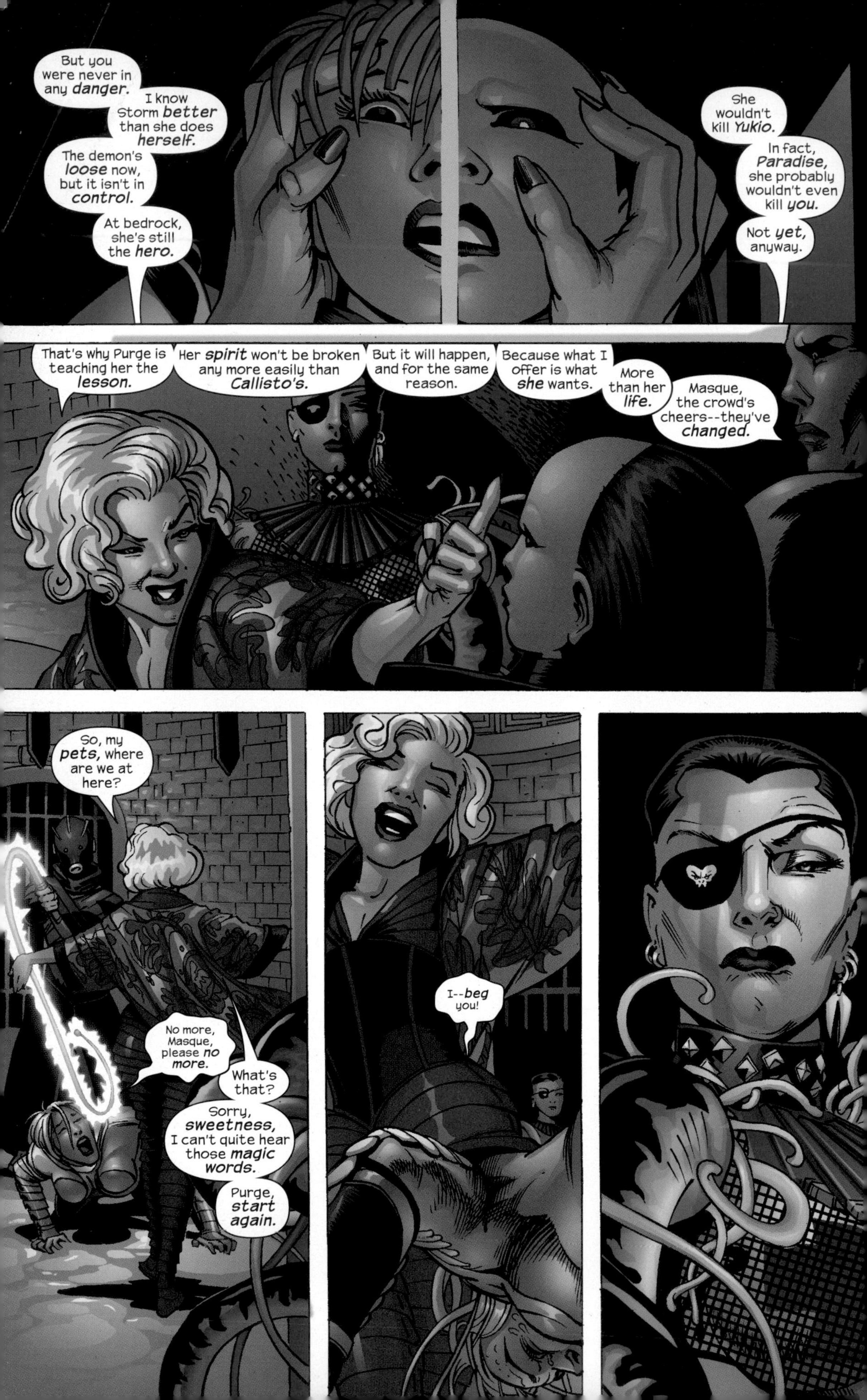
But you were never in any danger.
I know Storm better than she does herself.
The demon's loose now, but it isn't in control.
At bedrock, she's still the hero.
She wouldn't kill Yukio.
In fact, Paradise, she probably wouldn't even kill you.
Not yet, anyway.
That's why Purge is teaching her the lesson.
Her spirit won't be broken any more easily than Callisto's.
But it will happen, and for the same reason.
Because what I offer is what she wants.
More than her life.
Masque, the crowd's cheers--they've changed.
So, my pets, where are we at here?
No more, Masque, please no more.
What's that?
Sorry, sweetness, I can't quite hear those magic words.
Purge, start again.
I--beg you!

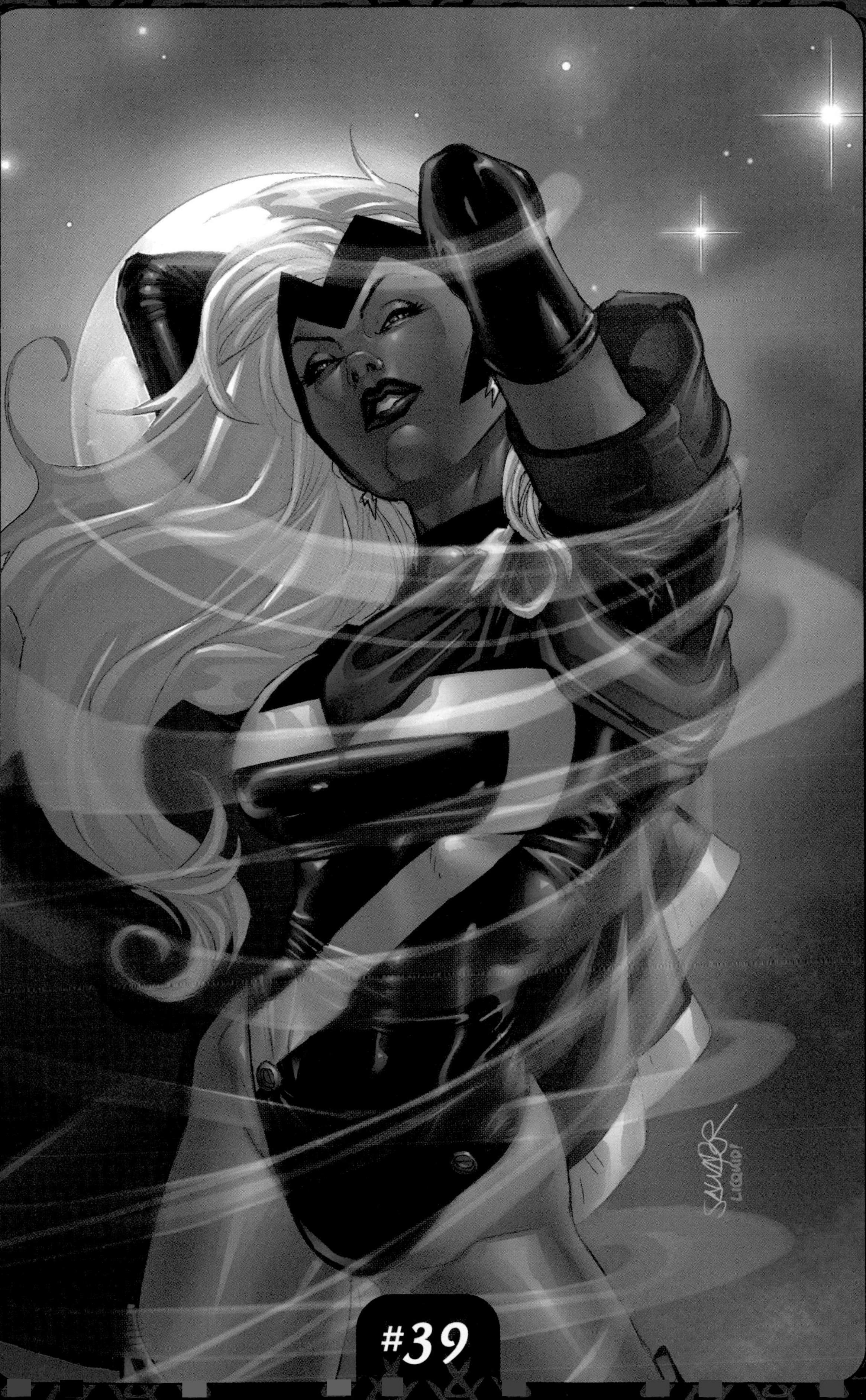
#39

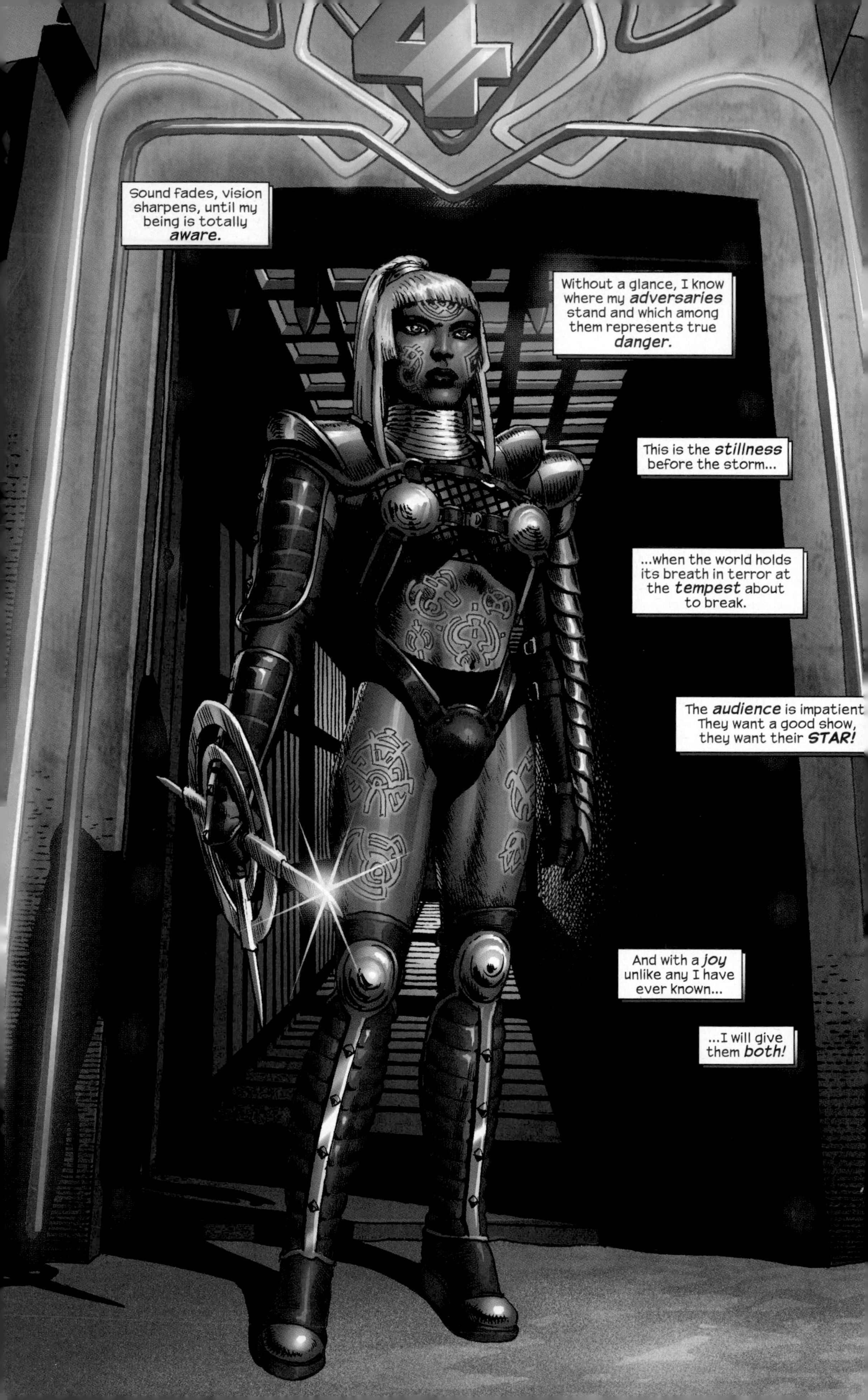
Sound fades, vision sharpens, until my being is totally *aware.*
Without a glance, I know where my *adversaries* stand and which among them represents true *danger.*
This is the *stillness* before the storm...
...when the world holds its breath in terror at the *tempest* about to break.
The *audience* is impatient They want a good show, they want their *STAR!*
And with a *joy* unlike any I have ever known...
...I will give them *both!*

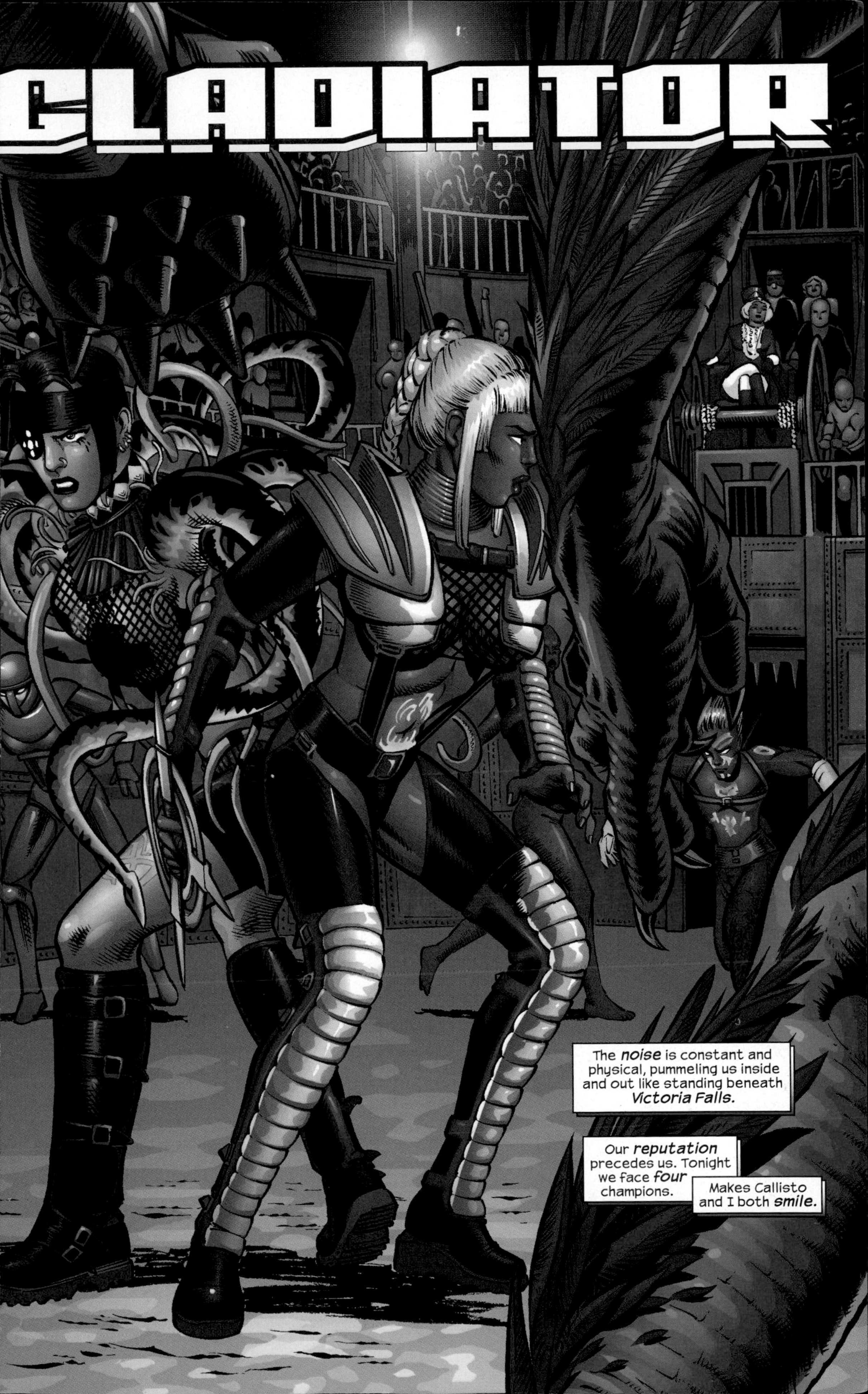
GLADIATOR
The noise is constant and physical, pummeling us inside and out like standing beneath Victoria Falls.
Our reputation precedes us. Tonight we face four champions.
Makes Callisto and I both smile.

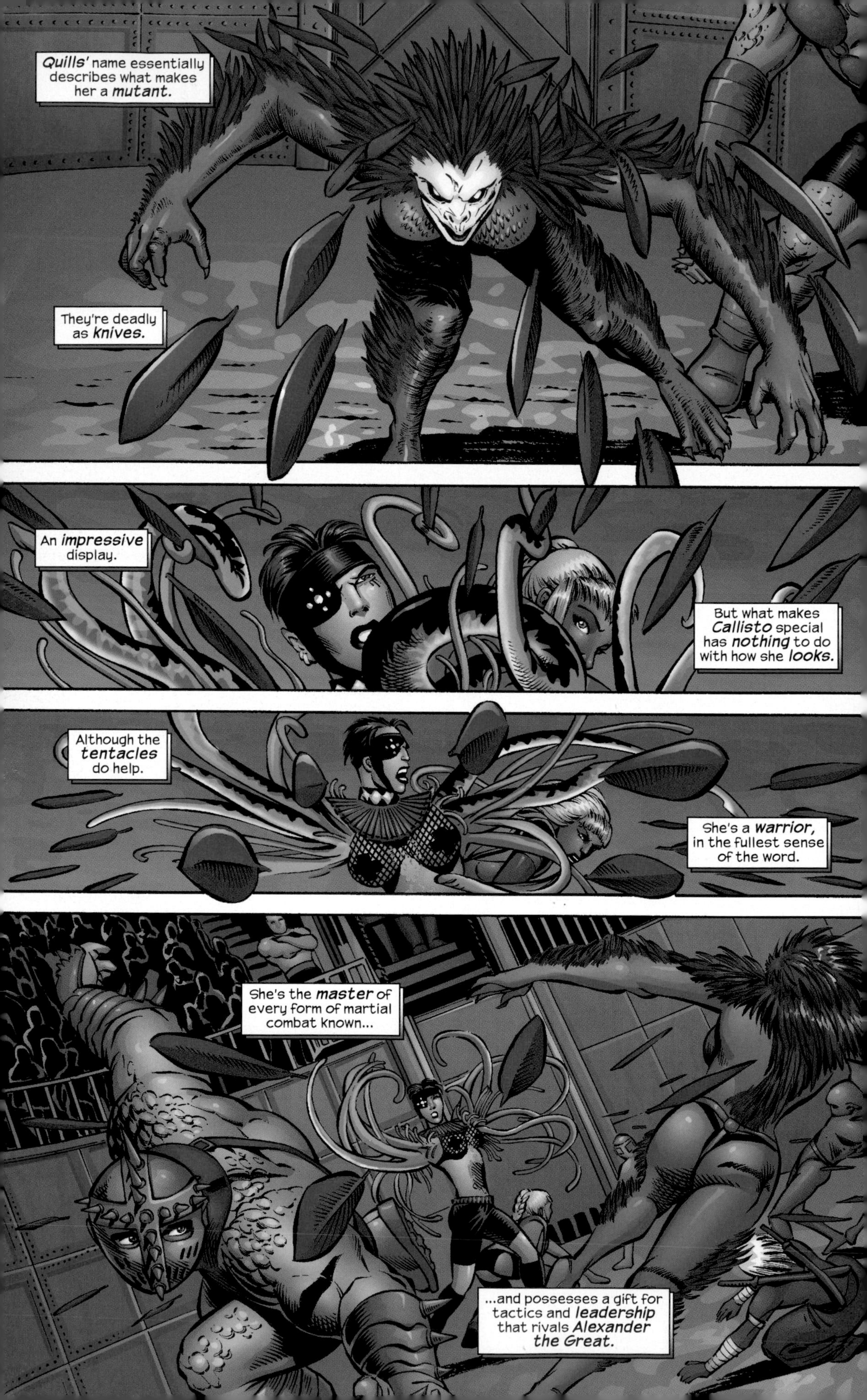
Quills' name essentially describes what makes her a mutant.
They're deadly as knives.
An impressive display.
But what makes Callisto special has nothing to do with how she looks.
Although the tentacles do help.
She's a warrior, in the fullest sense of the word.
She's the master of every form of martial combat known...
...and possesses a gift for tactics and leadership that rivals Alexander the Great.

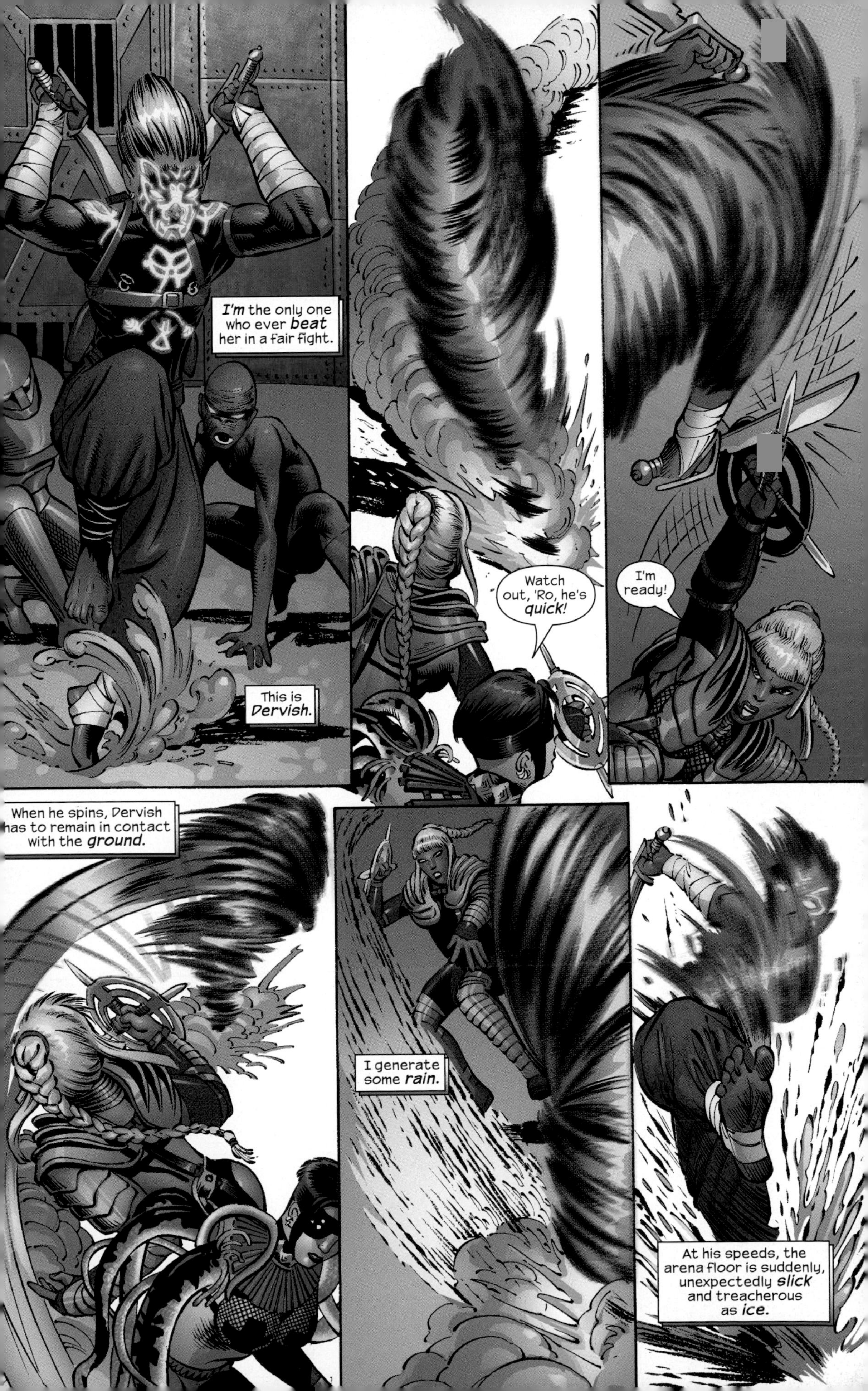
I'm the only one who ever beat her in a fair fight.
This is Dervish.
Watch out, 'Ro, he's quick!
I'm ready!
When he spins, Dervish has to remain in contact with the ground.
I generate some rain.
At his speeds, the arena floor is suddenly, unexpectedly slick and treacherous as ice.

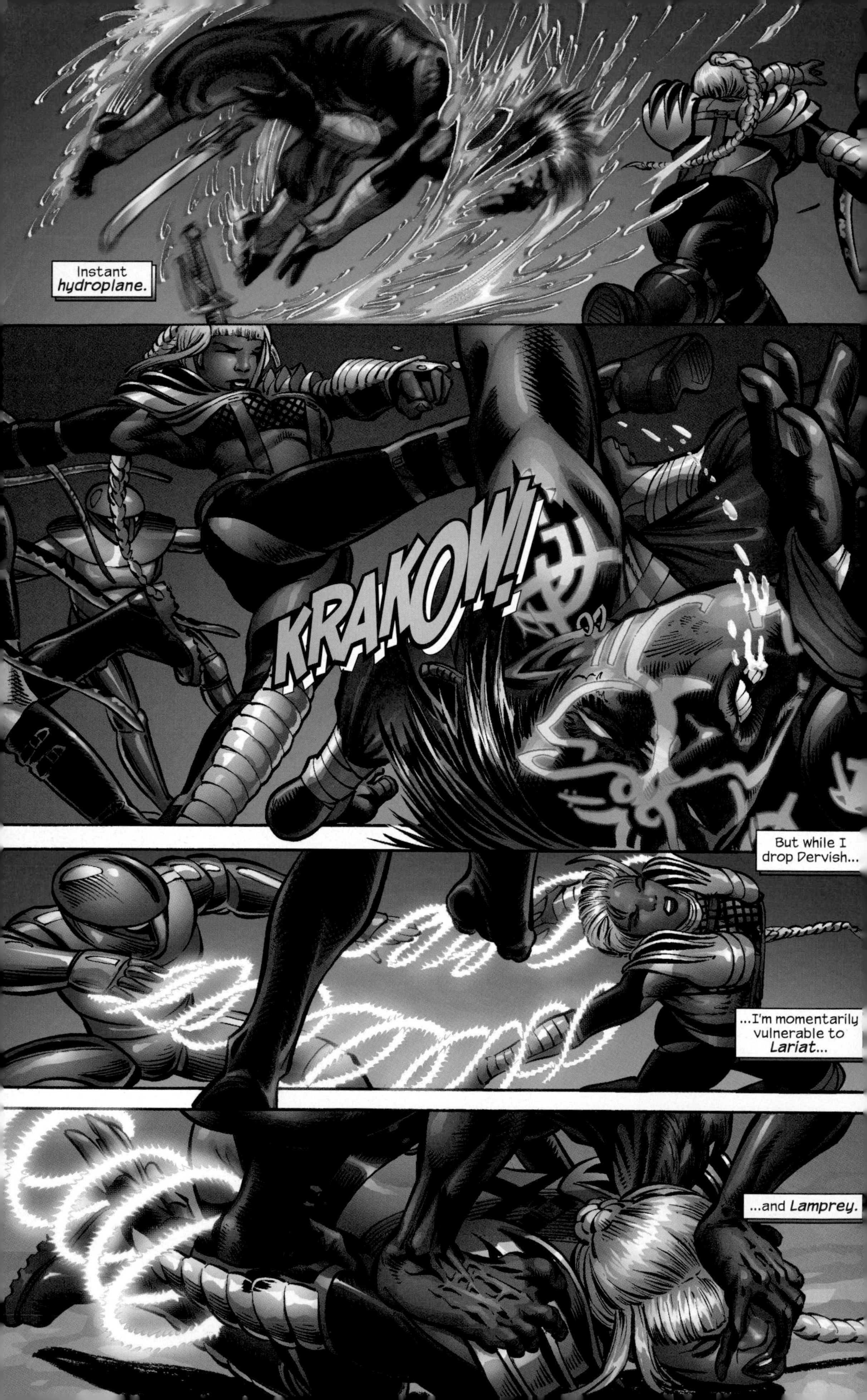
Instant hydroplane.
KRAKOW!!
But while I drop Dervish...
...I'm momentarily vulnerable to Lariat...
...and Lamprey.

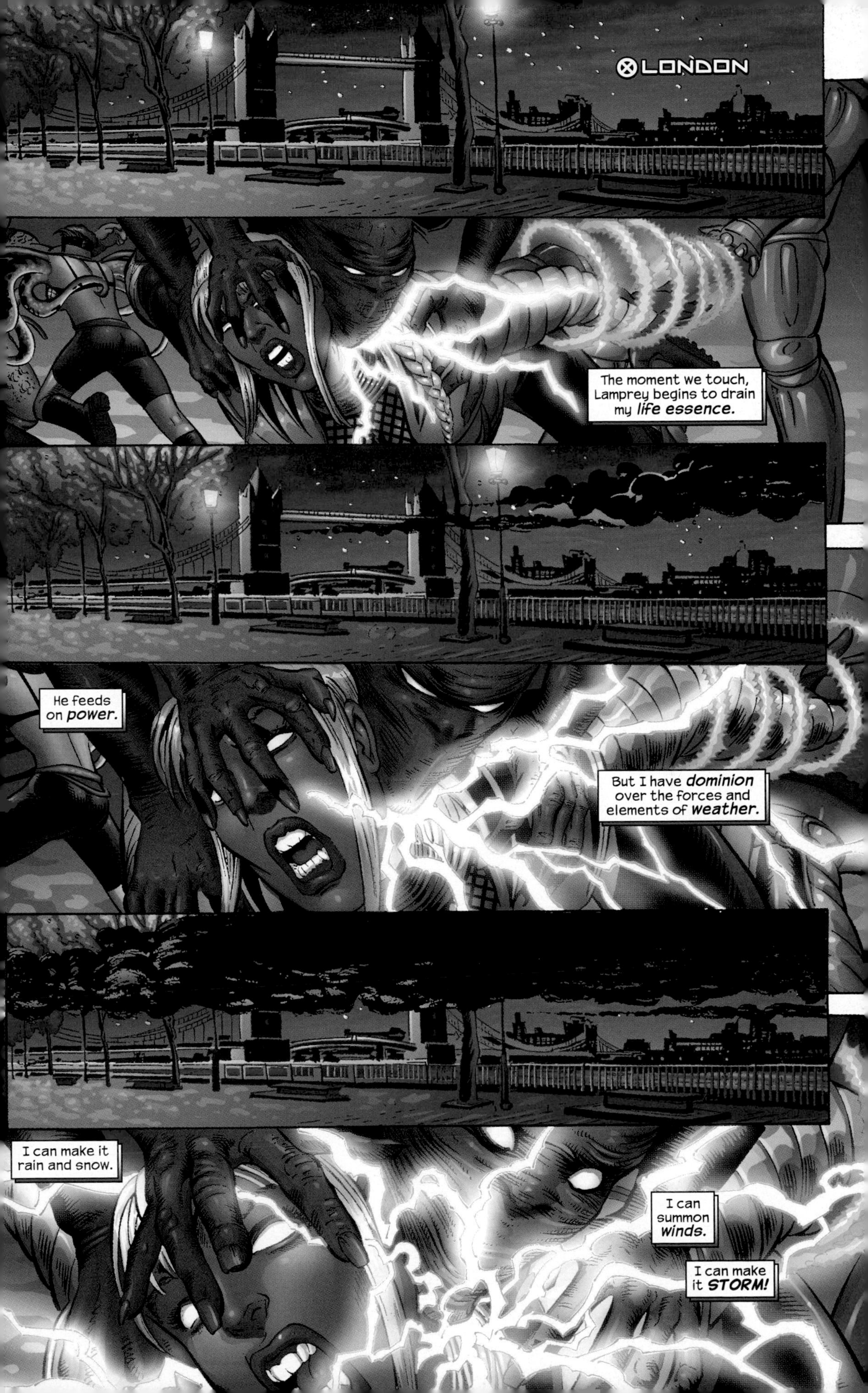
LONDON
The moment we touch, Lamprey begins to drain my *life essence.*
He feeds on *power.*
But I have *dominion* over the forces and elements of *weather.*
I can make it rain and snow.
I can summon *winds.*
I can make it *STORM!*

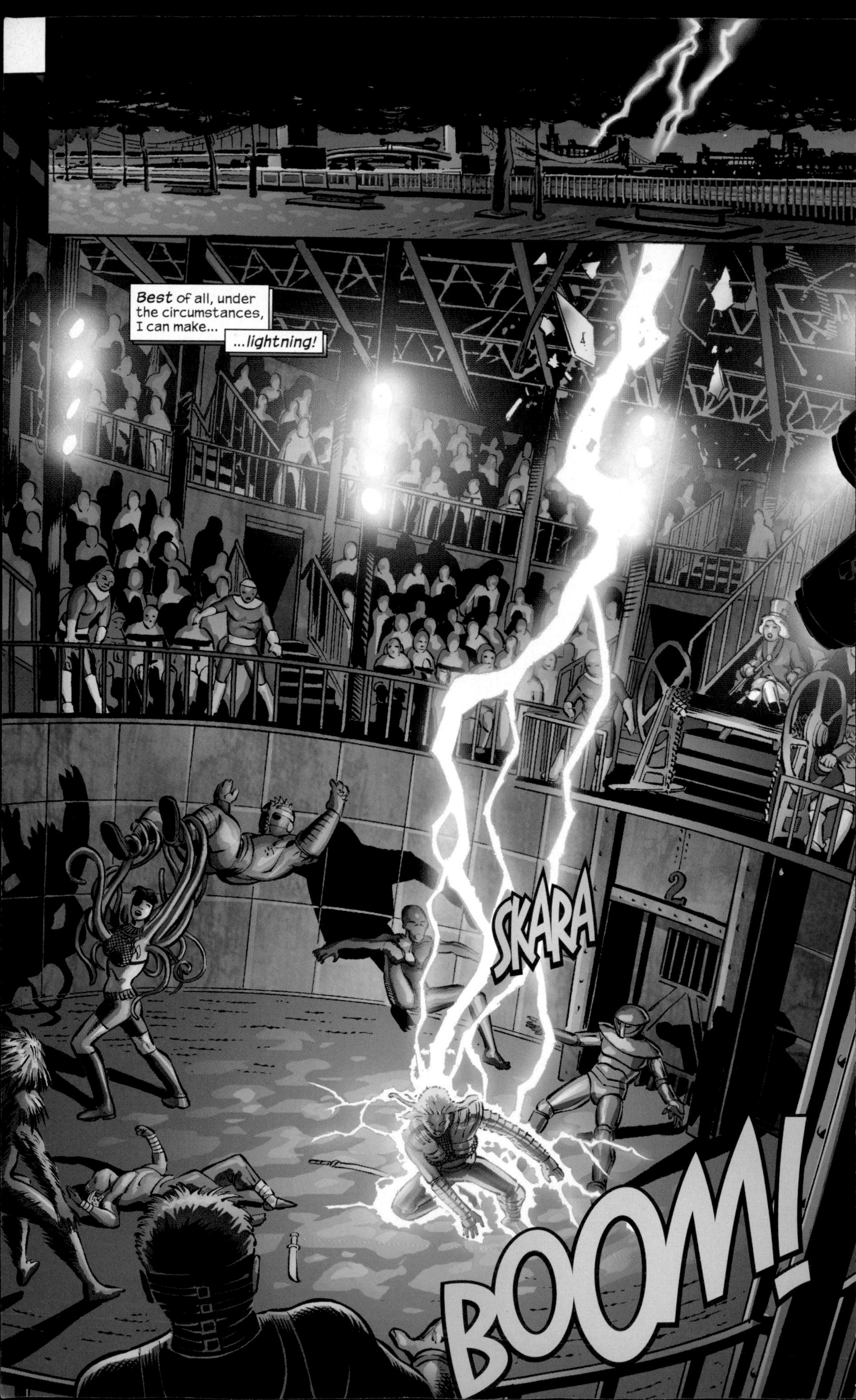

Best of all, under the circumstances, I can make...
...*lightning!*
SKARA
BOOM!

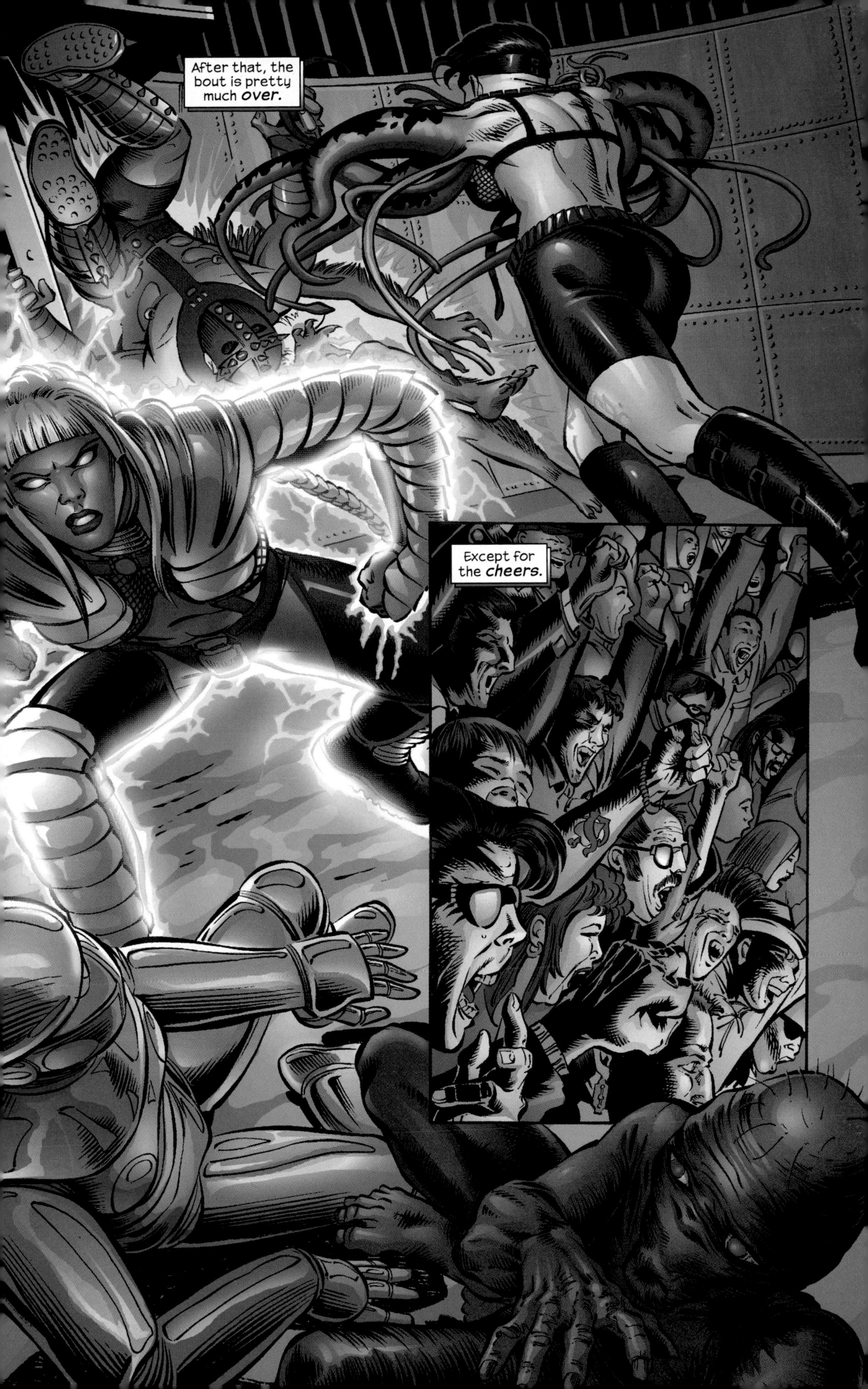
After that, the bout is pretty much *over.*
Except for the *cheers.*

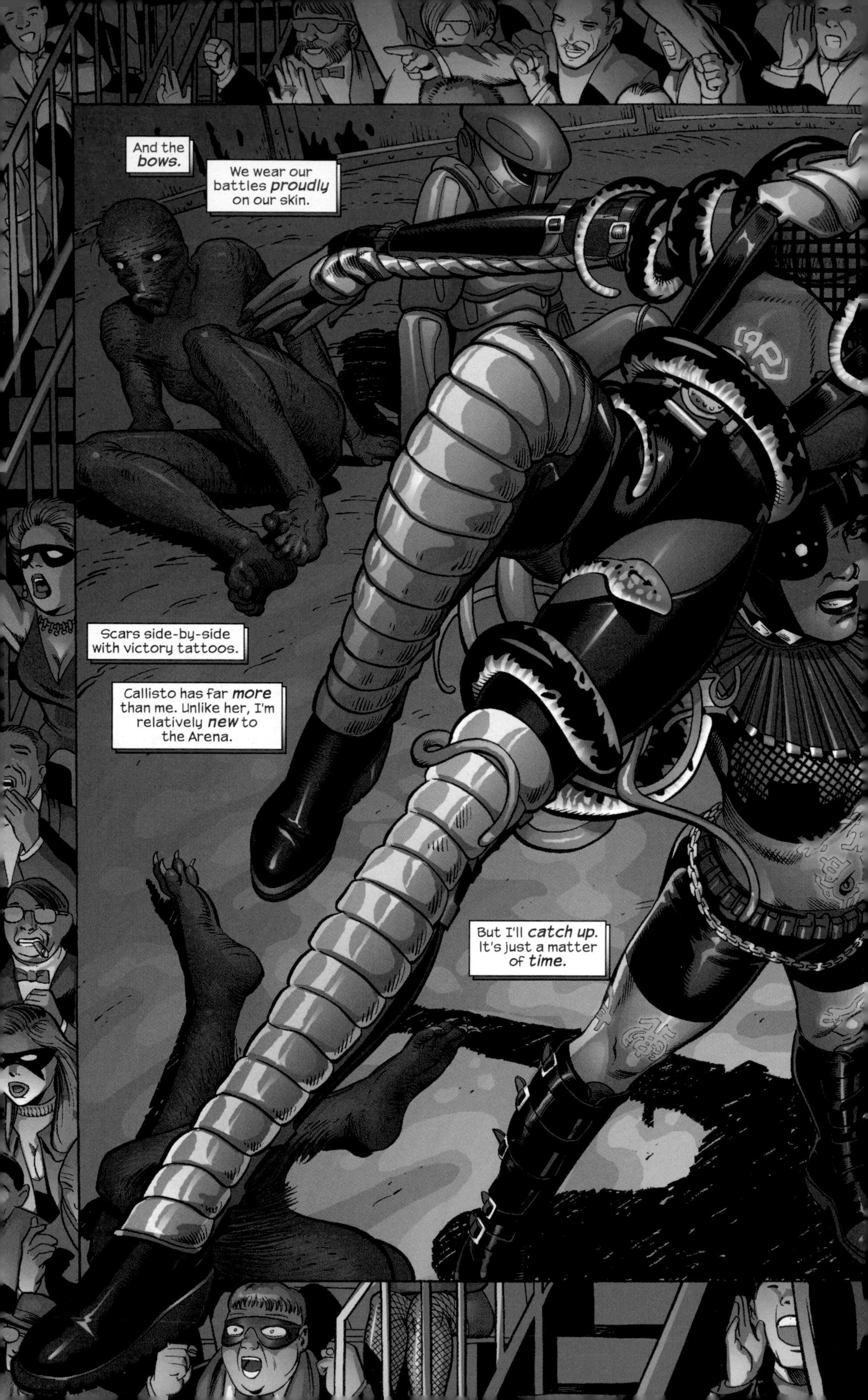
And the *bows.*
We wear our battles *proudly* on our skin.
Scars side-by-side with victory tattoos.
Callisto has far *more* than me. Unlike her, I'm relatively *new* to the Arena.
But I'll *catch up.* It's just a matter of *time.*

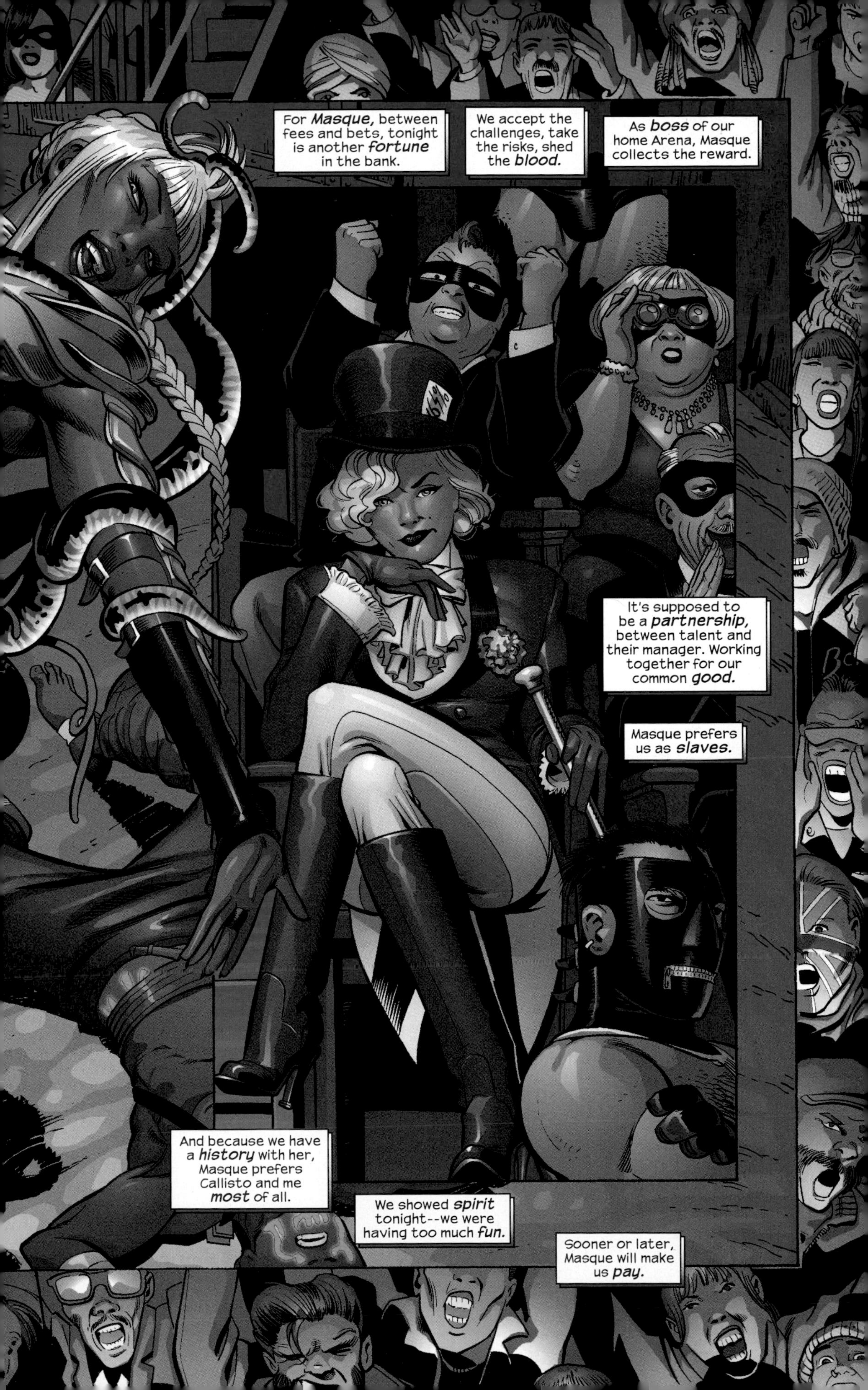
For Masque, between fees and bets, tonight is another fortune in the bank.
We accept the challenges, take the risks, shed the blood.
As boss of our home Arena, Masque collects the reward.
It's supposed to be a partnership, between talent and their manager. Working together for our common good.
Masque prefers us as slaves.
And because we have a history with her, Masque prefers Callisto and me most of all.
We showed spirit tonight--we were having too much fun.
Sooner or later, Masque will make us pay.

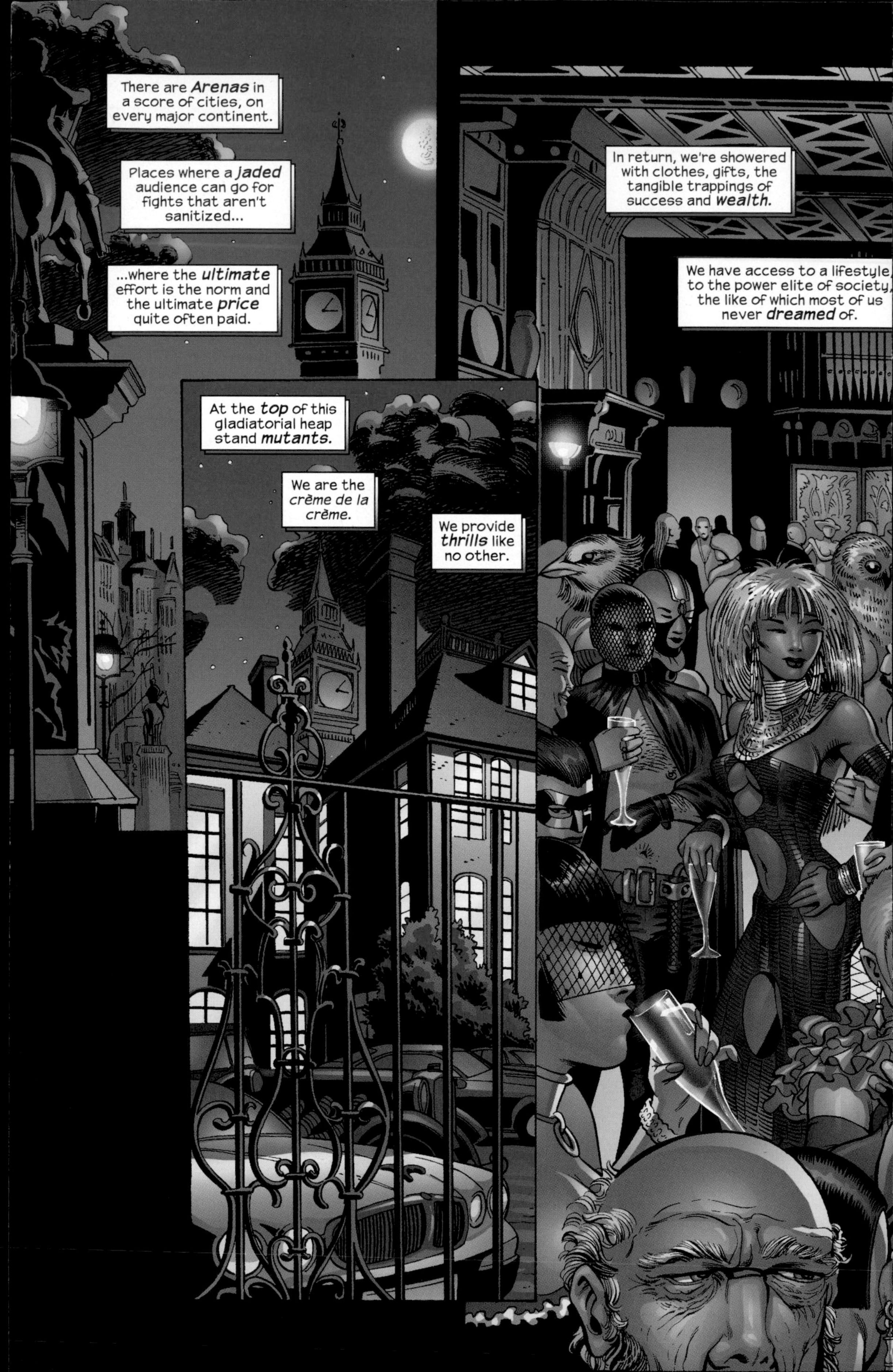
There are *Arenas* in a score of cities, on every major continent.
Places where a *jaded* audience can go for fights that aren't sanitized...
...where the *ultimate* effort is the norm and the ultimate *price* quite often paid.
In return, we're showered with clothes, gifts, the tangible trappings of success and *wealth.*
We have access to a lifestyle, to the power elite of society, the like of which most of us never *dreamed* of.
At the *top* of this gladiatorial heap stand *mutants.*
We are the *crème de la crème.*
We provide *thrills* like no other.

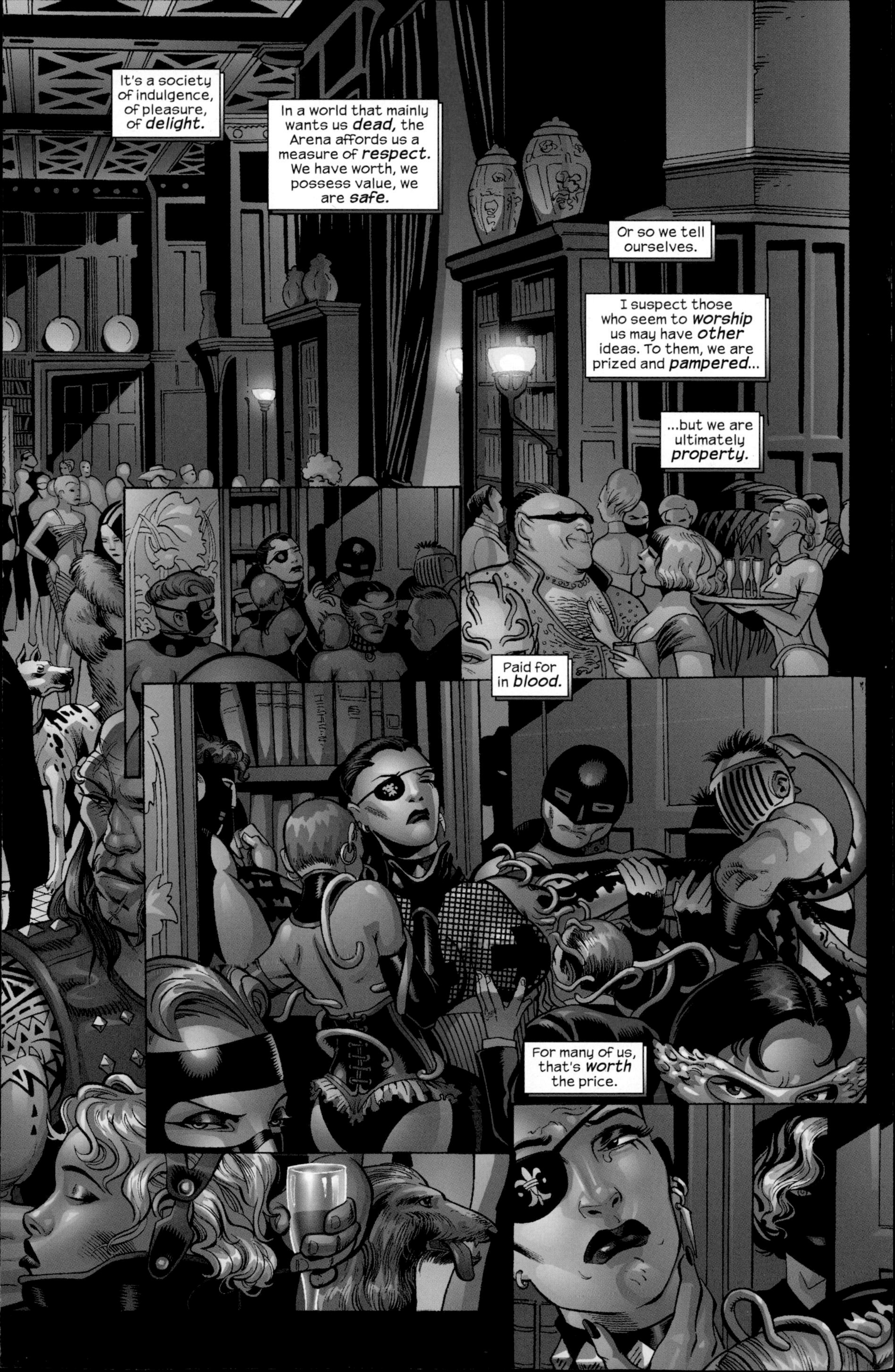
It's a society of indulgence, of pleasure, of delight.
In a world that mainly wants us dead, the Arena affords us a measure of respect. We have worth, we possess value, we are safe.
Or so we tell ourselves.
I suspect those who seem to worship us may have other ideas. To them, we are prized and pampered...
...but we are ultimately property.
Paid for in blood.
For many of us, that's worth the price.

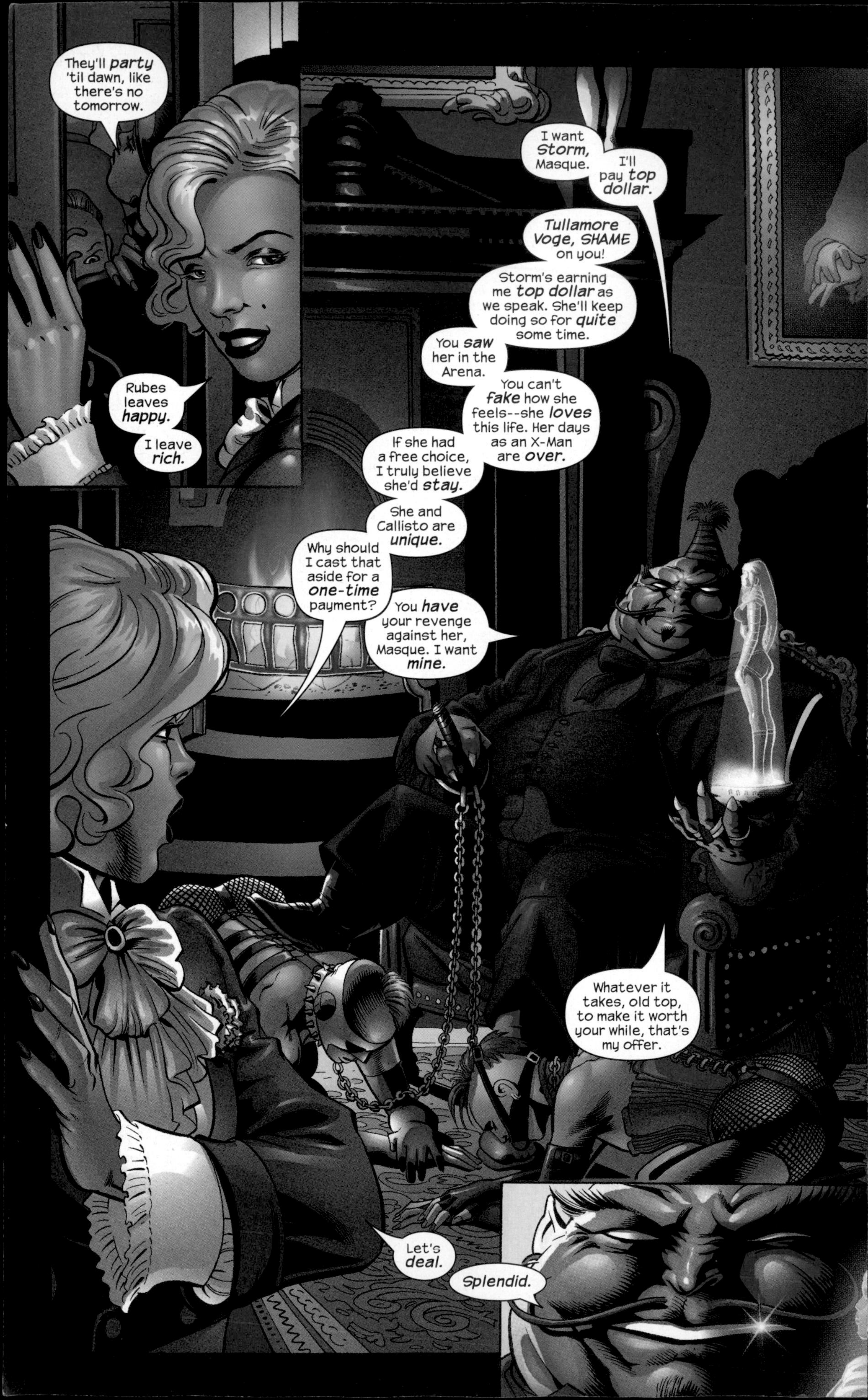
They'll party 'til dawn, like there's no tomorrow.
Rubes leaves happy.
I leave rich.
I want Storm, Masque.
I'll pay top dollar.
Tullamore Voge, SHAME on you!
Storm's earning me top dollar as we speak. She'll keep doing so for quite some time.
You saw her in the Arena.
You can't fake how she feels--she loves this life. Her days as an X-Man are over.
If she had a free choice, I truly believe she'd stay.
She and Callisto are unique.
Why should I cast that aside for a one-time payment?
You have your revenge against her, Masque. I want mine.
Whatever it takes, old top, to make it worth your while, that's my offer.
Let's deal.
Splendid.

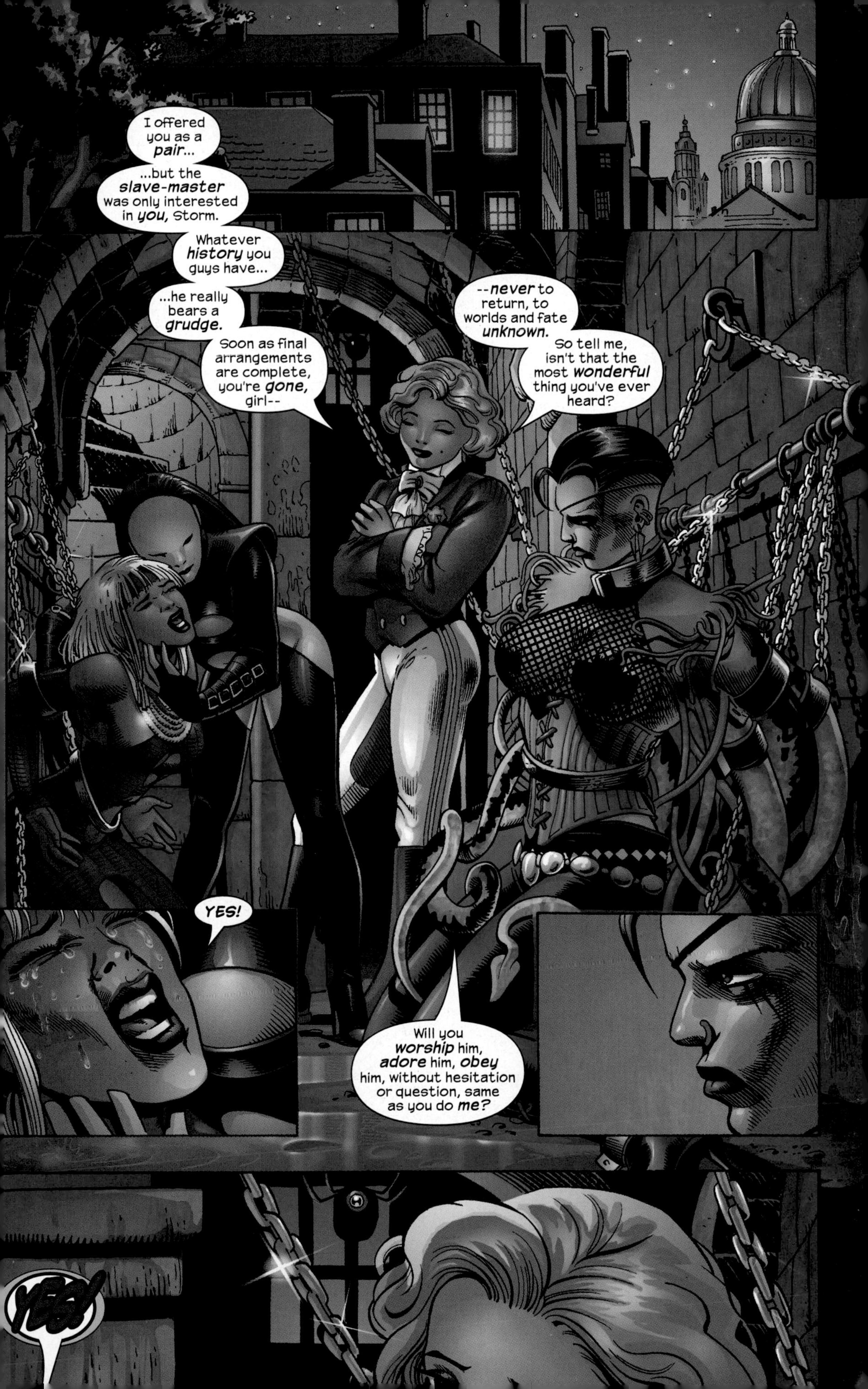

I offered you as a pair...
...but the slave-master was only interested in you, Storm.
Whatever history you guys have...
...he really bears a grudge.
Soon as final arrangements are complete, you're gone, girl--
--never to return, to worlds and fate unknown.
So tell me, isn't that the most wonderful thing you've ever heard?
YES!
Will you worship him, adore him, obey him, without hesitation or question, same as you do me?
YES!

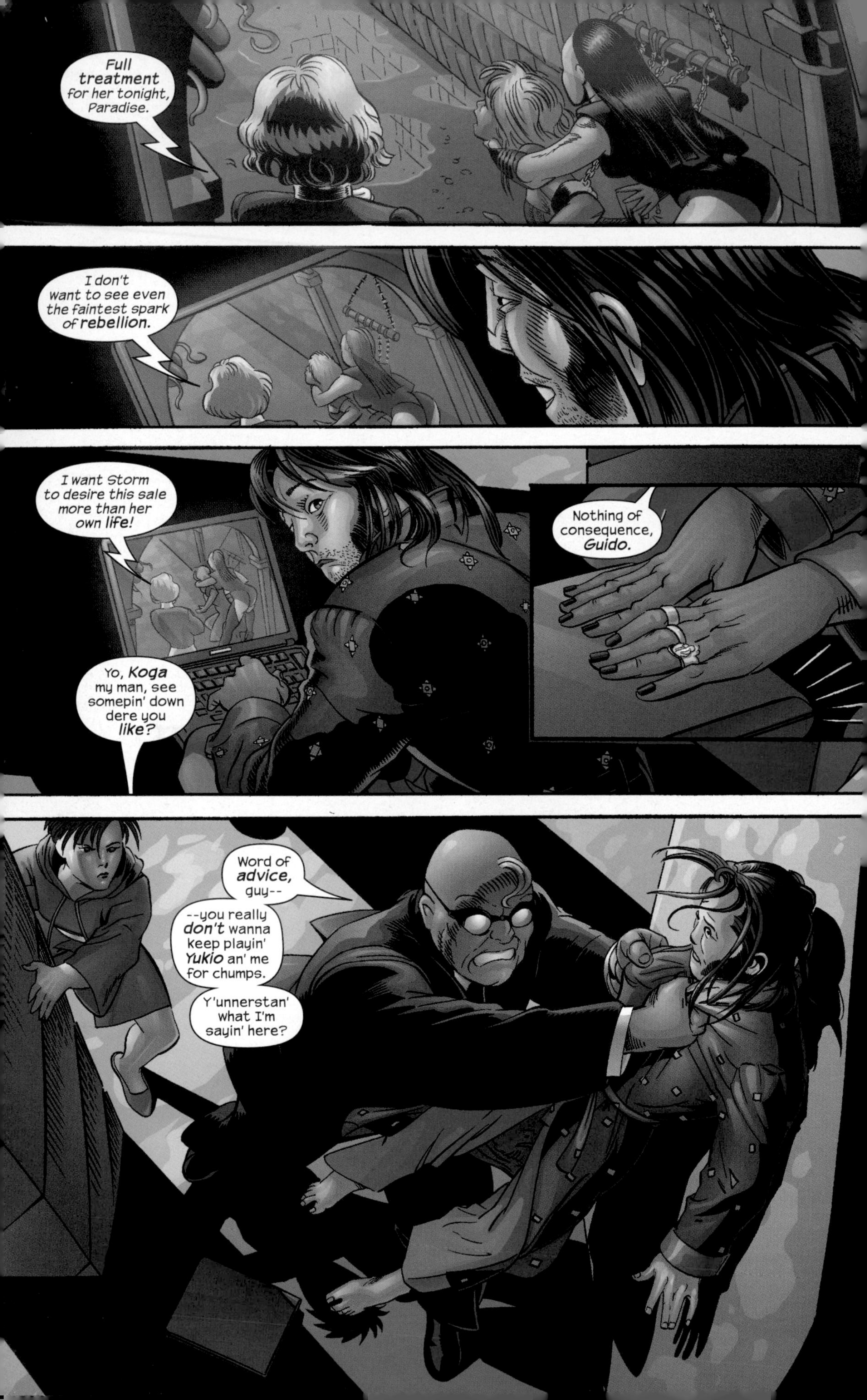
Full treatment for her tonight, Paradise.
I don't want to see even the faintest spark of rebellion.
I want Storm to desire this sale more than her own life!
Nothing of consequence, Guido.
Yo, Koga my man, see somepin' down dere you like?
Word of advice, guy--
--you really don't wanna keep playin' Yukio an' me for chumps.
Y'unnerstan' what I'm sayin' here?

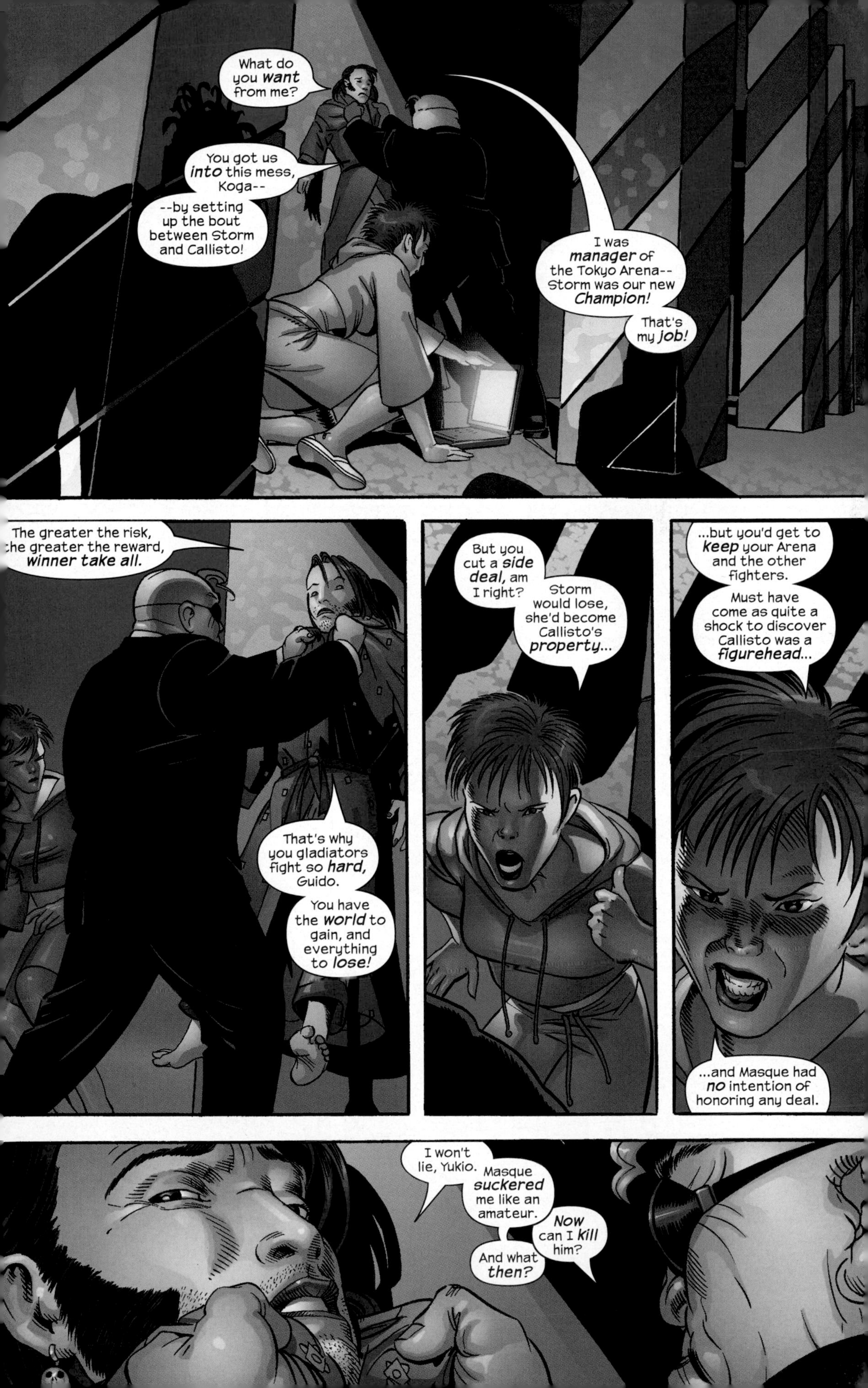
What do you want from me?
You got us into this mess, Koga--
--by setting up the bout between Storm and Callisto!
I was manager of the Tokyo Arena-- Storm was our new Champion!
That's my job!
The greater the risk, the greater the reward, winner take all.
That's why you gladiators fight so hard, Guido.
You have the world to gain, and everything to lose!
But you cut a side deal, am I right?
Storm would lose, she'd become Callisto's property...
...but you'd get to keep your Arena and the other fighters.
Must have come as quite a shock to discover Callisto was a figurehead...
...and Masque had no intention of honoring any deal.
I won't lie, Yukio.
Masque suckered me like an amateur.
Now can I kill him?
And what then?

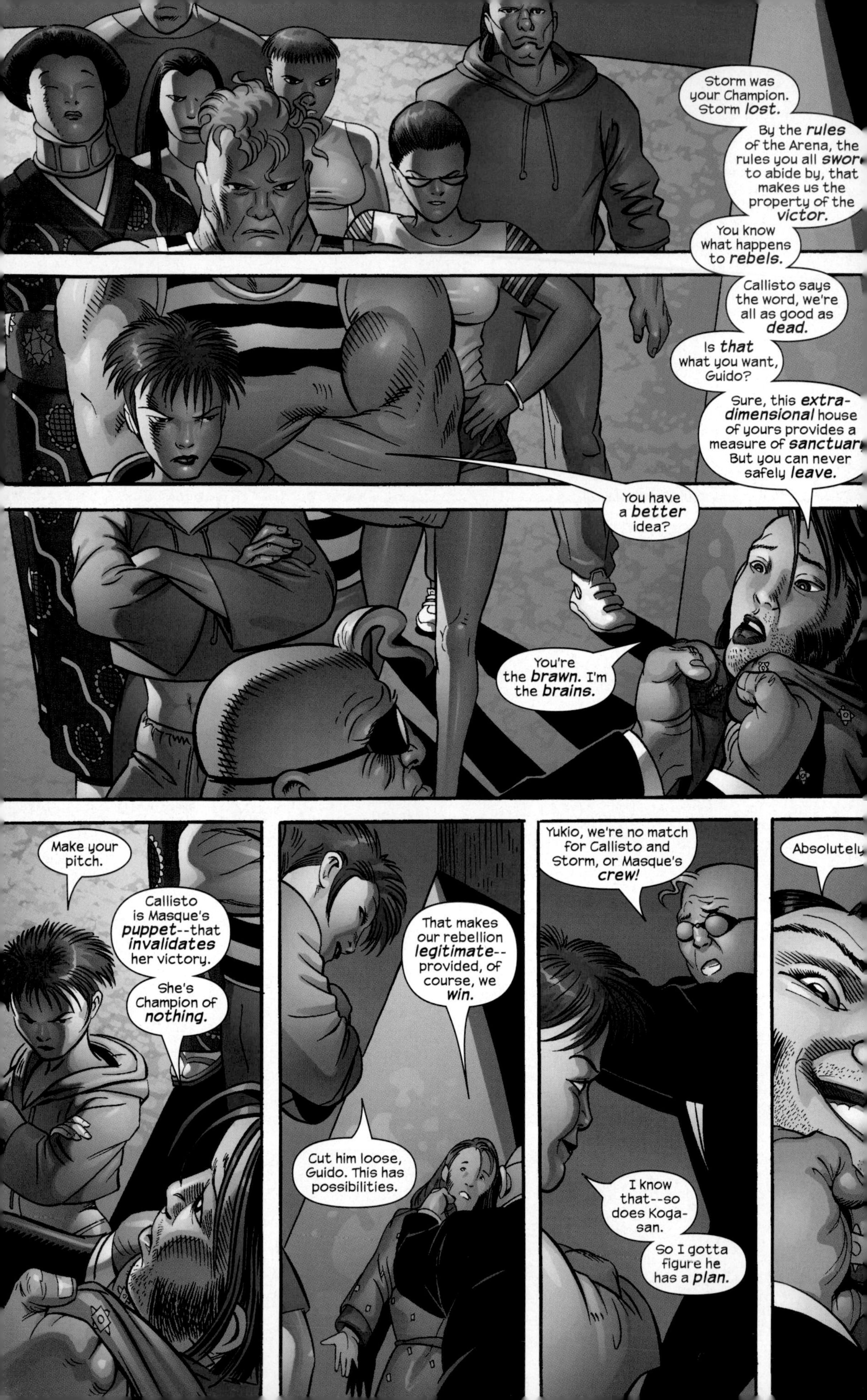

Storm was your Champion. Storm lost.
By the rules of the Arena, the rules you all swor to abide by, that makes us the property of the victor.
You know what happens to rebels.
Callisto says the word, we're all as good as dead.
Is that what you want, Guido?
Sure, this extra-dimensional house of yours provides a measure of sanctuar But you can never safely leave.
You have a better idea?
You're the brawn. I'm the brains.
Make your pitch.
Callisto is Masque's puppet--that invalidates her victory.
She's Champion of nothing.
That makes our rebellion legitimate--provided, of course, we win.
Cut him loose, Guido. This has possibilities.
Yukio, we're no match for Callisto and Storm, or Masque's crew!
I know that--so does Koga-san.
So I gotta figure he has a plan.
Absolutel

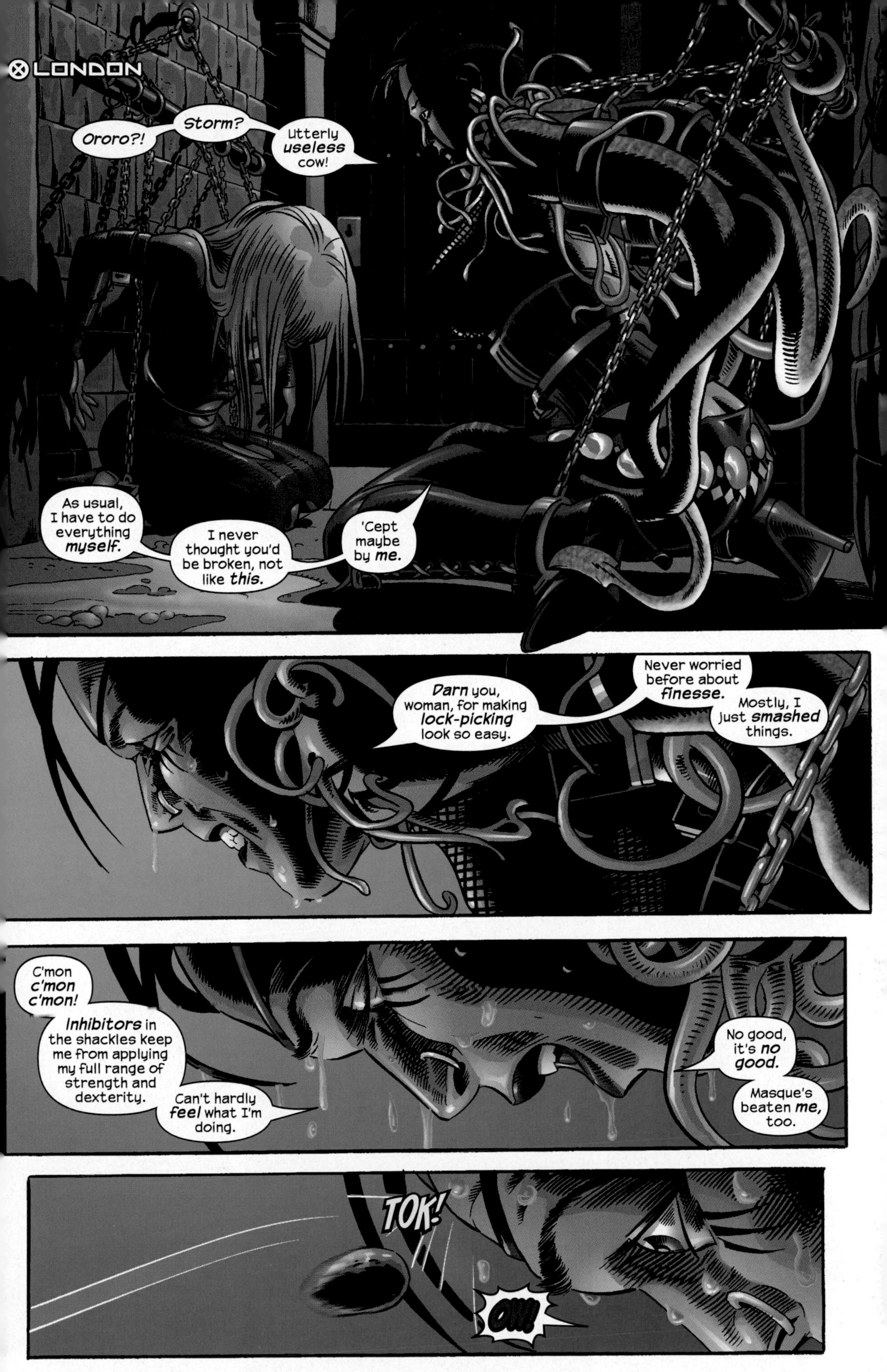
LONDON
Ororo?!
Storm?
Utterly useless cow!
As usual, I have to do everything myself.
I never thought you'd be broken, not like this.
'Cept maybe by me.
Darn you, woman, for making lock-picking look so easy.
Never worried before about finesse.
Mostly, I just smashed things.
C'mon c'mon c'mon!
Inhibitors in the shackles keep me from applying my full range of strength and dexterity.
Can't hardly feel what I'm doing.
No good, it's no good.
Masque's beaten me, too.
TOK!
OW!

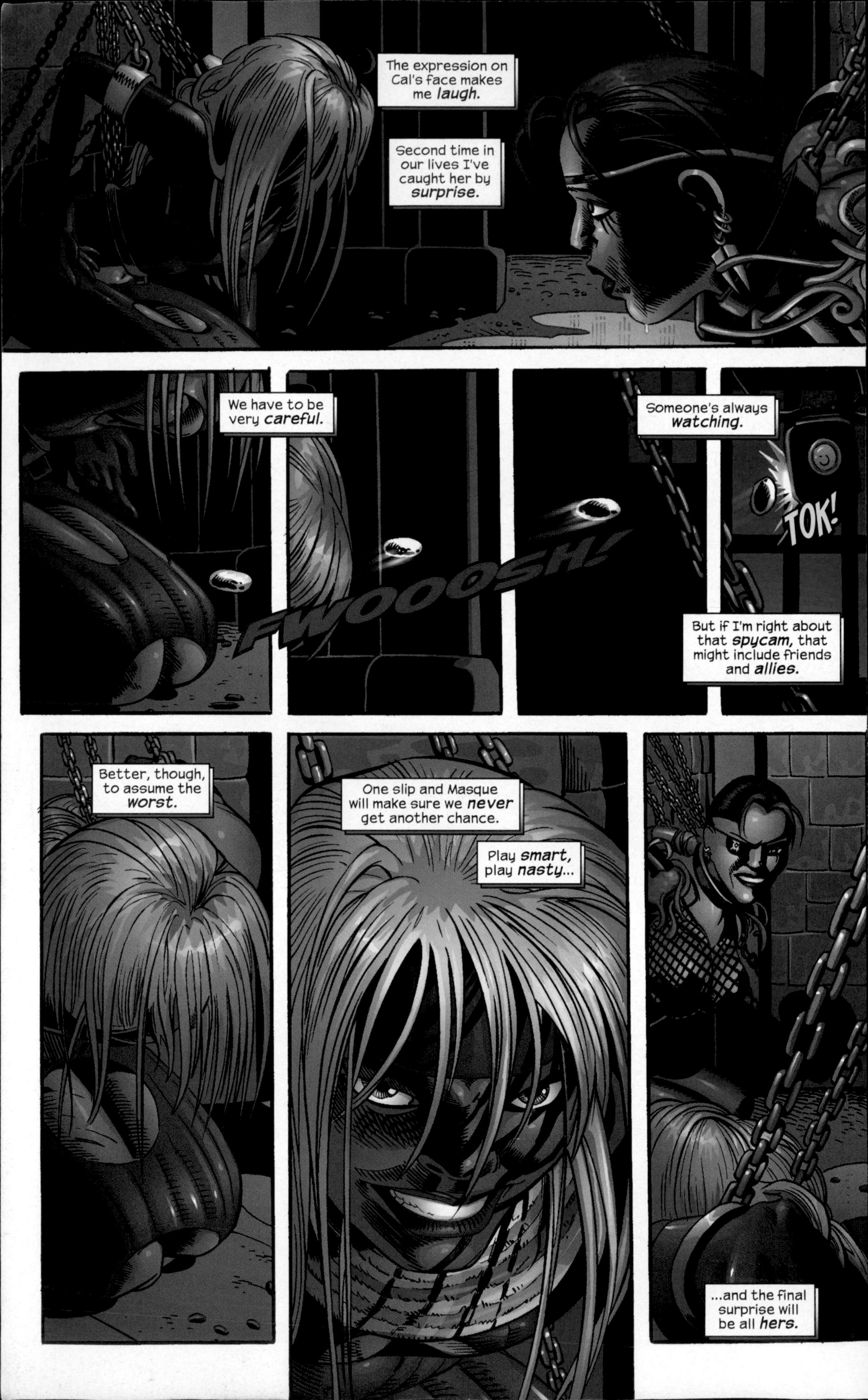
The expression on Cal's face makes me *laugh.*
Second time in our lives I've caught her by *surprise.*
We have to be very *careful.*
FWOOOSH!
Someone's always *watching.*
TOK!
But if I'm right about that *spycam,* that might include friends and *allies.*
Better, though, to assume the *worst.*
One slip and Masque will make sure we *never* get another chance.
Play *smart,* play *nasty...*
...and the final surprise will be all *hers.*

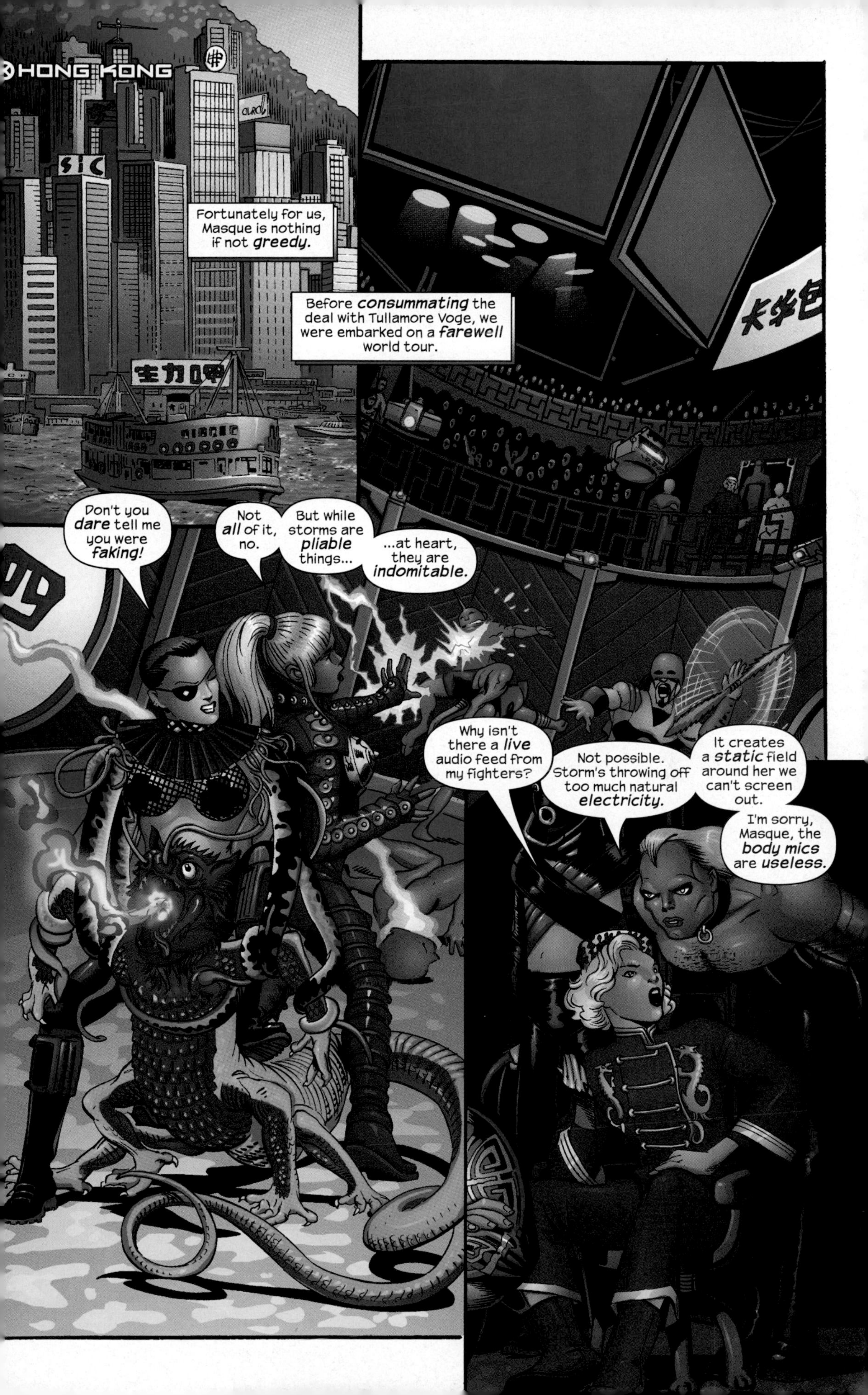
HONG KONG
Fortunately for us, Masque is nothing if not greedy.
Before consummating the deal with Tullamore Voge, we were embarked on a farewell world tour.
Don't you dare tell me you were faking!
Not all of it, no.
But while storms are pliable things...
...at heart, they are indomitable.
Why isn't there a live audio feed from my fighters?
Not possible. Storm's throwing off too much natural electricity.
It creates a static field around her we can't screen out.
I'm sorry, Masque, the body mics are useless.

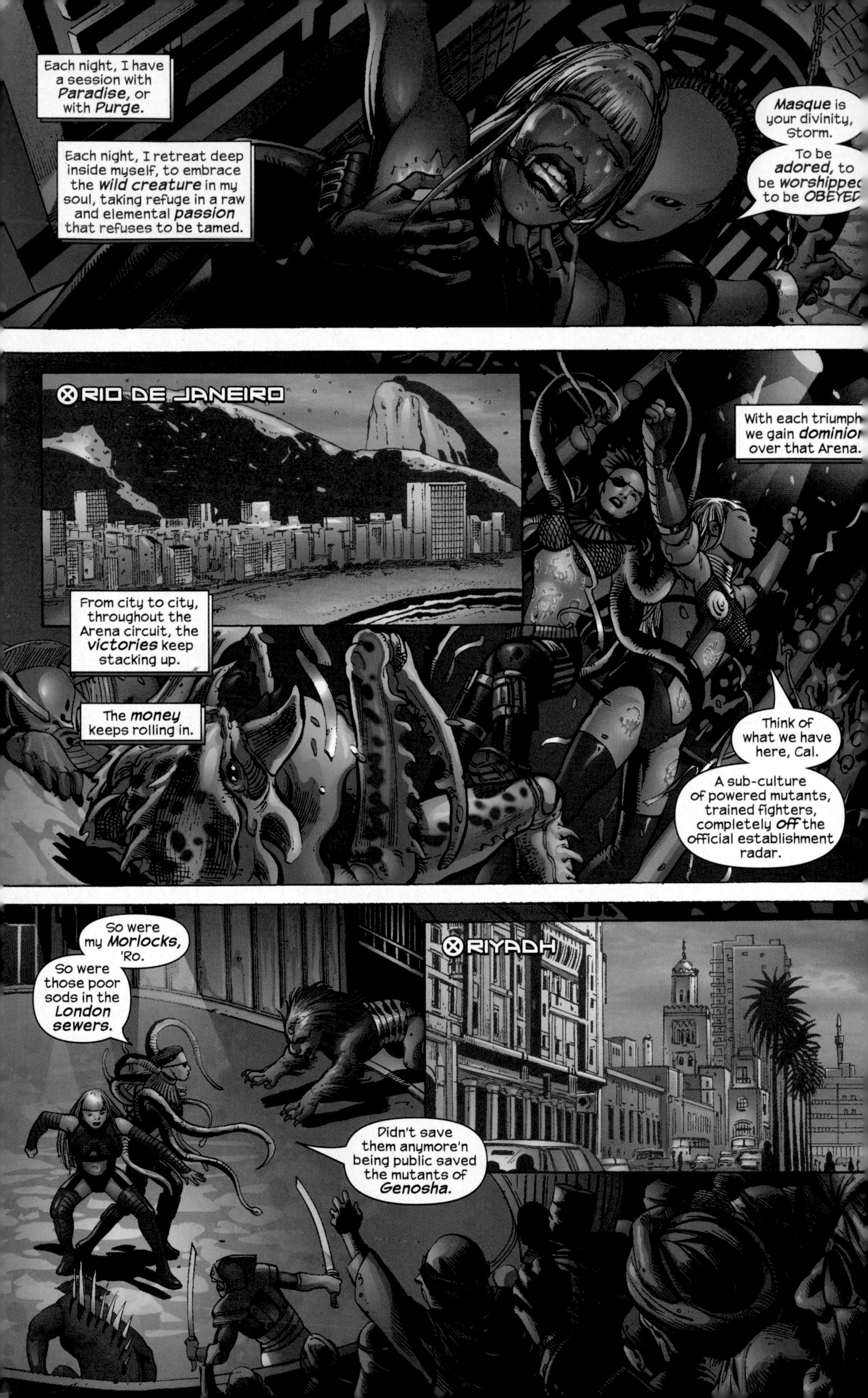
Each night, I have a session with Paradise, or with Purge.
Each night, I retreat deep inside myself, to embrace the wild creature in my soul, taking refuge in a raw and elemental passion that refuses to be tamed.
Masque is your divinity, Storm.
To be adored, to be worshippe
to be OBEYED
RIO DE JANEIRO
From city to city, throughout the Arena circuit, the victories keep stacking up.
The money keeps rolling in.
With each triumph we gain dominio
over that Arena.
Think of what we have here, Cal.
A sub-culture of powered mutants, trained fighters, completely off the official establishment radar.
So were my Morlocks, 'Ro.
So were those poor sods in the London sewers.
RIYADH
Didn't save them anymore'n being public saved the mutants of Genosha.

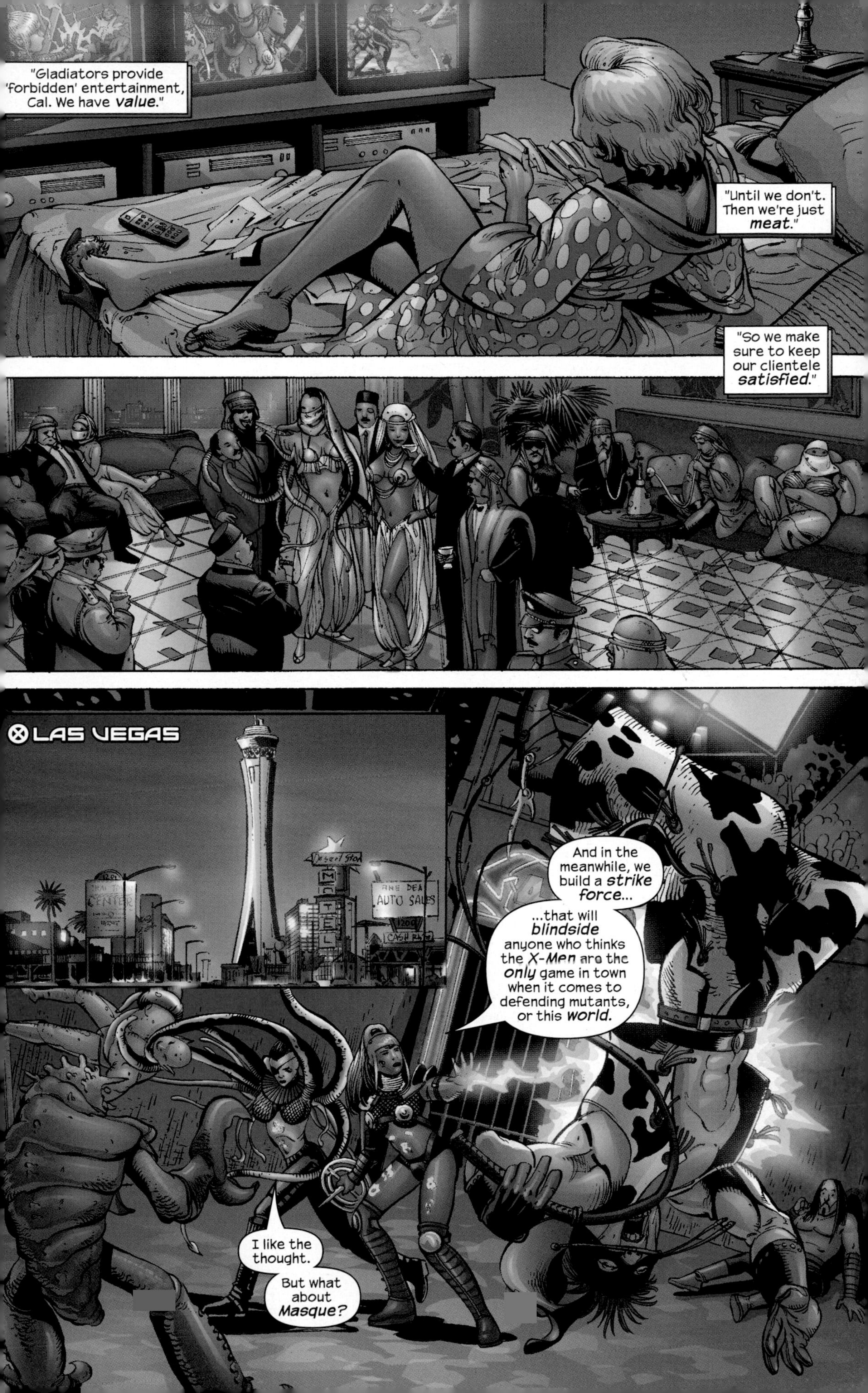
"Gladiators provide 'forbidden' entertainment, Cal. We have *value*."
"Until we don't. Then we're just *meat*."
"So we make sure to keep our clientele *satisfied*."
LAS VEGAS
AUTO SALES
And in the meanwhile, we build a *strike force*...
...that will *blindside* anyone who thinks the *X-Men* are the *only* game in town when it comes to defending mutants, or this *world*.
I like the thought.
But what about *Masque*?

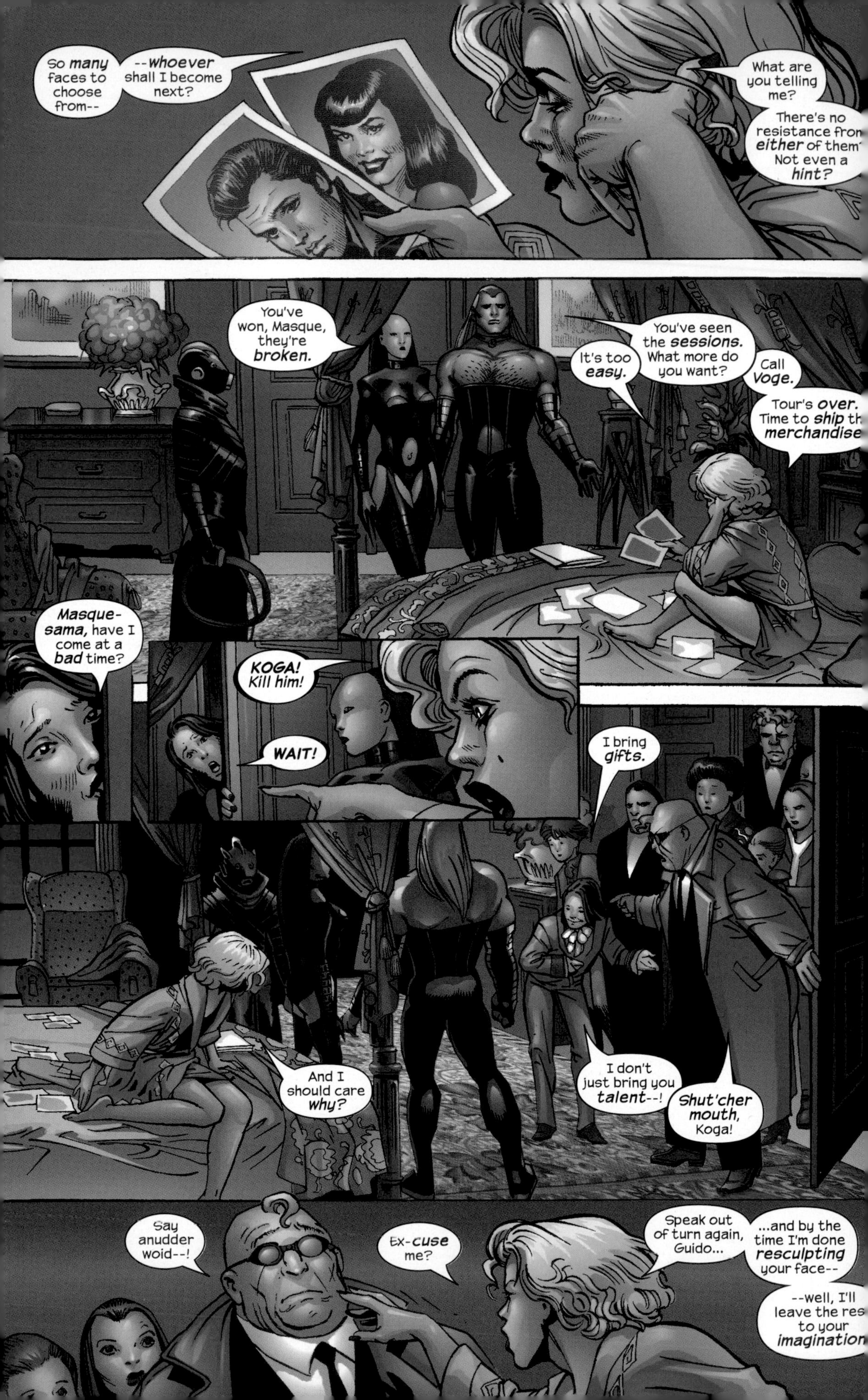
So many faces to choose from--
--whoever shall I become next?
What are you telling me?
There's no resistance from either of them? Not even a hint?
You've won, Masque, they're broken.
It's too easy.
You've seen the sessions. What more do you want?
Call Voge.
Tour's over. Time to ship the merchandise.
Masque-sama, have I come at a bad time?
KOGA! Kill him!
WAIT!
I bring gifts.
And I should care why?
I don't just bring you talent--!
Shut'cher mouth, Koga!
Say anudder woid--!
Ex-cuse me?
Speak out of turn again, Guido...
...and by the time I'm done resculpting your face--
--well, I'll leave the rest to your imagination.

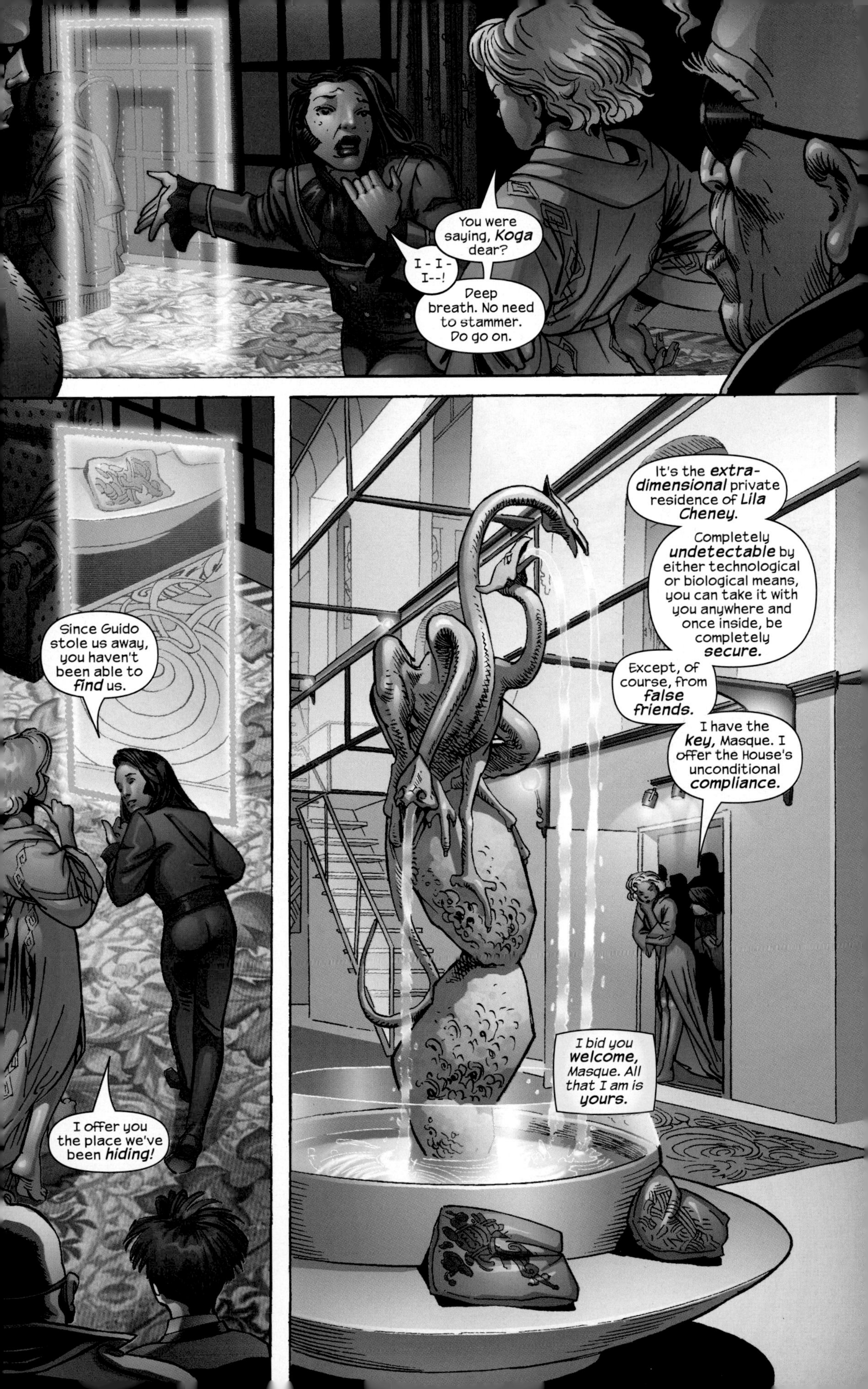
You were saying, Koga dear?
I - I - I--!
Deep breath. No need to stammer. Do go on.
Since Guido stole us away, you haven't been able to find us.
I offer you the place we've been hiding!
It's the extra-dimensional private residence of Lila Cheney.
Completely undetectable by either technological or biological means, you can take it with you anywhere and once inside, be completely secure.
Except, of course, from false friends.
I have the key, Masque. I offer the House's unconditional compliance.
I bid you welcome, Masque. All that I am is yours.

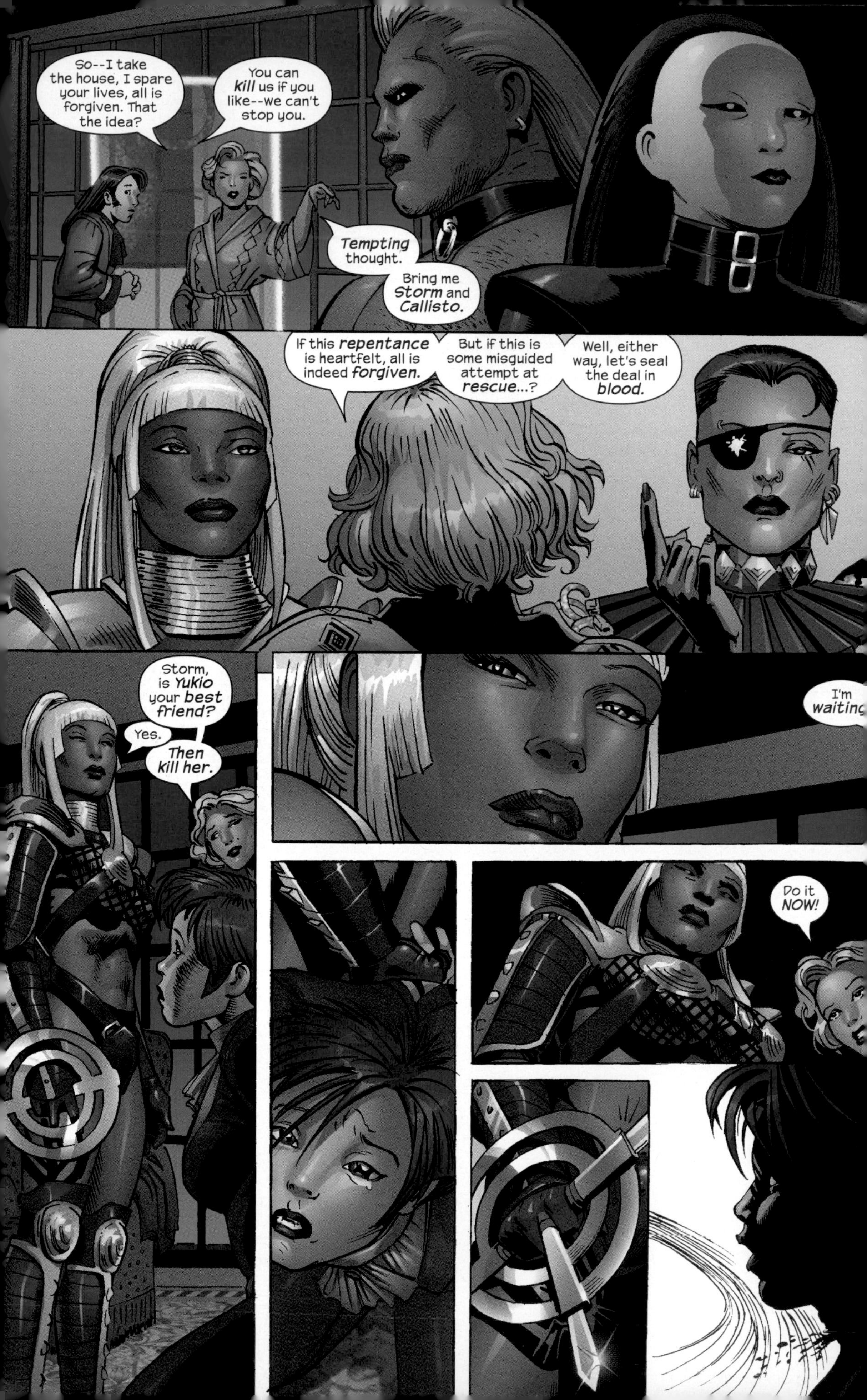
So--I take the house, I spare your lives, all is forgiven. That the idea?
You can kill us if you like--we can't stop you.
Tempting thought.
Bring me Storm and Callisto.
If this repentance is heartfelt, all is indeed forgiven.
But if this is some misguided attempt at rescue...?
Well, either way, let's seal the deal in blood.
Storm, is Yukio your best friend?
Yes.
Then kill her.
I'm waiting
Do it NOW!

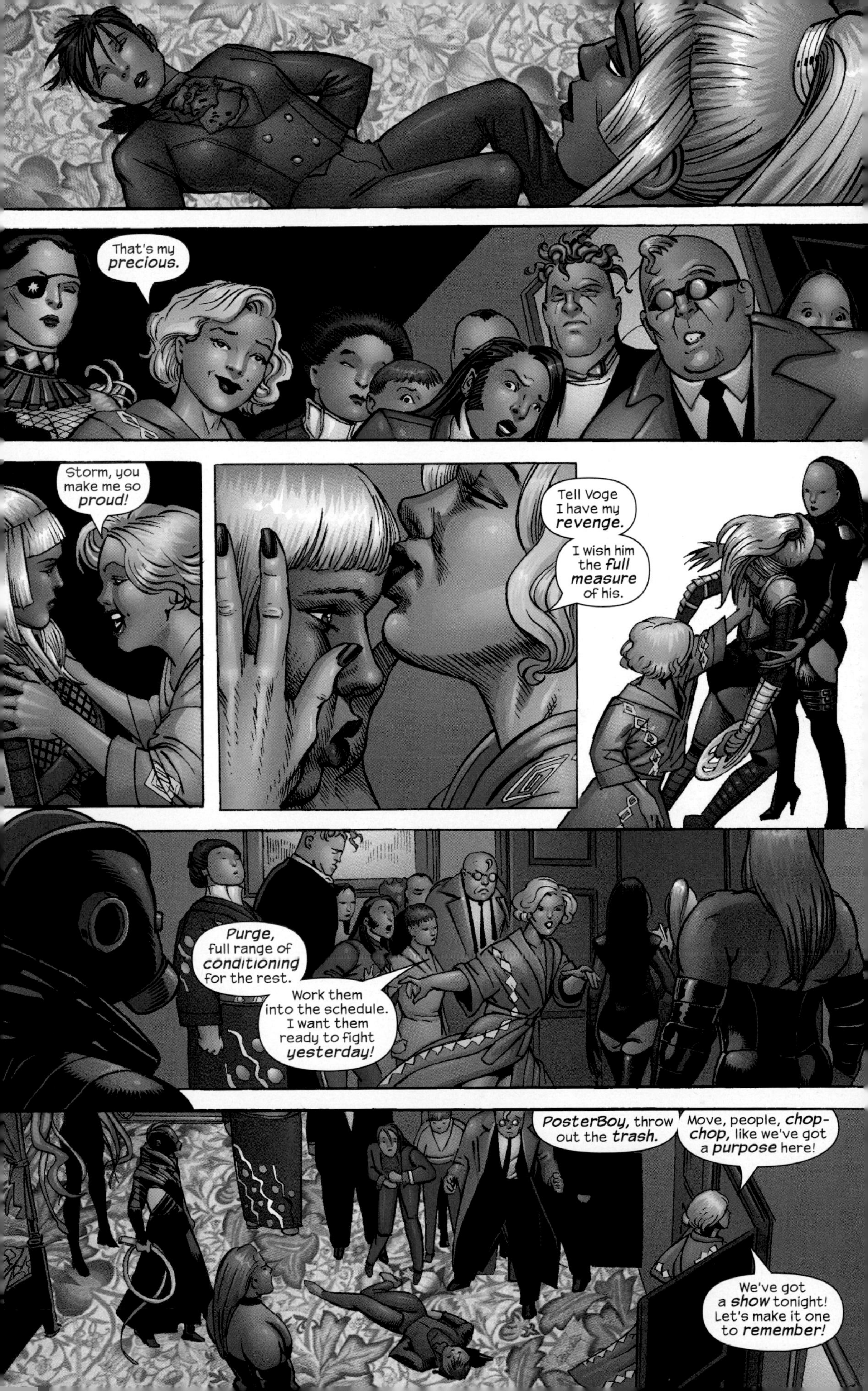
That's my precious.
Storm, you make me so proud!
Tell Voge I have my revenge.
I wish him the full measure of his.
Purge, full range of conditioning for the rest.
Work them into the schedule. I want them ready to fight yesterday!
PosterBoy, throw out the trash.
Move, people, chop-chop, like we've got a purpose here!
We've got a show tonight! Let's make it one to remember!

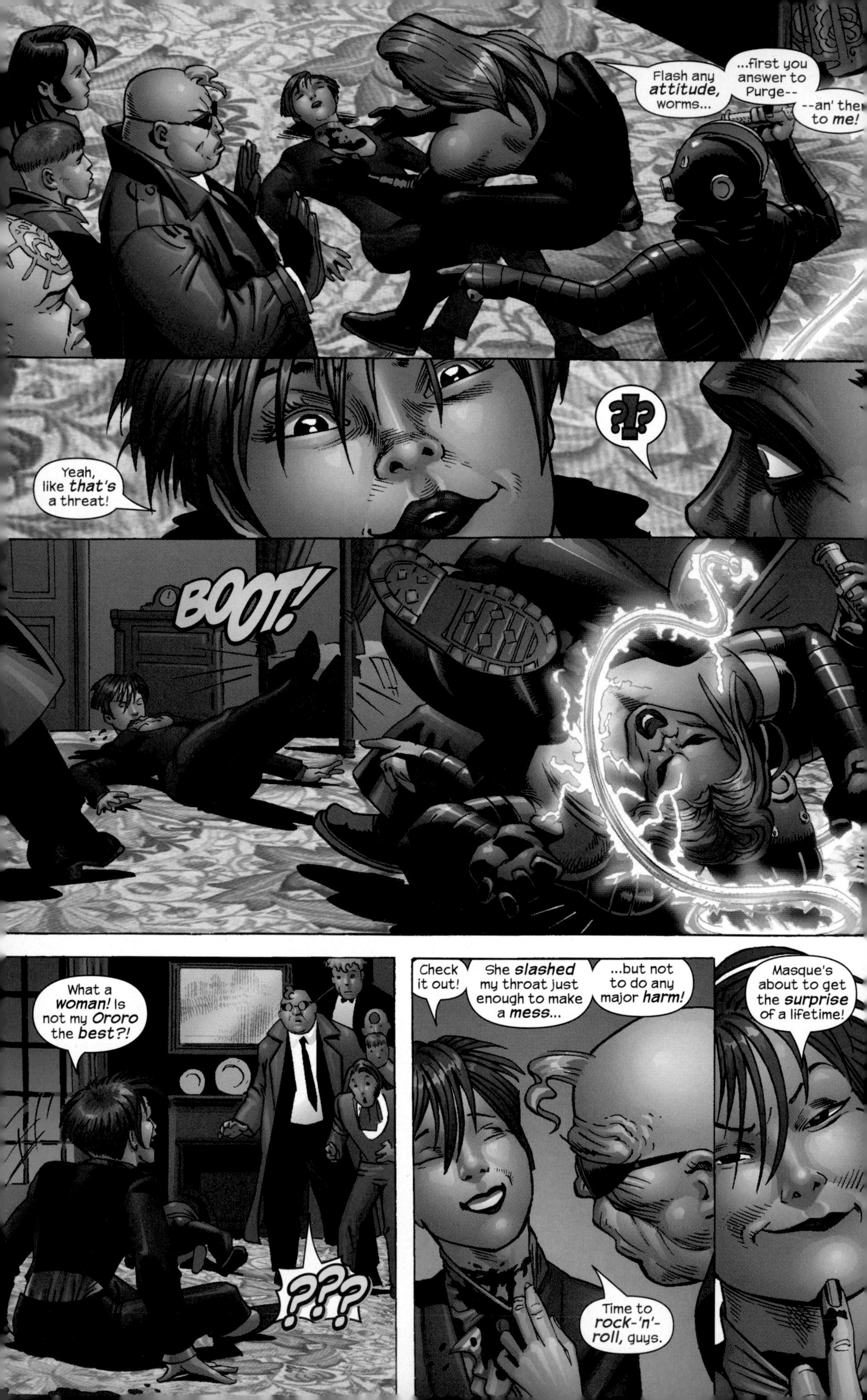
Flash any attitude, worms...
...first you answer to Purge--
--an' then to me!
Yeah, like that's a threat!
?!?
BOOT!
What a woman! Is not my Ororo the best?!
???
Check it out!
She slashed my throat just enough to make a mess...
...but not to do any major harm!
Masque's about to get the surprise of a lifetime!
Time to rock-'n'-roll, guys.

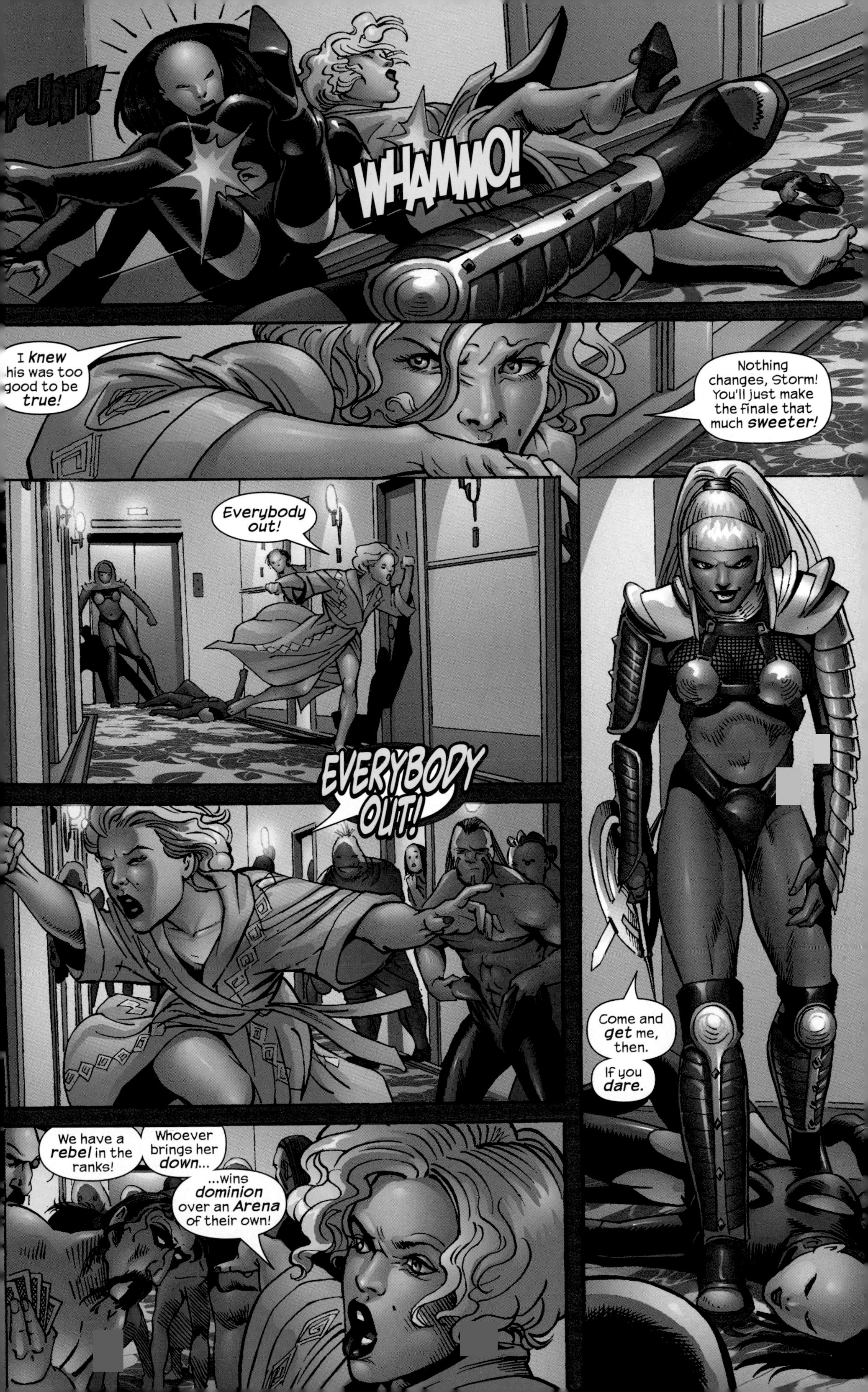
PUNT!
WHAMMO!
I knew his was too good to be true!
Nothing changes, Storm! You'll just make the finale that much sweeter!
Everybody out!
EVERYBODY OUT!
Come and get me, then.
If you dare.
We have a rebel in the ranks!
Whoever brings her down...
...wins dominion over an Arena of their own!

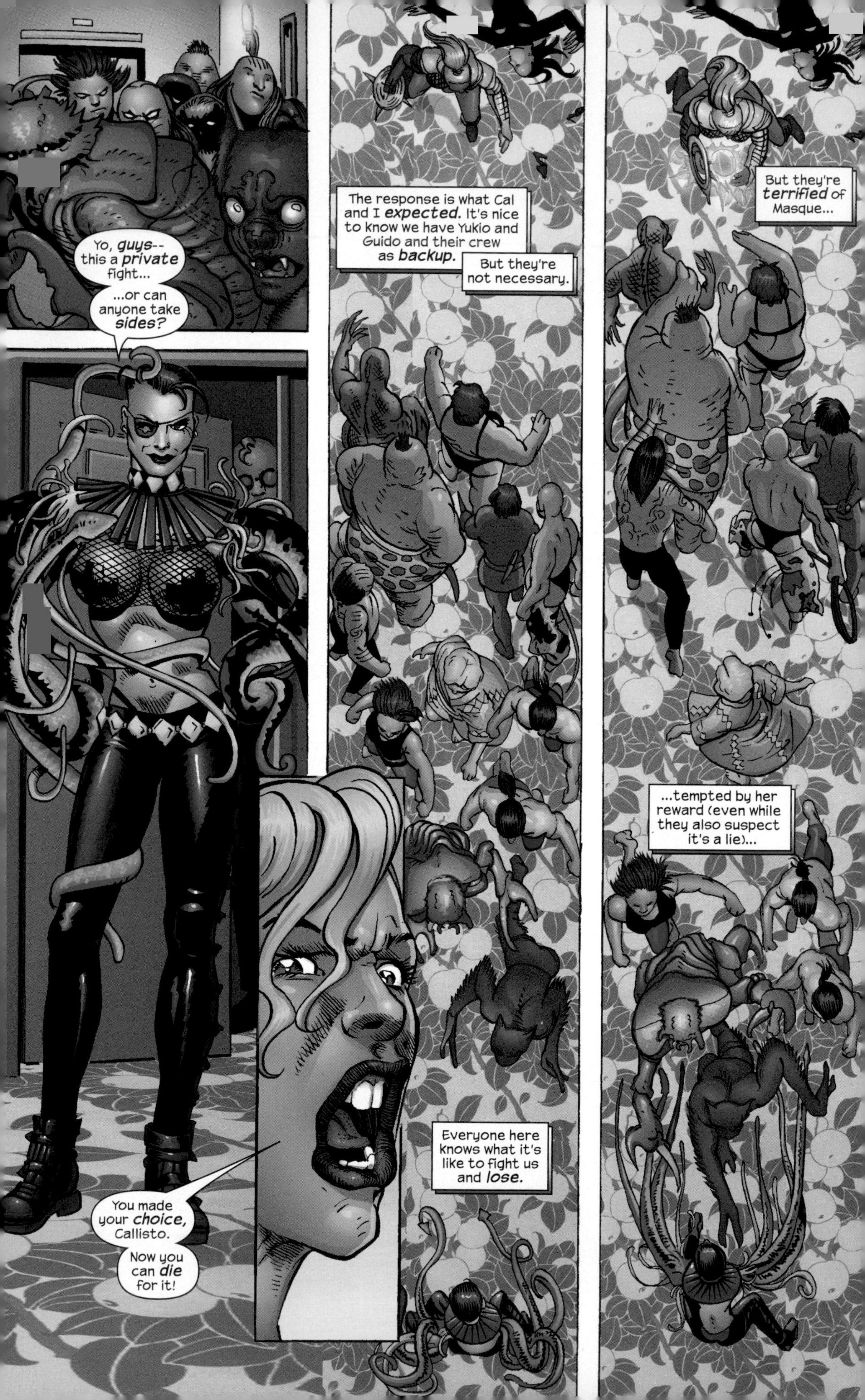

Yo, guys-- this a private fight...
...or can anyone take sides?
You made your choice, Callisto.
Now you can die for it!
The response is what Cal and I expected. It's nice to know we have Yukio and Guido and their crew as backup.
But they're not necessary.
Everyone here knows what it's like to fight us and lose.
But they're terrified of Masque...
...tempted by her reward (even while they also suspect it's a lie)...

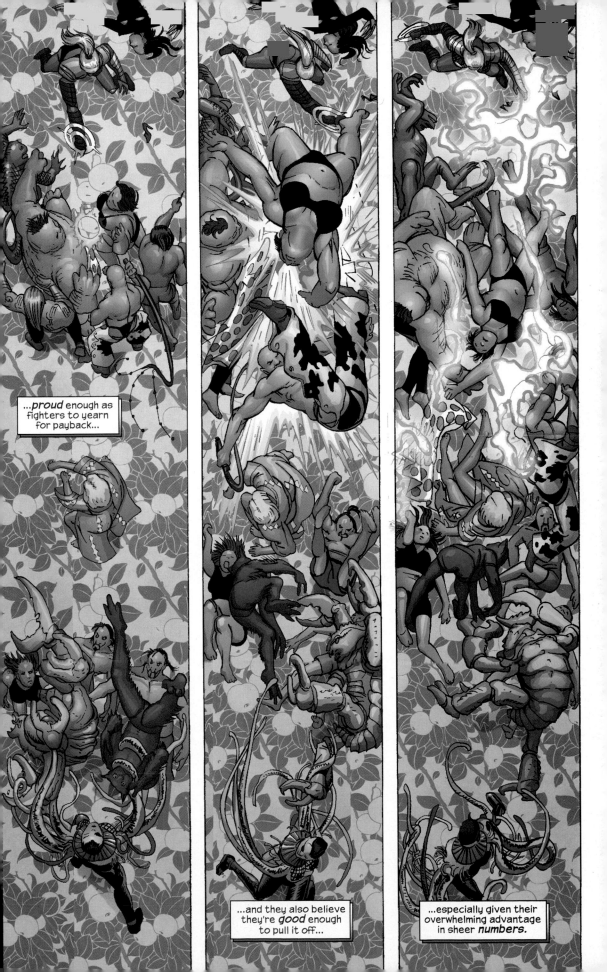

...*proud* enough as fighters to yearn for payback...

...and they also believe they're *good* enough to pull it off...

...especially given their overwhelming advantage in sheer *numbers.*

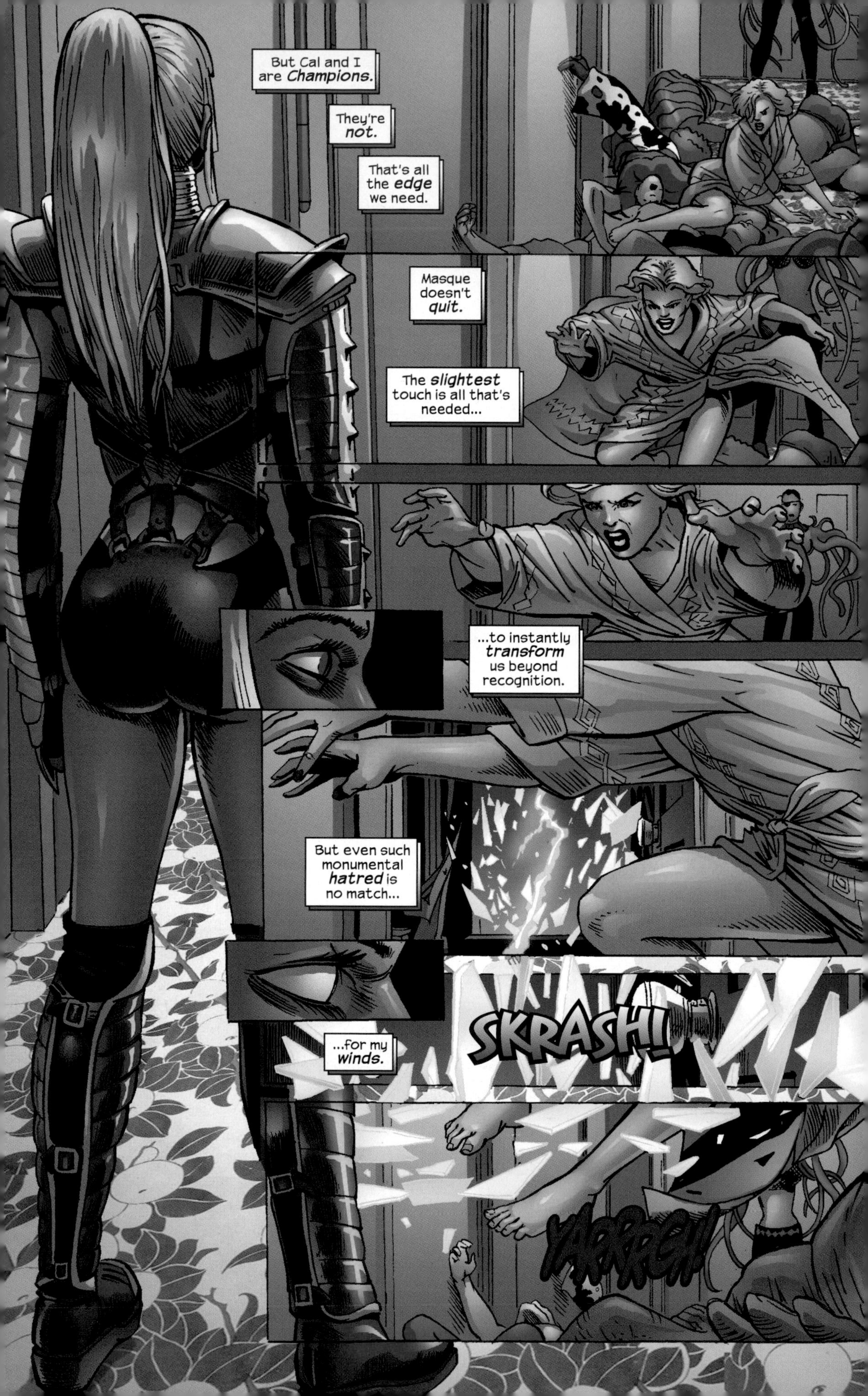

But Cal and I are *Champions.*
They're *not.*
That's all the *edge* we need.
Masque doesn't *quit.*
The *slightest* touch is all that's needed...
...to instantly *transform* us beyond recognition.
But even such monumental *hatred* is no match...
SKRASH!
...for my *winds.*
YARRGH!

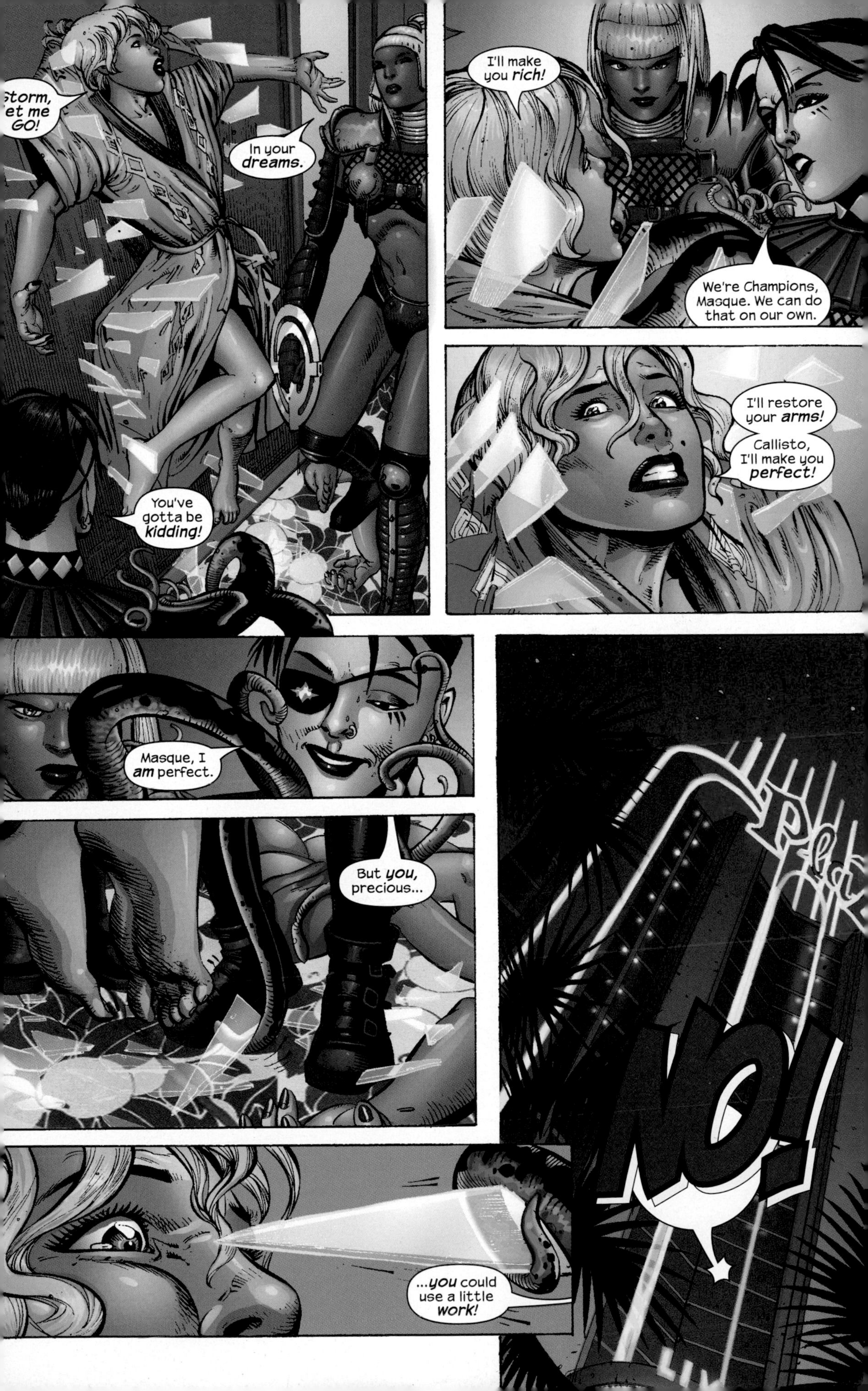
Storm, let me GO!
In your dreams.
You've gotta be kidding!
I'll make you rich!
We're Champions, Masque. We can do that on our own.
I'll restore your arms!
Callisto, I'll make you perfect!
Masque, I am perfect.
But you, precious...
...you could use a little work!
NO!

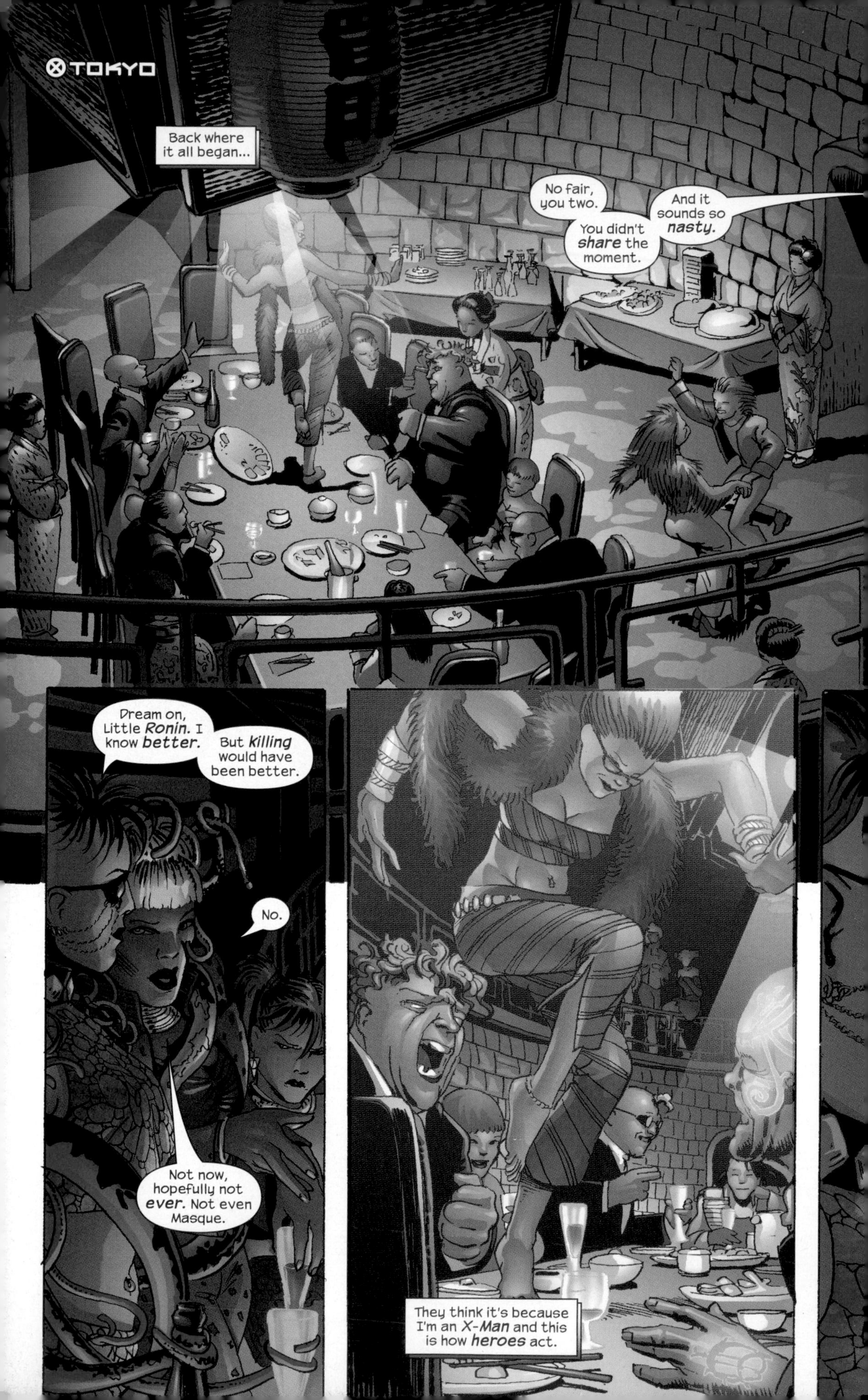
TOKYO
Back where it all began...
No fair, you two.
You didn't share the moment.
And it sounds so nasty.
Dream on, Little Ronin. I know better.
But killing would have been better.
No.
Not now, hopefully not ever. Not even Masque.
They think it's because I'm an X-Man and this is how heroes act.

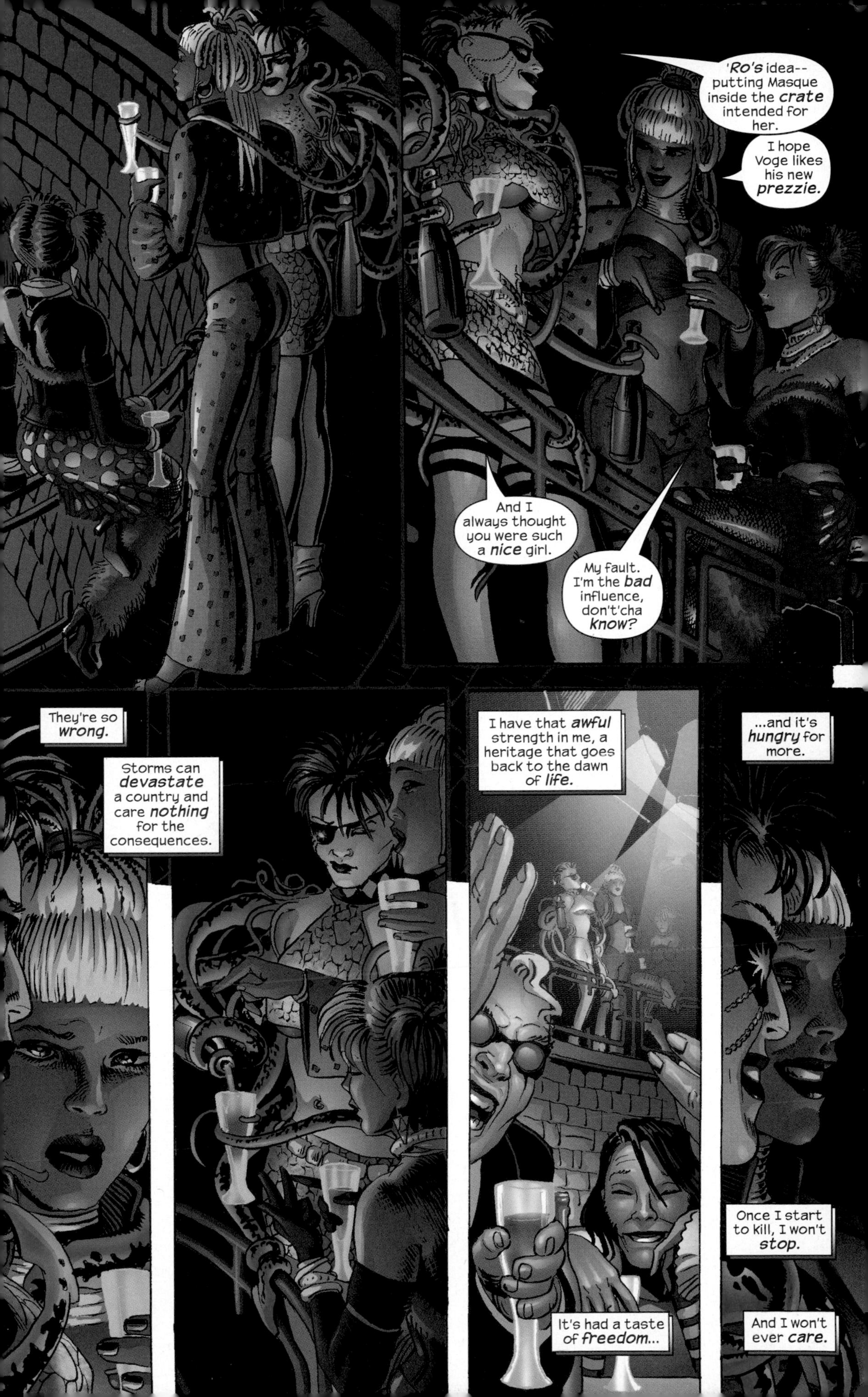
'Ro's idea-- putting Masque inside the crate intended for her.
I hope Voge likes his new prezzie.
And I always thought you were such a nice girl.
My fault. I'm the bad influence, don't'cha know?
They're so wrong.
Storms can devastate a country and care nothing for the consequences.
I have that awful strength in me, a heritage that goes back to the dawn of life.
It's had a taste of freedom...
...and it's hungry for more.
Once I start to kill, I won't stop.
And I won't ever care.

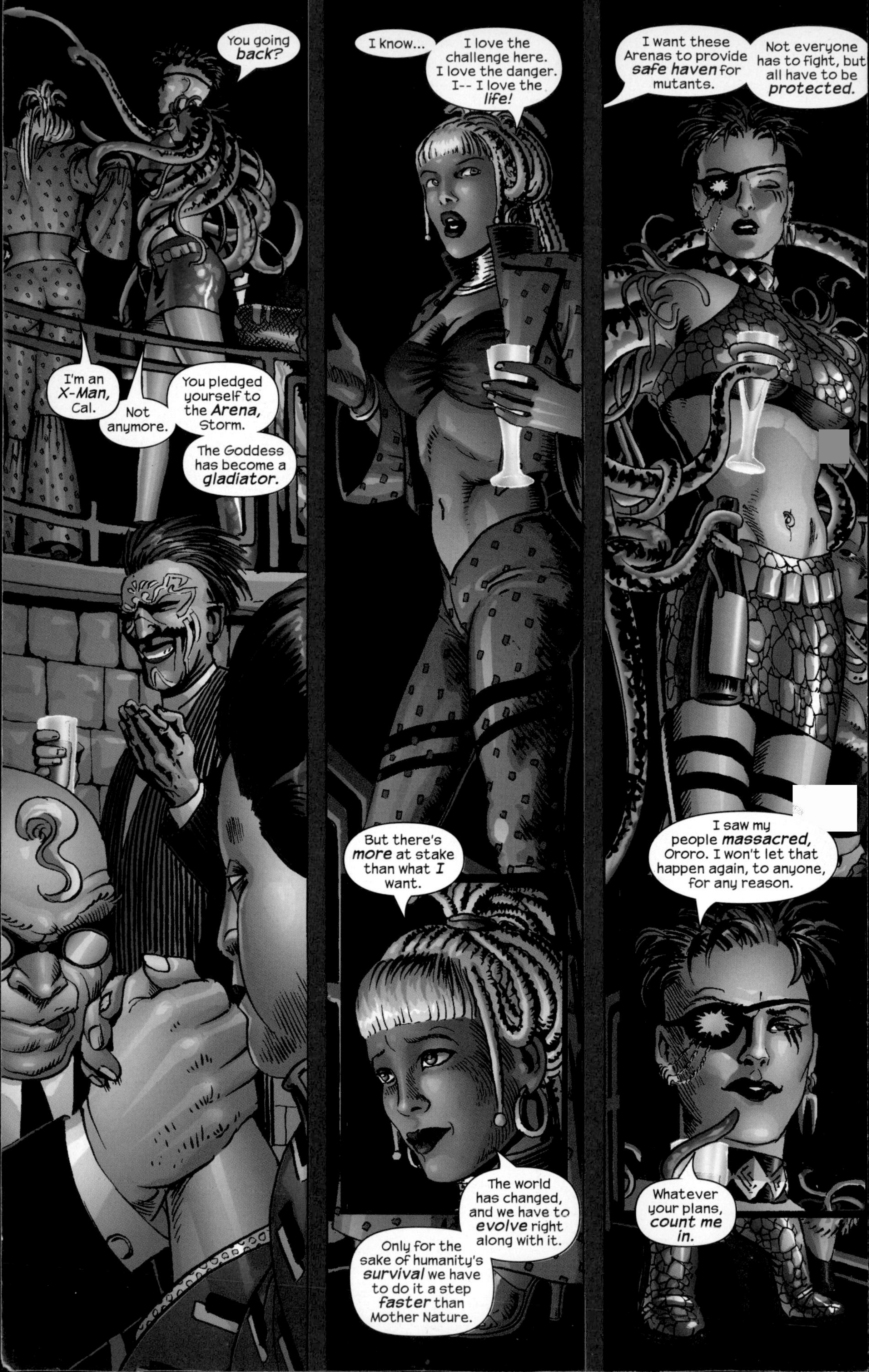
You going back?
I'm an X-Man, Cal.
Not anymore.
You pledged yourself to the Arena, Storm.
The Goddess has become a gladiator.
I know...
I love the challenge here. I love the danger. I-- I love the life!
But there's more at stake than what I want.
The world has changed, and we have to evolve right along with it.
Only for the sake of humanity's survival we have to do it a step faster than Mother Nature.
I want these Arenas to provide safe haven for mutants.
Not everyone has to fight, but all have to be protected.
I saw my people massacred, Ororo. I won't let that happen again, to anyone, for any reason.
Whatever your plans, count me in.

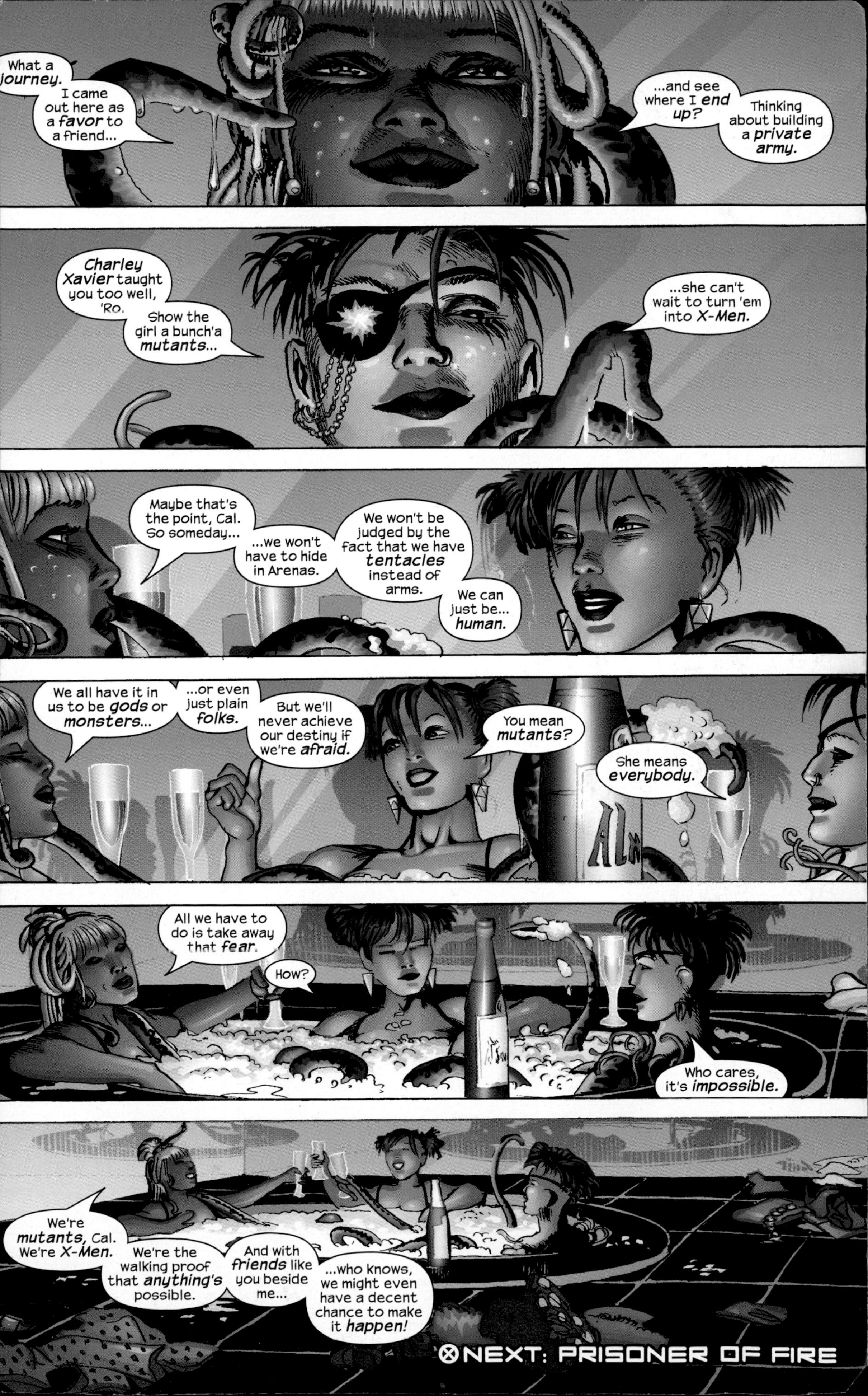
What a journey. I came out here as a favor to a friend...
...and see where I end up?
Thinking about building a private army.
Charley Xavier taught you too well, 'Ro.
Show the girl a bunch'a mutants...
...she can't wait to turn 'em into X-Men.
Maybe that's the point, Cal. So someday...
...we won't have to hide in Arenas.
We won't be judged by the fact that we have tentacles instead of arms.
We can just be... human.
We all have it in us to be gods or monsters...
...or even just plain folks.
But we'll never achieve our destiny if we're afraid.
You mean mutants?
She means everybody.
All we have to do is take away that fear.
How?
Who cares, it's impossible.
We're mutants, Cal. We're X-Men.
We're the walking proof that anything's possible.
And with friends like you beside me...
...who knows, we might even have a decent chance to make it happen!
NEXT: PRISONER OF FIRE

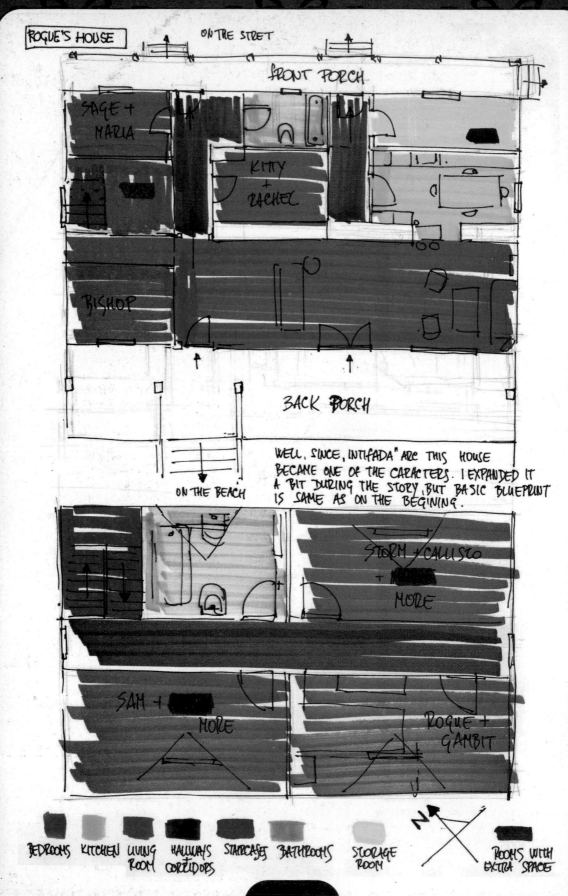

ROGUE'S HOUSE

ON THE STRET

FRONT PORCH

SAGE + MARIA

KITTY + RACHEL

BISHOP

BACK PORCH

ON THE BEACH

WELL, SINCE "INTIFADA" ARC THIS HOUSE BECAME ONE OF THE CARACTERS. I EXPANDED IT A BIT DURING THE STORY, BUT BASIC BLUEPRINT IS SAME AS ON THE BEGINING.

STORM + CALLISTO + MORE

SAM + MORE

ROGUE + GAMBIT

BEDROOMS   KITCHEN   LIVING ROOM   HALLWAYS CORRIDORS   STAIRCASES   BATHROOMS   STORAGE ROOM   ROOMS WITH EXTRA SPACE

N

Sketches by Igor Kordey